The Last Wilderness

To Pete Wilkinson, for persuading me that going to the Antarctic was a good idea; Maureen, my wife, for suggesting the daily journal on which the book is based; and the crew of the *Gondwana* for giving me plenty to write about.

The Last Wilderness

Eighty Days in Antarctica

PAUL BROWN

HUTCHINSON

London   Sydney   Auckland   Johannesburg

This edition first published in 1991
by Hutchinson

Random Century Group Ltd
20 Vauxhall Bridge Road, London SW1V 2SA

Random Century Australia (Pty) Ltd
20 Alfred Street, Milsons Point, Sydney, NSW 2061, Australia

Random Century New Zealand Ltd
PO Box 40–086, Glenfield, Auckland 10, New Zealand

Random Century South Africa (Pty) Ltd
PO Box 337, Bergvlei, 2012, South Africa

British Library Cataloguing in Publication Data
Brown, Paul
The last wilderness: eighty days in Antarctica.
1. Antarctic. Description & travel
I. Title
919.8904

ISBN 0-09-174423-7

Set in Baskerville by 🦅 Tek Art Ltd, Addiscombe, Croydon, Surrey
Printed and bound in Great Britain by Mackays of Chatham PLC.

Contents

List of Illustrations

The author and the publishers would like to thank Steve
Morgan and Greenpeace for their kind permission to
reproduce some of the illustrations that appear in this book. All
other illustrations are the author's own.

1

Man's Last Test

SITTING OVER A pub lunch in the Horseshoe in Farringdon Road in London, Pete Wilkinson was telling me that the future of the human race could depend on our not despoiling Antarctica. A former director of the environmental group Greenpeace UK, Pete had three times led the organisation's expeditions to that vast, inhospitable continent. He was now trying to convince me of its importance to readers of *The Guardian*, the paper I worked for. It was the summer of 1988, and at that time the urgency of the problems of the area had not yet filtered through to me, but, as always when Pete campaigned on an issue, he had a masterly grasp of facts and figures and he quickly educated me.

First he described the hole in the ozone layer above the southern hemisphere, how it had come about, and the effects it was already having – people there were now afraid to sunbathe on account of the increased infrared radiation. Then he moved on to global warming. He started with the dangers of the icecap melting. I knew so little about the subject that I had no idea even that the icecap over the South Pole was much bigger than the icecap in the north.

To someone living on a small island like Britain, the sheer scale of the Antarctic is hard to comprehend. Still unmapped in many areas, the continent is one-tenth of all the world's earth surface, the size of all of Europe. The statistics poured out of him: 'Nearly the whole land area and a lot of the sea is covered by a gigantic icecap, in some places three miles thick. The icecap contains seventy per cent of the world's fresh water. What makes this important is that all this ice is above sea level. If man's activities cause even some of it to melt, sea levels will rise and swamp large areas of some countries like Holland and eastern England. Perhaps even more important, it would have a catastrophic effect on the world's climate. So far we are not quite sure how this

1

works, except that the existence of this huge area of ice controls ocean currents and weather patterns over most of the world. We have lots of theories about it, some of them frightening possibilities of what may happen if it all goes wrong. We still have no concrete answers about what is really happening.'

Pete was telling me it was my responsibility to play a part in awakening the world's attention. What he really wanted was for *The Guardian* to chronicle Greenpeace's next expedition to Antarctica. Only publicity could alert people to the appalling dangers. Only if the public was alarmed and demanded action would money and expertise be poured into understanding and preserving Antarctica's delicate ecological balance.

But he knew it was not enough simply to take a national newspaper journalist down to the Antarctic – there had to be some kind of action. Also, for *The Guardian*, a political element was important. He explained, therefore, that at the same time as the scientific community was getting alarmed about changes in Antarctica, politicians were suddenly taking a dangerous interest in the last great unexploited wilderness.

As scientific exploration continued and technology improved, claims were now being made that immense mineral riches lay beneath the ice, and untapped oil and gas reserves in the seas around. Many countries, some without natural resources of their own, now saw Antarctica as a new Klondyke. Since no one 'owned' Antarctica, they believed they should all have a share in the cake.

So, Pete said, the last continent to be discovered – and at first glance the least important – now faced a cut-throat political contest over its future. Although no one owned the vast land mass, and no native people had ever lived there, there were now fifty or more scientific stations along its coastline, and an intense battle was being waged for influence over it. The battle went on in international conferences, often shrouded in secrecy, where diplomatic language hid the protagonists' real motives. As a campaigner for the environment he had learned to treat governments with deep suspicion. He believed that where there was a possibility of financial gain, the natural world usually came well down the list of politicians' priorities. He said he could not yet predict what would happen in Antarctica, but Greenpeace was putting a large part of its resources into trying to save the continent from exploitation. He said the fate of the continent represented the last great test for humankind. Would greed or enlightenment triumph? I remembered what I liked about Pete – he always saw things in black and white.

For him it all boiled down to a simple fundamental choice. Being unspoilt, with no local pollution, the Antarctic provided an ideal open-air laboratory for scientists, where they could measure the spread of greenhouse gases from the whole globe. The continent might be the only reliable barometer left which could tell us what was happening to our climate. If we pollute it by digging up the minerals and drilling for the oil, then we lose all chance of understanding the climatic changes that are taking place. If we do not understand what is happening, and cannot measure the effects of corrective measures, how can we hope to prevent global warming getting out of hand?

His flow was stopped by the need to get another beer. It brought a change of tack. He had to admit that the Greenpeace Antarctic campaign had a serious problem. It was not that the three expeditions so far had failed in their research aims: the difficulty had been to catch public attention. The area was so remote from the concerns of ordinary people that publicity on a vast scale was needed if Greenpeace was to influence world opinion on the issue of preserving its environment. And as far as the British were concerned there was another snag: the summer of 1988 being very cold and wet, the threat of global warming was unlikely to arouse much general anxiety.

Pete's next expedition to the Antarctic was to be his last, he said. He was determined to make it a success in public relations terms, and for that he needed me, backed by *The Guardian*, to go with him. He accepted therefore that he had to convince me I wanted to go. Then it would be up to me to convince *The Guardian* there would be enough newsworthy material to justify a trip of around three months.

He then pointed out that, with so many other pressing environmental concerns, Greenpeace must be pretty convinced of the importance of the Antarctic if it was willing to spend so much of its resources down there. Not only was the campaign by far the most expensive, it also carried enormous physical risks for the crew, and demanded a continuity of effort that could weaken the effectiveness of the organisation in other spheres.

Pete moved on to the trip itself. The campaign ship intended to visit and confront the French at a base they were enlarging on the Antarctic mainland despite vigorous international protests.

Greenpeace planned to drop in on the Russians' mountaintop retreat by helicopter, to take on the Japanese whaling fleet on the high seas, and to demonstrate against United States behaviour on Antarctica's biggest base.

I perked up. That was much more the sort of activity that appeals to newspapers, I said. Both of us knew that this sort of swashbuckling was a thorn in the side of the establishment, and that my newspaper would be forced to ask and then to answer the question 'What the hell is Greenpeace up to?'

Having been on Greenpeace expeditions before, I knew that the crews were motivated by a genuine concern for the environment. This did not stop them being a pleasant bunch to travel with, full of spirit and a self-mocking sense of humour. They come from widely differing backgrounds, but all have the same lack of respect for the establishment that allows them to justify breaking its rules. Normally they present a sloppy or, more charitably, a carefully cultivated casual appearance, but when in action on behalf of the natural world they are very sharp.

Eventually Pete's intensity of feeling about the importance of the Antarctic began to be infectious. I also realised what a tremendous adventure it would be to go to this wild place, the last wilderness. Then again, there was the happy thought of being 12,000 miles away from the news desk.

Before the lunch was over I told Pete I would try to persuade *The Guardian* to send me on the next Greenpeace expedition to Antarctica.

To put the issue in context, our pub lunch had taken place before the British Prime Minister, Mrs Margaret Thatcher, spoke to the annual gathering of Britain's foremost scientists, members of the Royal Society, in November 1988. At that time the ozone layer and the threat of global warming were not taken seriously outside academic circles. Green organisations which worried about it were still regarded as fringe pressure groups. But on that red-letter day for the Green movement, Mrs Thatcher took Green politics to the top of the agenda simply by endorsing the view that man had created a crisis in the world's environment. Perhaps she did not realise fully what she was doing, but her speech marked a turning point in the British political scene. Shortly afterwards, in 1989, when the Green Party from nowhere took twenty per cent of the votes in the European elections, it became a political necessity for all people in public life to be environmentally friendly, or at least to appear to be.

Sitting at my desk the previous summer, however, I tried to compose a convincing memo to my editor, Peter Preston. There is always an element of David versus Goliath about Greenpeace campaigns which is attractive for newspapers and, judging by the organisation's now huge membership worldwide, a winner with the public. Even so, and despite my rush of enthusiasm, it seemed a tall order to persuade *The Guardian* to let me go, so, to make it sound a more attractive proposition to Peter Preston, I threw an overdue month-long sabbatical into the equation – the paper would then only be losing two months of my time.

The memo remained unanswered for a couple of weeks, so I plucked up my courage and went to see him. It was a great shock to be told I could go. Much later Peter confessed that he had harboured grave misgivings about the expedition – but he agreed because I seemed so enthusiastic. Pete Wilkinson had obviously done a good job on me.

At any rate, since Greenpeace saw the coming voyage as part of their campaign of saving the Antarctic from the men who sought to exploit it, I now had to find and interview these ogres. And the curious thing about this was that everyone I contacted or read about claimed to have the same motives – they all had the best interests of the Antarctic and its wildlife at heart. They also all agreed that the Antarctic was at a crossroads. Science and technology had advanced far enough for the Antarctic to be exploited for its natural resources in the foreseeable future. It need no longer remain a frozen and inaccessible curiosity at the bottom of the world. What was at issue was how to deal with this new situation, which had created new international rivalry and tension.

A diplomat's first instinct is always to paper over the cracks, and I discovered that this was the policy of the men delegated by their governments to deal with this particular continent. Many had served in their departments of polar affairs for decades and had been responsible for the admirable international consensus which had kept the Antarctic free from conflict for so long. This consensus was enshrined in the Antarctic Treaty, an international agreement to keep the peace and engage in scientific cooperation, signed by thirty nations with an interest in the Antarctic.

These nations had formed themselves into what Greenpeace

describes as a cosy club. It began in 1959 when twelve nations, including the superpowers, signed a treaty to regulate activity in the continent. Over the years other nations have joined and a series of committees have been formed. Club members now include all the major industrial nations and the countries close to the Antarctic, including South Africa – making the club one of the few where that unhappy nation has remained an unchallenged member.

Perhaps the best demonstration of the unique rules that apply in the club occurred during the Falklands war, when Britain and Argentina sat round the same table and discussed the affairs of the Antarctic while a few miles outside the treaty boundary their armed forces were locked in mortal combat. It was the only diplomatic contact between the two sides during hostilities, and yet neither side mentioned the war. For thirty years this has been the pattern. Outside international conflicts have not been allowed to interfere with the large measure of agreement that has existed in running the Antarctic. Problems inside the Antarctic Circle have all been dealt with amicably while the Cold War continued in warmer climes.

Greenpeace say that this desire to keep the peace, so laudable in many respects, has nevertheless contributed towards damaging the treaty's effectiveness. Nations may not always have behaved perfectly in the Antarctic, yet they have escaped censure because no one wants to disturb the peace. Greenpeace say many of the rules which the club drew up to protect the region from environmental damage have been broken without challenge. This is because the importance of maintaining international harmony among governments of all political hues has outweighed the risks of pointing out each other's indiscretions.

One of the rules of the treaty is that all debates are held in private, without the press or any outside interested bodies having any say. The supporters of this system claim that all the political tub-thumping which mars other international forums has in consequence been absent from treaty meetings. On the other hand, as a journalist I suggest it also means that matters which could be of extreme public importance have never been given a public airing. Members of the club have defended this by saying that it would not be possible to achieve in public discussion the consensus that the club has always managed in private.

But now, in any case, stresses in the cosy arrangement have

begun to show. Members of the club who fall out in private meetings have started making public statements. And the principal issue which has caused this increased tension is the presence of valuable minerals and the possibility of their exploitation. This and the parallel but conflicting need for the scientific study of the Antarctic and its link with the survival of the human species are now the crux of the matter. The club rules are still being broken by nations taking actions in the Antarctic which break the provisions of the treaty, but those who care to ignore the convention of secrecy have now taken the political debate outside the conference chamber in order to gain public support. Greenpeace, and the rest of the environmental lobby, which now includes an increasing number of politicians both in and out of power, believe this public debate is necessary and healthy. For Greenpeace, however, the reason is simple – they do not trust politicians, left to their own devices, to make the right decisions.

The story of the 1988/89 Greenpeace expedition, the people involved in it, and the issues and arguments which arise are examined in the following chapters. The misunderstandings, the different perceptions of scientists and politicians, are part of the story. In fact, of course, the muddle of motives and the conflicting ideas which mark the current debate have been part of the continent's history from the beginning. Once man had discovered Antarctica, and seen how cold and inhospitable it was, it would have been left alone but for the seal hunters. The sealers were the first wave of European and North American hunters cashing in on the plentiful supplies. The seals were so tame they could be killed without the necessity of a chase. The penguins only survived the slaughter because the hunters could not think of a commercial use for them. Instead they used their fatty bodies as bonfires to keep warm.

Such excesses have admittedly ceased, but basic conflicts over the wildlife still remain. The battle to save the whales continues; the seals are only temporarily not hunted; and stocks of fish have been virtually wiped out in some areas. All three issues are dealt with by separate international conventions, and neither the whales nor the fish are effectively conserved by the treaties which were specifically set up to do so.

Greenpeace believe that issues of conservation and exploitation can only be resolved if they are brought out into the open. They believe that pretending there is no tension is short-sighted and can only make things worse in the long run, and it was to further their campaign of bringing the issues out into the open that Greenpeace had planned a series of 'actions' for the voyage in which I had agreed to take part. They were aimed at forcing countries to explain what they were doing on the continent and make public their policy decisions.

The confrontational Greenpeace voyage I sailed on has certainly influenced world opinion on the Antarctic. Even so the future of the continent and the creatures that inhabit it, and indeed the future of our own race, still hangs in the balance. And meanwhile the continuing struggle over the future goes on in a series of conferences which take place thousands of miles away from the continent in the capital cities of countries which are parties to the treaty. The conferences all have much in common: they are secretive, closed to journalists, and very seldom reach a decision. The future of the entire continent depends on what the delegates eventually do, but no one wants to cause friction by pushing too hard.

Ultimately, as Pete said in the pub, Antarctica could be humanity's greatest test. Is it time to conserve rather than exploit? After all, the scientists tell us the future of mankind could be in the balance. This book is intended as a contribution to the important and increasingly fierce debate about the future of Antarctica. It is also about the future of the planet.

2

Teething Troubles

FOUR MONTHS AFTER the conversation in the Horseshoe I left London from Gatwick airport for the gruelling twenty-seven-hour journey to New Zealand to join the expedition. Pete had made the same journey two months previously. There was a large amount of organisation necessary to get the ship and crew ready. One of his jobs was to select a replacement team for the four people who were already spending a year in the Antarctic carrying out a long-term plankton study, among other scientific experiments, at the camp which Greenpeace had built there on previous expeditions. The camp was part of Greenpeace's effort to be recognised as a genuine scientific organisation as well as a pressure group, and the team needed the right personnel to carry on the work.

The selection was a very difficult process: members of such a small team sharing a tiny base need to get on well together, particularly in the three months of total darkness they have to endure. They rely on each other for survival and cannot afford to fall out. They need to be fit, but of prime importance must be a personality stable enough to cope with the conditions. This, fortunately, was Pete's problem, and he had started to tackle it well before he left England. All Greenpeace activities are based on multiracial, mixed-sex crews and this added another complication to team selection. Pete took all this on with no expertise except his common sense. Greenpeace expect a lot from their campaigners.

Pete is the son of a Bermondsey bench fitter and grew up in Deptford in South East London. He left school in 1963 at the age of sixteen 'because everyone else did'. He had six O levels but no idea what to do. He took seventeen jobs in three years but earned most money driving lorries. When a chum, John Martin, gave him a Friends of the Earth publication called *The Environmental*

9

Handbook it changed his life. Up to then the only grass he contemplated regularly was on the Millwall football club pitch. He said the FOE booklet made him realise he was living an artificial life, in an artificial economy, divorced from the environment on which the human race ultimately depended. He went to work for Friends of the Earth in 1971 and stayed until 1975, when he married and got a job as a Post Office clerk.

He joined the infant Greenpeace in 1978 at the invitation of David McTaggart, the powerful Canadian behind the organisation. McTaggart was then anxious to establish branches in Europe. Pete worked half the week for Greenpeace, earning £25 a week, and the other half for the Post Office, making a total of £50. He became accomplished on the radio and television, and eventually Greenpeace took over his life, with painful personal repercussions. On one occasion, for example, he went to Iceland for three weeks on a campaign against whaling, was sent on to Japan, and came home four months later. On his return to London he went straight to the office, and then to the BBC for an interview, missing the last train home and the reunion with his wife. His marriage did not survive such shocks and eventually he was divorced.

When my 747 finally touched down in Auckland, New Zealand, his familiar figure was waiting to meet me as he had promised. I could smell the pine trees in the warm drizzle, a semi-tropical feel after the bleak December I had left behind. Pete thought the weather was a bit grim – it was supposed to be summer – but after all my time in the stale air of planes and airports I found it very pleasant.

The van which Pete had brought was typical of the Greenpeace I had known years before when the organisation was young. The driver's door did not open properly so we both had to get in the passenger side. Pete explained that the best van was not working because no one had put any petrol in it. He had the air of someone surrounded by incompetence. Time was running out if the new expedition ship, the *Gondwana*, was going to be ready to sail before Christmas.

But even Pete's obvious irritation did not prepare me for the shambles which greeted me at the ship. She resembled a scrap yard or heavy engineering shop. Men with welding equipment, electricians and workmen of all sorts swarmed over her. The *Gondwana* was ice-strengthened, an oil platform supply vessel brought from Finland especially for the purpose, but needed extensive modification to make her an expedition ship. Conditions were so dreadful on board that only two of the crew were living there. Some were still ashore at home or staying with friends, but the rest were living in another ship, the *Greenpeace*, which lay alongside. This had been the organisation's Antarctic vessel for the previous three seasons but had been replaced because she could not deal with the ice.

The *Gondwana* looked a tough, not to say brutish vessel. She was not an icebreaker but could push her way through ice up to two metres thick and, with her two engines totalling 8,000 horsepower, could penetrate broken pack ice which would have defeated the *Greenpeace*. She had already been through months of refitting in Europe. This included having a hangar built on the rear deck to take two small helicopters, and new crew accommodation behind the bridge. Although much of the major structural work had been completed before the ship got to New Zealand, much work had been left unfinished.

The extended sea trial that the voyage south allowed had shown up some other problems. One of them was that the *Gondwana* had not been built for giant southern seas. She had been used in quieter northern waters, probably the Baltic, and shipped huge quantities of green water even in moderate weather. Greenpeace was therefore having a series of vertical steel plates welded on to the foredeck to direct the worst of the water back over the side. We would not know if they worked until we hit the first storm.

Pete explained all this to me as he showed me to my cabin. It was in the new accommodation and turned out to be a surprisingly big room with four bunks, two wardrobes and a chest of drawers. He told me I would be sharing with an English film crew who had not yet arrived. He said it was the biggest cabin on the whole ship: the film crew had been given so much space because they had the most luggage. He left me to unpack. The noise outside the cabin was like a factory in full swing. I tried the bunk, which was very comfortable, and instantly passed out despite the noise. After all those hours sitting bolt upright in a full jumbo jet I was exhausted. When the hammering finally woke me again it was time to explore the ship and a new country.

From the bridge I could see the ship was on a quay only a few minutes' walk from the city centre, so I decided on a walk into Auckland to get away from the noise and fumes.

Having just come from London crushed under the weight of Christmas shoppers, I found Auckland practically deserted. The small skyscrapers of downtown Auckland did not have a great deal of charm, however, and I soon retraced my steps to the shipyard, where I rang a friend who had emigrated a year previously and worked on the news desk of the *New Zealand Herald*. John Gardner, former deputy News Editor on *The Guardian*, introduced me to the Press Club and the government press officer, who opened the door to the interviews I needed with his country's Antarctic specialists.

John insisted I evacuate the boat and come and stay with him while the expedition sorted itself out. Still better, he had a friend with a yacht and a weekend off. The temptation was too much, and the three of us and John's two sons sailed off into the sunset.

Before leaving London I had decided to keep a daily journal of my trip. The first entry was for Tuesday 20 December, a week after I arrived:

Five days before Christmas for normal people, but to us on the Gondwana *two days before we sail for the Antarctic.*

Spray painters have now sealed up the portholes to put a fresh coat over all the decks and new constructions. It will make things look a lot better and cover up the welding marks. The crew have now moved on board because the Greenpeace *has departed to resume campaign duties elsewhere, and things are at last beginning to take shape.*

There was a press conference on board this morning to talk about the 1989 campaign. A rather uninterested bunch of reporters were escorted into the lounge, slightly alarmed at the noise of the generators and the paint-spraying activities on deck. I have acquired a commission to write a piece for the New Zealand Herald *on the trip – a welcome chance to try out one of the ship's computers and printer.*

The film crew have arrived to share the cabin, and Pete was right – they have a staggering amount of luggage which completely fills the entire floor space. They seem a jolly pair: Tim Fraser, a sound man, and Sean Leslie, with the camera, both English and anxious to be friendly, so we should get on all right.

The sewage plant on the ship went wrong this morning and as a result the water was turned off. It was impossible to wash. In this climate, which is so humid, this could make life unpleasant quite quickly.

Thursday 22 December: This is the great day when we are finally off. It seemed impossible to me that all the work would be completed, and it was not. The paint was still wet and the woodwork unvarnished – but Pete elected to sail anyway. The carpenters worked until midnight last night and were back at seven this morning. I spent a couple of hours this morning filling dustbin bags with the rubbish which has accumulated on deck in the last few weeks. We tried to get rid of anything we did not need before we left.

There is a roll call at 5 pm before we cast off to make sure no one has got lost or changed their minds. Every one of the thirty people supposed to be on board is a vital cog, or should be. We are still stowing things as we cast off, including the office filing cabinets with the campaign material in. They are still being used until the last minute and are not roped down until we have actually left the harbour. For me the leaving is a relief after a miserable week, but for some of the others there are tears.

Four years ago I had sailed for a month on the Greenpeace flagship the *Rainbow Warrior* during its epic last voyage across the Pacific – before it was blown up by the French at the same quay from which we were now sailing. In the Marshall Islands Greenpeace evacuated the inhabitants of a remote atoll called Rongelap which had been contaminated by nuclear fallout from the United States Bravo bomb tests. The people had appealed again and again to the United States, which administered the Marshalls as a United Nations Trust territory, to be taken to a new safe home, but were ignored. Greenpeace had answered their call for help. In between reporting the evacuation I had spent three weeks helping to carry the 300-odd people, mostly women and children, their corrugated iron homes, school and all their worldly goods, to their new island, 110 miles away. We had no hope of getting all the people and their possessions on one ship load and had to make repeated journeys.

On that voyage one member of the crew had been Henk Haazen, from the Netherlands, a blond giant of a man who had travelled all round the world helping Third World peoples. Henk, who was a mechanical wizard, was now the logistics officer for this Antarctic campaign. It was he who had to decide on the quantities and type of food both for the voyage and for the overwintering team. He also had to organise the fuel supplies and contend with the refitting of the ship, and the dozens of details such an expedition entailed. He knew where everything was and exactly how much of it we had.

When the *Gondwana* cast off there were about two hundred people on the Auckland quayside. There seems to be a great fund of good will for Greenpeace in New Zealand. We had a fierce rainstorm just at the point of departure, swamping the crew and well-wishers alike, but it did not dampen the enthusiasm. Tim and Sean, my cabin mates, got soaked trying to film the departure. Pete meanwhile had organised a send-off picture, with the ship's two small four-seater helicopters to escort us out into the harbour, and her inflatables buzzing alongside to give an impression of her resources against the whalers we were hoping to intercept. The whole lot was filmed from a third helicopter by Steve Morgan, the expedition's official photographer.

Finally, as Auckland began to fade into the sunset, the *Gondwana* felt for the first time more like a ship than a building site. The sea was calm and the ship was ploughing along, heavy laden but sturdy, ready for the task ahead. Since I had no idea how to sail such a complex vessel I was a bit like a passenger on a cruise, standing idly by while the professionals got on with it. But this was not a holiday, merely a pause before the action started.

3

Towards a New Klondike

A DETAILED ITINERARY of the coming voyage had been given to me and all the other new arrivals on the ship. It had a list of places to be visited with approximate length of stay and journey time in between. According to the itinerary we had six days at sea before reaching Hobart in Tasmania. The ship was due to spend two to three days there and then head due south for Antarctica. Eight to nine days later we should reach Dumont d'Urville, the French base on the Antarctic mainland. This was one of the main targets of the Greenpeace expedition and for me, at that stage, the most likely to produce a good story.

The visit to Dumont d'Urville was to challenge the French over the airstrip their government had ordered to be built there. The issues surrounding this airstrip are critical to the whole question of how the Antarctic is run, and what its future holds, so it is important now to set the scene.

Greenpeace's stated objective in going into the Antarctic campaign in the first place had been to save it from development and turn it into what they called a World Park. This seemed to me a clumsy title, but the best alternative I could come up with was 'wilderness reserve', which was not much better. What both terms try to convey is an Antarctic free from destructive development by man. This does not rule out scientific study in Antarctica, or the bases necessary to house the scientists while they do their work. Greenpeace was prepared to criticise how the bases were run and to insist that all human waste and rubbish should be returned to the country of origin, but was not against the science. Indeed, the purpose of Greenpeace having its own base on the continent was to establish the pressure group's own scientific credentials, and to become accepted into the political forum which controls the continent.

The Antarctic Treaty system which developed in the 1950s was set up against a background of international tension, a series of disputes over territorial claims which threatened to spill over into open warfare. The solution was a unique programme of international scientific cooperation called the International Geophysical Year of 1957/58. This laid the foundations for a treaty which put aside petty squabbles and allowed this scientific cooperation to continue. Negotiated at the height of the arms race, this treaty was a remarkable achievement. It secured the cooperation of the twelve participating nations and stopped the Cold War spilling over into the cold continent.

Seven nations had actual territorial claims: France, the United Kingdom, Argentina, Chile, Australia, Norway and New Zealand. They were joined as signatories by the United States, the Soviet Union, South Africa, Japan and Belgium. Under the treaty all territorial posturing was set aside, all existing claims were frozen and no new ones were allowed. Furthermore, the treaty permitted free access to any nation or individual anywhere in the Antarctic: it was truly international territory.

Over the years since 1958 a number of other countries interested in the Antarctic have decided to join this club. To gain admittance they had to set up their own scientific bases on the continent. Having a proper scientific programme in Antarctica remains the one essential condition before a nation can be voted in to treaty membership and so be granted attendance at its secretive conferences. The club now includes all the largest and most heavily industrialised countries, representing around eighty per cent of the world's population, but its meetings remain the most secretive of international forums.

When Greenpeace tried to gain at least observer status within this club, which the organisation's ruling council decided was essential if they were to influence events, they were faced with a blank refusal. Many other international bodies with a conservation role, like the International Whaling Commission, have granted Greenpeace observer status. This status, depending on the organisation, allows lobbying, and sometimes speaking rights at conferences, but never voting rights. Greenpeace, as always, were not prepared to accept being excluded from any conference, and decided to try and prise open the door of the Antarctic Treaty meetings by establishing a scientific base. Because the Antarctic is international territory no permission was required for this. The organisation had the whole continent in which to find

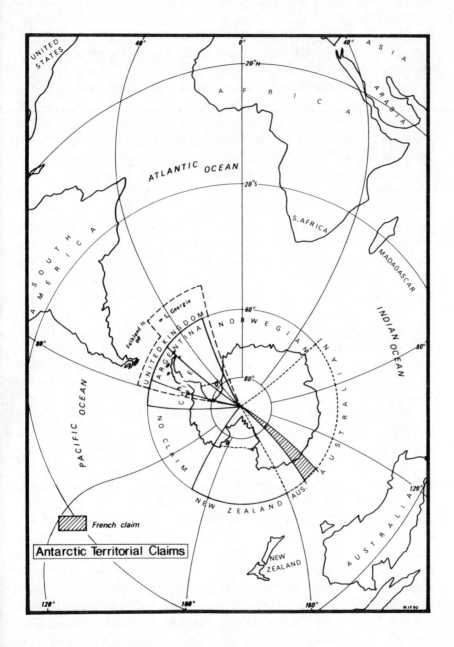

Antarctic Territorial Claims

a suitable site and eventually chose Ross Island, partly in order to keep an eye on the nearby United States base at McMurdo Sound, the biggest on the continent.

Because of the need for countries to establish a base in Antarctica to qualify to join the club, and a genuine increase in scientific interest in the continent, new bases had sprung up in many places since the 1960s. Some countries – Britain, the United States and the Soviet Union in particular – have as many as five each. The countries who had previously been territorial claimants, and in theory had put in abeyance their claims, still kept them up by maintaining bases on their previous 'territory'. As can be seen from the map of these territories (see page 17), some countries have overlapping claims, notably the United Kingdom, Argentina and Chile. This was one of the principal reasons why the Antarctic Treaty was brought into being. The potential for conflict still remains, however, and all three of these claimants are holding their ground.

France's claim in Antarctica is to a narrow slice unclaimed by others, running from the coast right to the centre of the continent. From the map (see page 48) showing the other main bases, it can be seen that most of them are close together in the Antarctic Peninsula area or on the Ross Sea. The single French base is completely isolated. This is because almost all this part of the continent is covered in a thick ice sheet: Dumont d'Urville is the one point in this whole area which is ice-free. The way the ice sheet covers the continent also explains the distribution of the other bases. They are nearly all grouped in places where exposed rock is available to build on. But this also creates one of the fundamental administrative problems of Antarctica and brings man and nature directly into conflict. The reason is that this same land that man needs to give firm foundations for his bases is also the essential breeding ground for seals and penguins. The rock provides the stability birds and seals need to rear their young and, even more important, the sun makes these areas considerably warmer than the ice, where the sunlight is reflected back, making the temperature much lower than on the heat-absorbing rocks. When scientists require new bases to be built anywhere in the Antarctic, therefore, the fragile wildlife that clings on to the same rocky outcrops invariably gets pushed aside.

This was what the row over Dumont d'Urville was all about. The French, who had built their scientific base there in the 1950s to study the wildlife, acknowledged that they had displaced a large number of nesting birds in order to do so. But that was all past history. The problem was that no one knew exactly what the French were now up to. The Antarctic is such a vast continent and travel is so difficult that there is no real scope for friendly neighbourhood visits. In the Antarctic Treaty there are provisions which allow governments to go on inspection visits to their neighbours, but since reaching and supplying even their own bases is so laborious, governments do not generally exercise these rights under the treaty, and instead just rely on one another to behave themselves.

It was into this comfortable system that Greenpeace had decided to trespass, having learned that the French were blowing up some of the remaining ice-free islands at Dumont d'Urville, with painful consequences for the already overcrowded wildlife. It seemed that the French government had decided to build an airstrip in the Antarctic, ostensibly so that its base could be supplied by air rather than by ship. The existence of an airstrip would give the scientists earlier access to the base in the summer and a longer season for study.

Under the terms of the Antarctic Treaty the French were supposed to keep the other treaty nations informed of what they were doing. They were also supposed to produce something called an environmental impact assessment before the work began. There were detailed agreements between the treaty parties which prevented the disturbance of the wildlife except in life-threatening circumstances or to achieve scientific aims which could not be accomplished in any other way. The French had informed no one of what they were doing and appeared to have made no study of the effect that construction of the airstrip would have on the wildlife.

Greenpeace were leaked information on this secret construction project by an outraged French scientist on the site. He revealed that when construction workers began blasting to level part of the archipelago, called Lion Island, some of the colony of Adélie penguins breeding there were killed. He gave Greenpeace emotive photographs of penguins lying dead on bloodstained patches of snow after the explosions, as proof that the French were breaking the treaty terms.

French officials had the grace to admit that the allegation was true and that France had fallen down in its treaty obligations. An international protest resulted, and France suspended work on the airstrip while a committee of scientists was appointed to assess the project. The French argued that the airstrip would allow access to the base for scientists for five months instead of the two now possible. The problem for the French was that the sea ice which surrounds the Antarctic in winter takes almost the whole summer to melt. This means that bases supplied by ship sometimes have only a short period of ice-free conditions before the winter closes in again.

The committee of scientists, mostly French, were not convinced by this argument and came out against the project, saying the damage to wildlife could not be justified and an alternative method of reaching the base should be found. The French, like the Americans at their bases, could for example use aircraft on skis and helicopters. In any event, no work on the airstrip was carried out in 1984 and 1985. But then the French government, without explanation, ordered a resumption of its construction.

When this decision leaked out, the French claimed the work was not to be on the runway itself but on a breakwater and embankment, to study the effects of the movements of winter ice. The next year, however, large quantities of explosives were shipped out to the Antarctic. Clearly the airstrip project was on again.

To Greenpeace this sequence of events illustrated all that was bad about the Antarctic Treaty system. While in theory the wildlife was protected, in practice the rules did not work. Furthermore, Greenpeace considered that the French had not put forward any convincing reasons for the airstrip. Constructing an airstrip in such an inhospitable climate cost an enormous amount of money. Highly paid construction workers had to be shipped all the way from France each year and earned the equivalent of an annual salary in two months. It seemed to Greenpeace an improbable amount of money to spend just for non-commercial scientific research. The organisation decided that the French might not have told the whole truth about their plans.

Other events had been taking place in parallel with the French airstrip construction project which Greenpeace thought could not be coincidental. There was talk of the Antarctic having great undiscovered mineral wealth. This had been creating a stir among the treaty nations, including France. The problem was that the Antarctic Treaty, originally intended to stop territorial claims, had now become a stumbling block to exploitation. The treaty said there were no owners of any of the land, so equally there could be no mechanism for staking a claim, since there was no one to register it with. Interest in the commercial search for minerals persisted, but the treaty system is unwieldy and no progress was made. This was partly because the last thing anyone wanted was to start an unseemly gold rush and inflame old territorial rivalries. Inside the club, nations were unwilling to admit that their laudable scientific interest was now sullied by the possibility of mineral wealth. Nevertheless, some method had to be found to sort out the impasse. Talks between the treaty nations began in earnest in 1982, with the expectation that a formula allowing mineral exploitation would soon be developed.

Greenpeace noted that it was at the time these talks began that the French decided to build their airstrip. Greenpeace felt the coincidence was too much. They suspected the French were trying to gain an advantage on their treaty partners. They could be creating an airstrip to fly in heavy machinery, and thus be in a position to exploit the Antarctic for its mineral wealth as soon as the negotiations reached a successful conclusion.

In keeping with the treaty members' overriding desire to keep the peace, this accusation was never openly made and therefore never refuted. But Greenpeace remained suspicious. Years passed without much happening. Then, suddenly, on 25 November 1988, the minerals issue appeared to be resolved. The next day I wrote an article for *The Guardian* which attracted the headline 'Pact paves way for mining Antarctic riches'. It described how nine countries had opened the door for commercial exploitation of the continent by signing a Minerals Convention which provided a set of rules to control mining and drilling for oil. This convention, an addition to the Antarctic Treaty, had taken six years to negotiate between the thirty-eight nations which were by that time part of the treaty organisation. My piece said that conservation groups, including Greenpeace, had fought the convention throughout: they saw it as 'the beginning of the end for the last wilderness'.

Those who supported the convention pointed to its extremely strong environmental regulations and the power of veto of claimant nations to any mining plans they disagreed with on 'their own patch'. It was said by its proponents to be a powerful weapon to control mining and prevent environmental damage. The growing conservation lobby's response was to point to other conventions, also part of the Antarctic Treaty, which had copious rules but failed to live up to expectations.

While the Minerals Convention was being negotiated, for example, prospecting remained officially banned under the treaty. A number of nations, including Japan and Britain, had ignored this and had been actively looking at the geology of the region to see if there was potential for oilfields. The justification for this activity was that it was all scientific research, but where was the line drawn between scientific research and prospecting? Under the treaty a gentleman's agreement seems to have grown up among member nations that this distinction was not to be enquired into too deeply.

At the time the *Gondwana* was about to set off for the Antarctic, in December 1988, only four of the sixteen signatures required for the convention were lacking. It seemed to me, therefore, that it would very soon be in operation.

As it turned out I was wrong, and the argument about mining is still raging. As yet no mining has taken place in Antarctica, nor is the necessary machinery there. During that November the prospect seemed imminent, however, and it was in this atmosphere that Greenpeace had decided to take a close look at the work going on at Dumont d'Urville. Apparently a chain of six islands, all of them vital nesting grounds for birds, was being levelled. The excavated rock was being used to fill the gaps between them and create an airstrip. During the construction, explosions would be frequent, and it was hard to see how the wildlife could be protected. Greenpeace knew that the French were building a runway long enough to take giant Hercules transport planes. These were exactly the type of plane that would be needed if heavy drilling machinery was to be brought in.

Greenpeace suspicions had been fuelled by a document dated 10 June 1987. This showed that a consortium between the French government and private industry had been formed for a pilot project for the development of the Antarctic for industrial purposes. The precise nature of the project was not explained, but the companies included the country's oil and mineral giants. Greenpeace also had a copy of the French environmental impact study. It showed that the airstrip was being built across the access to the emperor penguins' main breeding colony. It was these rare birds that the French scientists originally went to study. Emperor penguin numbers had dropped from 7,000 to less than 3,000 in the time the French had been at the site. The airstrip would cut off the birds from their breeding grounds, and Greenpeace feared for the future of the colony.

Additionally the French study showed that the breeding grounds of an estimated 3,100 pairs of Adélie penguins, 269 pairs of snow petrels, 291 pairs of Cape pigeons, 270 pairs of Wilson's petrels and 9 pairs of Antarctic skuas would be destroyed.

And of course, the deep suspicion between the French and Greenpeace caused by their chequered history could not be ignored. Greenpeace had really been born out of an encounter in the Pacific between the father figure of the organisation, David McTaggart, and the French in June 1972. He had sailed his yacht, the *Vega*, with two companions right to Moruroa Atoll to protest about the continued use of the Pacific for atmospheric nuclear tests. Protests from all over the world had failed to stop the tests. McTaggart's yacht was rammed by a French minesweeper and towed for repairs to Moruroa before being escorted out of the area.

His example created enthusiastic support for the idea of 'direct action', and the following year a small flotilla went to Moruroa. McTaggart this time sailed right into the heart of the atoll just before detonation. On this occasion heavily armed French commandos boarded his ketch and beat up McTaggart. He was hit in the eye with a truncheon and his sight permanently damaged. The crew were strip-searched, but pictures of the attack were smuggled out of French territory by a woman crew member who hid the film in her vagina. The pictures were subsequently shown on television worldwide and had considerable effect on international opinion.

The next year the French abandoned atmospheric nuclear testing. The battle over Moruroa, now over the underground tests, has continued ever since, but elsewhere Greenpeace has had plenty of clashes with the French on other issues.

In 1982, during protests over shipments of plutonium, the French had used stun grenades as riot police stormed a Greenpeace ship in Cherbourg and arrested it and the crew. And in New Zealand in July 1985, at the dock where I had first boarded the *Gondwana*, the French secret service blew up the Greenpeace flagship, the *Rainbow Warrior*, while she was at anchor, killing Fernando Pereira, the expedition photographer. The scandal rocked the French government and caused the resignation of the French Defence Minister, but there was no expression of regret. The French government knew Greenpeace had intended to send their ship to Moruroa Atoll in another protest about underground nuclear tests. The French wanted to stop this, so they labelled the unarmed, nonviolent Greenpeace protesters as terrorists and subsequently promoted and decorated the saboteurs even while they were in detention.

Some of the crew on the *Gondwana* had been on the *Rainbow Warrior* the night it was blown up and narrowly escaped with their lives. They found it hard to believe much good of the French. It was against that background that we were sailing to Dumont d'Urville.

4

South to the Ice

ABOARD THE *GONDWANA* these past conflicts with the French were not discussed. One of the strange things about being on a Greenpeace ship is that there is little or no debate of the issues, past or present. It seemed to me that everyone knew exactly why they were on the voyage and therefore there was no point in discussing it. There was certainly no sense of impending danger. In the folder given to us which contained the itinerary there was plenty about the safe way to get in and out of helicopters, but no mention of how to deal with French paratroopers wielding truncheons.

All my journal entry for Friday 23 December shows is that we were beginning to get into the ship's routine:

A beautiful sunny day. This morning saw a school of about thirty dolphins heading towards the ship. They loped across the water, plunged into our bow wave, and then they were gone. At 1 pm we were the furthest north of the whole trip, going round the top of the North Island of New Zealand and then turning west for Tasmania. It is very hot, the sky is cloudless and most people are wearing shorts. According to the weather maps on the bridge there is an area of high pressure stretching right across the Tasman Sea; it could last the five days it takes us to get to Hobart.

On the board in the mess room the crew rosters have gone up for watches. The routine is four hours on, eight hours off, night and day. There are twenty-eight people on board altogether and so, excluding the three engineers, the two cooks and the captain, there are still more than enough to provide the four required for each watch. The three journalists on board – me, the Japanese Naoko Funahashi, and an American freelance, Mary-Ann Bendel – have been left off the list. As it happens, one of those on the rota, Dave Walley, the senior helicopter pilot, is away from the ship. He will be joining us in Hobart for the journey south. I have volunteered to do his 4 am to 8 am shift because I do not want to feel like a drone and maybe I will appreciate watching the sun coming up.

The general tidy-up of the ship continues during this good weather. The decks are being hosed down and scrubbed. It is important that we get everything cleaned up in time for Hobart because the visit includes an open day. It seems very important for Greenpeace to get the public relations right. Anyway we are carving our way through the Tasman at eleven knots. A good cruise so far.

Christmas Eve: Did my first 4 am to 8 am shift this morning. Watched the full moon sink in the west as the sun rose in the opposite sky. I felt slightly ill because there was a strong swell from some faraway and forgotten storm. When my shift finished I had breakfast and went back to bed to wake up in time for lunch.

On the rota list of crew jobs for the day I was down for cleaning the alleyways. This involved pushing the ship's vacuum cleaner up and down and trying to get all the muck out from between the stores, stacked up and roped securely wherever there was space in the corridors. Quite difficult humping the thing up and down the stairs in the swell, but I suppose I will get used to it.

Back on the bridge at 4 pm for my next watch, to find we are being followed by an albatross. These wonderful, graceful birds very rarely seem to flap their wings. They fly so close to the waves that they sometimes disappear from view behind a crest, only to pop up again unscathed and effortlessly climb out of danger on an unseen current of air.

When the weather forecast came in there was a cyclone and gale warning from Wellington weather station. The ship has very sophisticated equipment and a weather map is faxed to us down the telephone via satellite. The cyclone and the gale are both hundreds of miles off, but the fact that both are on the same map as us is not very cheering. We have a problem with the ship's water. It has gone a dirty brown colour and seems to be full of rust. Fortunately we have plenty of beer on board, and since it is Christmas Eve, even though it does not seem like it, we all have a drink. I am missing my family.

Christmas Day: Woken up at 3.45 am for the 4 am watch by Henk. Decided to take a seasickness pill before going on the bridge because of the swell, but it made me so sleepy I was practically asleep standing up and regretted it. It was a beautiful night with the moon showing almost full. Tuned into the Australian World Service and heard for the first time news of the Lockerbie jumbo crash and the theory of a bomb having been placed on board in Frankfurt and transferred to the plane at Heathrow. It all seems very far away and unreal.

The weather map came across showing the cyclone close to the North Island of New Zealand where we had been sailing two days ago. Across our part of the map, where the isobars were nice and wide apart, the forecaster had scrawled 'Merry Christmas'. At 7 am Bob Graham, who was in charge, signed me off saying it was such good weather that he did not need my help.

Awoke at 11 am to find cocktail snacks and a buffet lunch were being served in the lounge. Christmas lunch would be later when the maximum number of crew were available. As we sat about wondering what to do with ourselves, the shout went up that there were whales. We all went on the bridge and we could see several blowing. The water was so clear that even under the water it was possible to see the whole of one whale as we passed by. This was wonderful.

We opened our Christmas presents at about 4 pm. When I opened my presents from my family, the parcel also contained cards from friends and touching messages. There were chocolates, biscuits from the children, and family photographs. I felt very close to them, missed them terribly, and wished I could see them.

At Christmas lunch, there was a great deal of unpacking of parcels provided by the Greenpeace office. There were bottles of rum, brandy, boxes of biscuits, crackers and paper hats. Greenpeace sent me a fine New Zealand nature diary with a note about there being no excuse for missing deadlines. They have certainly worked very hard to make it like a big family party.

Christmas lunch arrived amid all the paper and boxes. The food was excellent. There was turkey and all the trimmings, plus an excellent ham. It was all very enjoyable but I became increasingly conscious of the sea getting up – I had a headache, which was very unusual for me – and decided it would be wise to slip off to bed. After an hour or two of sleep I felt much better and came down to find I was not the only one who had suffered. Only the hardy partygoers remained. The twelve-hour time difference between us and London meant Christmas Day was only just beginning at home. At 10 pm I rang my family to wish them well – strange talking to people across 12,000 miles. My parents were so excited at the technology I could hardly get any sense out of them, but they just seemed happy to hear my voice. Went back downstairs and had a final drink of schnapps with the diehards. Sea travel, rich food, drink and my stomach do not get on well together.

Boxing Day: This was certainly the most miserable Boxing Day I can *remember. The wind got up in the night. I had stopped taking the seasickness tablets, having come to the conclusion that they were causing the headache. The headache went, but the sickness seems here to stay. I had also stopped drinking water because of the rust in it. This is caused by a totally unsuspected problem to do with the fact that the Gondwana has two water tanks connected by a balancing pipe. During the ship's fourteen-year life it seems that only one of the tanks has ever been used. With a small crew, and comparatively short supply voyages, the second one was not needed. When we left Auckland, with double the crew that had sailed from Europe to New Zealand, the two-tank system was brought into use for the first time. It was not until we got out into the swell that it was discovered that the second tank was full of rust. The sea stirred it up and mixed it up in both tanks.*

Fortunately Greenpeace had a back-up system – apart from the beer supply: there was a very efficient water maker installed below decks. This was operated the whole time we were out on the open sea, and turned sea water into pure fresh water at the rate of about a ton a day.

Wednesday 28 December: By breakfast time we were approaching Hobart up the wide channel of the Derwent river that looked to me exactly like a Scottish loch. No wonder so many Scots had settled here. It was a beautiful sunny morning with no other shipping. We were slightly early, having arranged with the harbour master for a pilot boat at nine, so we dawdled up the channel. The pilot took us the last bit at a fine pace. In the harbour there were two men and a dog in a Zodiac inflatable, and a single canoe, waiting to greet us. It turned out they were the local Greenpeace supporters, who also possessed a van, and they stood ready to drive us about and look after us.

We had to wait a frustrating hour for the customs people to clear the ship before any of us could go ashore. On the quayside were a group of well-wishers and, more important from the Greenpeace point of view, two television crews. It was no coincidence that Greenpeace had chosen this time to visit Hobart. The Sydney to Hobart yacht race is one of the main sporting events of the Christmas holiday in Australia, and the press were out in force to cover the finish. Because of the terrible weather the yachts were at least a day late and the press corps was hanging around without a story to do. The Greenpeace arrival helped to fill the gap. On a quiet news day it was important enough to make the main bulletin. For Pete this kind of prime-time slot for Greenpeace was a vital part of the campaign – and justified the extra distance required in coming to Hobart.

These formalities over, there was a new round of loading to be done.

Meanwhile, with other members of the crew who had suffered from seasickness, I made an escape ashore, only to find the buildings swaying gently as I walked. I sat down in the middle of the town for a cup of tea. At last, having not eaten for two days, I began to feel hungry. We all agreed this was the moment to eat and began looking for a suitable place. We found a very English-style pub that did sausage, egg and chips. It was delicious.

Loading at the ship had stopped by the time we returned, and I went for a snooze. When I woke up, the ship was almost deserted. Phil Doherty, the quietly-spoken radio operator, and I decided to go for a walk and try and get beyond the town to the country. We had only a couple of days in Tasmania and we wanted to make the most of it. Phil was one of the four people Greenpeace had selected to overwinter at the base on the Ross Sea, and I was anxious to find out what had made him decide to spend a year of his life in Antarctica. We made our way from the shore through the suburbs and headed for the town park. The bush still seemed quite a long way off, so we settled for the park.

During the walk I gently interviewed Phil about his decision to spend a year in the Antarctic. He told me he had spent ten years working for the same employer in Auckland. It was something to do with the university, and he repaired and serviced all sorts of electrical machines, with a bit of biotechnology thrown in. He had also, in those years, done some studying and ultimately some teaching, and in his spare time built himself a house on Waiheke Island off Auckland. This was one of the still 'wild' places off the coast. Pat, the ship's cook, also came from there.

Phil said that after ten years in the same job he had felt he was in a rut, and he was looking for a way out of it when he had heard about the Greenpeace job. He had first put himself forward as base leader for the team. He said Pete had 'wisely' decided that he was not a leader and had offered him a job as an ordinary member of the party – which he was glad to accept. He clearly felt he was at a crossroads in his life: he was not advancing in his job, he was not married and he had no OE. This was a new term to me and meant overseas experience. It seemed that all young people in New Zealand who got anywhere went on the grand tour of Europe and the US to gain OE before coming back to New Zealand to settle down. A CV without OE, and most jobs were closed to you, he said.

It was a very pleasant walk, but at the end of it I was not sure I knew much more about what made Phil tick. Greenpeace people are hard to get to know. Although they never seemed to talk about it, they all felt very strongly about the way man was changing the environment for the worse. They all chose, at least for a period, an exciting but rootless and rough way of life with no prospect of long-term employment – and there was no money in it either. The days had gone when people worked for Greenpeace just for their keep, but the organisation was still not wealthy enough to pay commercial wages.

By the time we returned to the boat it was time to eat again. A man called Robert, who had come from the Sydney office to support us, took us to an extremely lively pub called the Doghouse where most of the rest of the crew were drinking jugs of ale. This Australian drinking custom involves buying a jug of beer and being given a glass for each member of the party. The jug is placed in the middle of the table and everyone helps themselves until it is time for a refill. A very simple system.

A Greenpeace party had been organised for later, on the other side of town, and some of us, guessing it would be a long night, went for a large Chinese meal in preparation. When we finally arrived at the party not many people were left, apart from members of the crew. There was some very loud music, and a lot of pent-up energy was being released on the dance floor. It was not long before tiredness caught up with me, and I walked down the hill to the dock. The town centre was deserted although it was only about midnight. Just as I neared the ship a police car came roaring round the corner and nearly ran me over. It turned round on the quay and stopped at the gangplank just as I reached it. The police were pleasant enough, but I did not think it was a courtesy call. The ship was in darkness, and I told them the crew were all asleep, although 'some of the lads' had gone for a drink. Quite so, they said. They began to relax, and we fell to discussing when we were sailing and where we were going. They told me they were very fond of England and were part of a pipe band which made regular visits to the Edinburgh tattoo. After ten minutes we parted the best of friends.

Sean was in bed reading quietly when I got to the cabin. He told me that a visit to Hobart casino had been a short one. The bouncers had taken one look at Pete and objected to his white shoes. A row ensued, but Sean managed to get everyone into a taxi and back to the ship before the police arrived.

The next day, 29 December, was open day on the ship. People started arriving when I was having breakfast around nine. Most of the crew had been up very early cleaning up in order to make the best possible impression and laying out Greenpeace T-shirts and other merchandise for the visitors. I did my bit showing families around.

That night was our last chance of dry land before the Antarctic. We were due to sail at 6 am to the bunkerage to refuel before the final exit. By the early evening the crew were again at the jugs of ale. The Doghouse pub was packed to the seams for a group called the Eureka Folk Band. With a flute, violin and penny whistle plus a variety of folk and rock instruments they were singing Irish songs and talking broad Aussie. It was a fascinating combination and an entertaining evening. They played until midnight, but the night was yet young. We managed to hitch a lift to the other side of town, where there was said to be late-night drinking. Steve Morgan the photographer and I went into a bar where a heavy rock band were playing. When my eyes got accustomed to the dim lights I noticed a number of men in kilts in another part of the bar. I peered at them through the gloom and realised that two of them were the policemen who had called at the ship on the previous night. Hobart is a small town.

We moved on and joined the others at the only other bar that seemed to be still open. By 2.30 am we had shouted ourselves hoarse trying to talk above the music and decided we could stand no more. Despite Pete's protests we decided to walk back to the ship. It appeared to be raining, although it was not, for we could see the stars. On the other hand, we were certain we were getting very wet. It turned out to be the Hobart irrigation system for trees and flower beds, which goes on automatically each night to keep everything green during the summer. It sobers you up trying to dodge the spray, and certainly speeds the drunks on their way home. We walked back to the boat along the waterfront. A television crew was still waiting there for the winner of the Sydney to Hobart yacht race to come in. The estimated time of arrival had slipped from before midnight to 3 am, and was now 4 am. It was later put back again, to 7 am. Such is journalism – all glamour, sitting on the waterfront all night, being irrigated by the town hall, waiting for two minutes of film for the next day's news.

At 6.30 next morning – only half an hour late – the ship sailed for the Hobart bunkerage, two miles upriver at a grim-looking oil terminal. I stayed in my bunk, not being needed. Some of the others who had to get up must have felt pretty rocky. I drifted back into sleep and did not get up until eight. We had to fill the ship right to the top with fuel and water for the journey south. Every last scrap of rubbish was removed, and everything else stowed and lashed down. After the previous night's jollity I was surprised to find I still had ten dollars left in my pocket and decided to blow it on chocolate, liquorice and peppermints. I got a lift to the local supermarket, which turned out to be brand new and sold everything, even having two bakeries on the premises. I walked back to the ship, taking a last long look at the greenery, which I knew I would miss. The gardens were very English.

Back at the ship there had been a disaster – a fuel spill. As the ship was being filled to the maximum there had been a blow back and fifty litres of fuel oil had spilled into the river. A mini oil slick was carried by the tide upriver and had been reported to the pollution inspectorate. Everyone was very distressed because it was against everything that Greenpeace stood for. Now Greenpeace was a polluter of the river – the worst kind of publicity as they set off to save the Antarctic. It made the lead item on the ABC news. By that time the fifty-litre spill had become 200 tonnes – so much for my fellow journalists. Personally I thought the incident so small as not to be worth reporting, but at the same time I wondered if I was losing my objectivity as I got to know these people.

The whole incident had cast Pete, and particularly Davey Edwards, the chief engineer, who blamed himself, into the deepest gloom. When we were finally ready to sail we were not allowed to do so because we would have had to go under the Tasman Bridge in the rush hour. This rule came about because an Indian tanker once rammed the bridge, just after it had been built, hitting one of the uprights and causing a piece of the roadway to collapse. Seventeen people had been killed, some of them in cars that had run off the edge. As a result ships were barred from going under the bridge during the rush hour – although from where I was standing the maximum number of cars I could see on the whole span of bridge and the motorway beyond was six. Some rush hour.

We were finally cleared for departure at 6 pm and went under the arch in fine style on a falling tide. When the pilot had finally

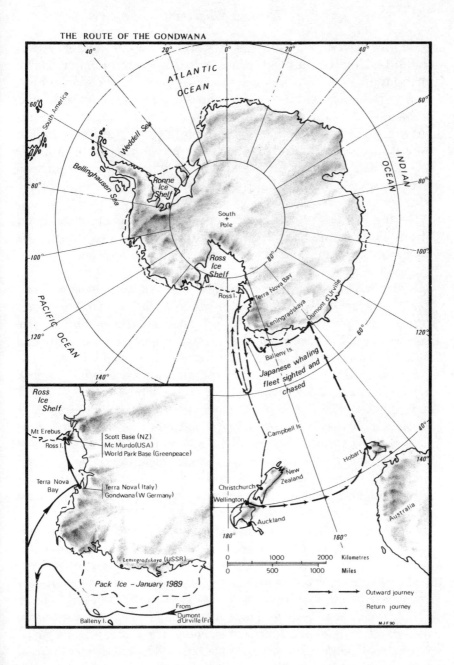

gone and waved us goodbye it was time for a late dinner. It was traditional on Greenpeace ships when a crew member had a birthday to make a cake and an occasion of it. Maggie McCaw, one of the deckhands, was thirty, and terribly shy and embarrassed by the whole thing. Up to now I had never seen her out of a boiler suit; she was always busy at the dirtiest jobs, hardly ever stopping work, and was virtually impossible to talk to. She was one of a minority of vegetarians on board and, it seemed, a Greenpeace veteran. I determined to interview her later in the trip.

During dinner, now that we were out at sea, everyone's mood lifted. The oil spill was forgotten; we were out on our own. The next stop was Antarctica.

Saturday 31 December: Woke in the night literally sliding round my bunk. The Southern Ocean swell never seems to let up, making sleep very difficult. The pitching was not too bad, but every few minutes the ship would roll enough to make me slide across the bunk and hit my head on the side. Eventually I picked up a book and read the night away.

On the bridge it looks very rough, at least by English Channel standards, although the sailors assure me it is just the ocean swell. I have decided to take a mild dose of seasickness tablets. The sea is coming on to the main deck and the foredeck as we plough our way south. Now we are away from ports for a long while, we pull in the tyres used as fenders round the ship. One of the lorry tyres which should have a hole in to let out the water is now full of sea water and it takes four of us a long battle to get it inboard. There is quite a danger of getting soaked because the sea washes right over the decks every few minutes.

Celebrations for New Year's Eve are subdued, partly because so many people are suffering from seasickness or dozy from taking too many tablets to prevent it. The other problem is that the buffeting of the sea makes it necessary to hang on all the time and so moving around is an effort. The can of beer I chose to celebrate with kept sliding up and down the table. By 12.30 am I was ready for bed. Quite a few people had decided not to move at all and planned to sleep in the lounge. The lounge is roughly in the centre of the ship, low down on the main deck, so the ship's roll is at a minimum. It is therefore more comfortable than bunks on the upper deck, or forward, but all the best spots were occupied by the time I decided to go to sleep, so I retired to my own cabin.

On New Year's Day I decided it was time to try and file a 'colour' piece to *The Guardian* about life on board, taking in the festive season. It was a struggle typing, even with my chair chained to the floor. I had to hang on to the furniture to prevent myself toppling over. Then the keyboard kept sliding about until I anchored it with a rubber mat. Another problem was getting the article back to London. The ship had the most modern equipment for all forms of communication, and in theory the ship's computer could be programmed to file direct into *The Guardian*'s computer in Farringdon Road in London so that, when the news editor switched on his desk-top screen in the morning, there would be my story waiting. But first a large number of numbers had to be fed into the machine at my end. The first two were to connect to the telephone, the next three were for the satellite, then there were two more for the Singapore station, three for the London land line and the last seven for *The Guardian*. Also there had to be the correct size gaps in between connections so that the chain of computers involved could adjust themselves to speak to each other. The gaps had to be the right length – if they were too long the computers lost interest and automatically cut off. Computer time is money.

Finally, tired, and battered by the sea, having tried every combination of gaps we could think of several times, I gave up and retyped the whole article into the telex machine. This was very much the second-best option because it was much slower to transmit and therefore much more expensive. At US $10 a minute for satellite time, this is not a minor problem.

We sent the copy finally, but like all reporters I am never happy until a human voice at the other end confirms receipt. But with the eleven hours' time difference it was the middle of the night in England and I had to wait several hours for someone to get in. And when they did, Pat Blackett, the news desk secretary, told me the copy had not arrived. I had no alternative but to send it again – at the cost of another $120. I waited a few minutes, and once again the transmission seemed to have gone astray.

With three months to go on the voyage this was not a happy start, but I could not give up – the problem had to be cracked. I fell back on the ship's third option, the fax, and Pat Blackett, sensing my anguish, said she would stand by the machine and coax it across the 12,000 miles. She rang a few minutes later: my piece was there, it was legible. By now it was 1 am *Gondwana* time and I was able to go to bed happy, knowing that at least some form of communication worked.

Monday 2 January 1989: Because of the swell the showers outside the cabins on our deck have been put out of commission. Every time someone has a shower and the ship rolls, the water does not go down the plug hole and overflows into the corridor. The lips on the showers have not been built high enough. But by taking the drain covers off we relieve the problem and decide we can risk quick showers while keeping an eye on the build-up of a tidal wave.

On the bridge Arne Sørensen, the Danish captain, gives me a geography lesson. He is a quiet, unassuming man who is said to be the Antarctic's most experienced captain, having spent seven successive seasons in these treacherous waters. He tells me that the sea temperatures have dropped five degrees Centigrade in four hours. This means we are nearing the Antarctic convergence where the cold waters from the icecap meet the warm waters of the Pacific. We are 700 miles from Tasmania and roughly halfway to the Antarctic continent. The air temperature is also dropping dramatically. For the first time, standing on the bridge wing, you can see your breath. Going outside now requires warm clothing. There are literally hundreds of birds in sight the whole time in this area. It appears that the Antarctic waters, despite the temperature, are full of fish, shrimps and plankton. The birds come from both north and south to reap this harvest, even though they have had to travel hundreds of miles from the nearest shelter.

We have now entered the northern limit of the icebergs, and there must be two lookouts at all times night and day. The danger is not the big icebergs – they show up on the radar miles before the ship reaches them – but the growlers. These are old, melted, nearly spent icebergs that have been rolling round the sea for as much as five years. After years at sea they are as hard as steel and translucent rather than white. They are so heavy that they barely show above the surface, so often the only sign of them is the waves breaking over them, as if over a reef. It is the lookout's job to spot the growlers. Hitting them at the eleven knots we are travelling would damage the ship badly, even an ice-strengthened vessel like ours. Arne says the main danger here is of hitting one at night: further south in the twenty-four-hour daylight we should always be able to spot them in time. Last night there was an hour of twilight between 11 pm and midnight, and about three hours before the light began to come back again. The night will be even shorter tonight.

Down in the mess there is a sweepstake on what latitude we will see our first iceberg; the prize is a ride in one of the ship's helicopters. The weather

*forecast is freshening winds and moderate seas. I thought they were fresh
and moderate enough already.*

*Tuesday 3 January: Learned enough about ice and icebergs to write and
file a piece for 'Young Guardian'. It took an hour to write and five hours
to send, not a happy arrangement, but at least this time I managed to get
it across by computer. Perhaps there is hope for the system. Rang the page
editor, Melanie McFadden, to check it had arrived, and she said it had
come twice. Needless to say, she had been too busy to read it.*

*Pete Wilkinson feels the moment has come to reopen communications
with the French. Greenpeace had formally notified the French Department
of Territoires d'Outre-mer after the* Gondwana *left Auckland in
December. Pete has the Dumont d'Urville telex number and sends the base
commander a message to say we are coming and would like a meeting. It
is a rather curious situation, in that the French cannot refuse our visit
since the Antarctic is open to everyone. Pete says the crew of the*
Gondwana *would like to express the Greenpeace organisation's dismay
at the building of the airstrip. He also informs the commander that the
crew are going to stage a nonviolent demonstration on the airstrip.*

*As Pete sends this off I wonder what the French reaction will be. They
must have known even before December's formal notification that we are
coming, so they have had plenty of time to make plans for our arrival –
but what can they do? Armed military personnel are not allowed in the
Antarctic under the treaty, they can only act as logistical support to civilian
expeditions. French police, on the other hand, would have no jurisdiction.
So how can they deal with Greenpeace? Do the French care about public
opinion? We shall have to wait and see.*

*We are now only forty-eight hours away from the continent and well
into the iceberg zone. It is now really cold out on deck, but as yet no sign
of ice.*

As I have mentioned before, the Greenpeace crew are a varied,
multinational bunch who have one thing in common: they are
very difficult to get talking about themselves. On previous
voyages with the organisation I had always worked alongside the
crew, endured hardships and shared triumphs, but left the ships
knowing little about the people who ran them, or what made
Greenpeace people tick. All I really knew was that some of the
crew had worked for Greenpeace on and off for years, being paid
so little that in between voyages they had worked at shore jobs to
make enough to join the next expedition. These foot soldiers for

the environment prided themselves on nonviolent
demonstrations they called 'direct action'. This meant using their
bodies as human shields, or targets, and organising the press so
the issue which prompted their action got into the public eye. In
our world, where voters' views do sometimes have to be
considered by people in power, these tactics seem to be as
effective for Greenpeace as the sword was for the Vikings.

I lay in my bunk contemplating how I was going to get the crew
to talk about themselves. Since ordinary chatting did not seem to
work, I decided I would have to try a more straightforward
technique. Greenpeace crew members are schooled into believing
that they must cooperate with journalists, because publicity is
good for the organisation, so I decided I would try the formal
approach.

Paul Bogart, a slow-talking but quick-witted American from the
East Coast, was the second-in-command on board and the obvious
person to start with, since I already knew Pete Wilkinson quite
well. I decided a formal interview with Paul was the right way to
start and he agreed – so I began with basics. Paul was from
Philadelphia, went to a Catholic school, was one of six children,
with three elder sisters and two younger brothers. His father
worked as a project manager for a construction company, and his
mother was a primary school teacher. So far so good.

He did political science at college, and this led him to join the
anti-nuclear movement, and then to move on to other
environmental causes. After college he did a year in the
construction industry but decided not to follow in his father's
footsteps. He moved to Washington, where he got a job in the
psychiatric wing of the National Children's Hospital. He had
some previous experience of child care, having taken similar work
during a year off college. He was with four- to thirteen-year-old
kids who were hyperactive, psychotic, had been physically or
sexually abused, or sometimes a combination of more than one
of these. He also worked with the parents of patients. Three years
later he offered his services to Greenpeace, who declined him
paid employment but said he could use his spare time to work for
them for nothing. He carried on at the hospital for another year,
spending his leisure as an unpaid toxics campaigner for
Greenpeace, principally trying to prevent the incineration of
dangerous wastes in ships off the East Coast of the United States,
a practice subsequently banned on health grounds.

One day another campaigner, due to participate in an action in Paul's home town of Philadelphia, dropped out and Paul grabbed the chance to take his place. The action involved breaking into a yard where toxic wastes were stored, in order to draw attention to the dangers they posed to people living in the area. Official reaction was angry, and he spent two days in jail before he was bailed. There were three attempts to prosecute before the toxics company backed off and dropped the charges. But Paul did not stop there, and he found himself in prison twice more as the companies fought back. I asked him whether having a criminal record worried him. He laughed it off: 'I decided a long time ago not to run for the Senate, so I do not have to worry about a criminal record.'

Despite the fact that he must by then have gained considerable street credibility in Greenpeace, Paul was still not offered a job, so 'in sadness' he decided to leave and find another outlet for his energies. Almost immediately he was telephoned by Kelly Rigg, then one of the US Greenpeace directors. He was asked over the telephone to become a US Antarctic campaigner. 'I knew nothing about the Antarctic except vaguely where it was, but I went to see her anyway and took it.' Paul said the new job proved much harder than toxics, or stopping radioactive waste dumping. There were no horror pictures to peddle, there was no instant support from people who were suffering dumping in their back yard. It was preventative work and education, trying to convince people of what would happen if they did not wake up and stop the destruction before it was too late. And this trip to the Antarctic he felt was a reward for all the groundwork he had done.

The interview was drifting away from Paul the person. How did his personal life fit into all this? I asked. He admitted that a private life and the Antarctic campaign were impossible to fit together. He had a girlfriend, Anne, who had formerly been with Greenpeace, so she understood the life and had been very supportive. Even so, this campaign meant spending six months a year away from home. He did not believe relationships could stand that sort of strain.

One thing very precious to him was his parents' support. He came from a close-knit Italian immigrant family where honour and principle were very important. His parents were 'very proud of him', and his father, who had little knowledge of the environment before his son joined Greenpeace, now worked for the toxics campaign. The plant which had led to Paul's first arrest was in the poor neighbourhood where his father grew up, and Greenpeace's defence of the district and the people who lived in it had led his father to give a tenth of his annual income to Greenpeace.

I talked to Paul about the organisation's tactics and suggested that he and the crew all had anarchistic tendencies. He firmly rejected that idea. The organisation was made up of people who simply looked at the establishment critically and questioned what it was doing. They then set out to alter what they thought was wrong, not shrinking from unorthodox tactics, even breaking the law, but always stopping short of violence and certainly never resorting to anarchy for anarchy's sake.

Paul was thirty, younger than most of the people on the ship. He was not sure what the future held. 'Let us see where this trip goes first,' he said. It was time for dinner; that was the end of the interview.

Wednesday 4 January: We have been sailing for six days due south from Hobart. We have not seen another ship, and now even the stately albatross has abandoned us as the temperature has steadily dropped to near freezing – a full twenty degrees Centigrade since we left Australia. There is a feeling that the great adventure is at last upon us.

The experienced sailors say we have been lucky – only moderate winds across the Roaring Forties and Screaming Fifties. It is almost unknown to make the crossing from Australia to the Antarctic without a gale, but we have done it. Not that the sea has been calm. This ocean is never still, and the great rollers that make our vessel seem tiny are still steep enough to make me slide about in my bunk at night. I have to wedge myself in to get some sleep. I have been promised all that will end when we get among the icebergs, but where are they? We have had an iceberg watch for two days now, and so far we have not seen one.

There was a crew meeting at 11 am. I only just made it. How can I contrive to be late for things when I live on the deck above?

The meeting started with a lecture about the heating. It seems that the old part of the ship is heated with radiators from a boiler which is getting overstretched. As the cold bites people keep turning the radiators up, and we are told this must stop. The boiler is vital to keep the engines warm when we are anchored: if the engines get too cold they will not start and we will be stuck.

Bruno Klausbruckner, an Austrian who is this year's leader of the overwintering team, gives us a lecture. He is an experienced mountaineer, has been to the Antarctic before, and gives us a briefing on the dos and don'ts of safety ashore. He tells us we should always carry spare gloves, a hat, a bar of chocolate as emergency rations and should never travel in parties of less than three. It all seems excessively cautious to me, but it is the people who have been to this continent before who seem most in awe of it. Perhaps we will soon find out why.

Lectures over, Pete Wilkinson tells us that according to the chart calculations we shall be at Dumont d'Urville at 5 pm tomorrow. This will give us plenty of time to find a safe anchorage and get rested before going ashore to meet the French commander at 10 am. Pete says it is important to explain to the French exactly why we are there, and to gather as much information about their real intentions as possible. He has drawn a large map of the area for the notice board.

Pete says once the meeting with the French is over, there will be twenty-four hours' preparation before the demonstrating begins. Weather permitting (and even in the Antarctic summer a blizzard can last for days), the plan is to erect a hut in the middle of the half-constructed runway. This will be occupied night and day by volunteers from the crew, and will prevent further work on the runway because it will stop the heavy machinery moving up and down.

There is a lot of tension in the air. People remember Moruroa and the fate of the **Rainbow Warrior**. *No one puts these fears into words at the meeting, but Pete emphasises more than once that the demonstration must be completely nonviolent. Details of the shore parties and who will do what have all been worked out in advance.*

After the meeting we have a telex from the French in reply to Pete's earlier announcement of the **Gondwana's** *arrival. It says in translation: 'We invite you to Dumont d'Urville base on 6th of Jan at 10.00 hours local time in our lounge building. During the course of our meeting we can settle by a common agreement, the conditions of your visit; give you explanations and technical documents on the construction of the airstrip; show you the protection measures for wildlife which we employ daily. We are ready to accept a peaceful demonstration if it is organised and planned as all demonstrations authorised at home* [en Métropole]. *We are also open to all technical questions which you may submit to us.' The message was signed by Jean François Houssin, Chef de District de Terre Adélie.*

This seems friendly enough.

We are now far enough south for it never to get completely dark, although the sun still drops below the horizon. At midnight there is a ripple of excitement through the ship because the bridge watch has spotted the first iceberg. There is not enough light for photographs, not on my camera anyway, but the iceberg is more spectacular than I could have believed. It is huge, maybe a hundred times the size of the ship. It looks like Beachy Head from half a mile away, with great caves and clefts worn away by the sea. It seems to give off a ghostly blue-green light from within. It is certainly lighter round the iceberg than anywhere else in the sea. It makes a big impression, and I feel compelled to watch it until it is out of sight. I go to bed happy that at last we have reached the Antarctic.

Thursday 5 January: It is pretty misty this morning. I am told we have reached a point on our journey when we are passing from the westerly current to the easterly. This takes the bridge some time to explain to me. The westerly current is caused by the wind roaring round and round the Antarctic continent in a series of low pressures. This is what causes all the rough seas and has given the Southern Ocean such a terrible reputation as there is no large land mass to break up the waves. Over the Antarctic continent itself it is a different story. A permanent high pressure over the icecap has an easterly airstream round the outside which in turn induces an easterly sea current.

On that morning we appeared to be crossing the bit of sea between the westerly and easterly currents, hence the stillness and mist. Very shortly after this conversation, and as if to confirm it, the wind began to blow from the east and it was noticeably colder. There was a blob on the radar which I was assured was another iceberg. When we got about a mile away it loomed out of the mist like a grey ghost. The ice these huge ice sculptures are made of is thousands of years old. It was formed from hundreds of years of snowfall which gradually compressed into the Antarctic ice sheet. Then eventually, as part of a glacier or from the sheer weight of ice further inland, the ice is pushed to the edge of the continent and snaps off. Icebergs last for five years or more, gradually melting, sometimes splitting, all the time slowly fading away. All day I was up and down to the bridge to view the icebergs and spot for growlers. As the icebergs became more numerous it was necessary to steer round them.

We were getting close to the coast now, and according to the charts were heading straight for the French base. Eventually it was possible to see a line on the horizon through the gradually thinning mist, but with so many icebergs around it was difficult to be sure it was really the continent.

Quite suddenly we came out of the mist, the sun was out and the air crystal clear. Icebergs were dotted all over the sea, shining white in the sun, and the Antarctic continent was a clear line right across the horizon. At first we could see no sign of the French base, even though the bridge was confident it was straight ahead. Eventually a thin vertical line appeared which turned out to be its radio mast. Below that we could now make out a series of steel boxes that looked like cargo ship containers. They were the living quarters and laboratories of the French base. I realised for the first time that the sea was now perfectly calm. Whether this was the result of all the icebergs or the calmer easterly airstream I was not sure, but it certainly felt better. We were now considering where to anchor.

This turned out to be a difficult matter. Pete wanted to be within sight of the airstrip so we could see all the time what was going on. Arne, on the other hand, responsible as captain for the safety of the ship, wanted primarily to be in a position where the ship would be pushed out to deep water and not towards rocks if a sudden storm blew up.

As we got closer to the base it became clear that the airstrip was some distance from the main base and had its own set of buildings for the construction workers. We nosed towards it, pushing aside the smaller pieces of ice. We could see trucks, bulldozers and JCBs. Men were standing in hut doorways looking at us and not waving a welcome. After a great deal of moving up and down in front of the airstrip, checking the readings on the depth gauge, Arne was satisfied, and we let down the anchors. The crew relaxed. Only the anchor watch were on duty. The rest of us had dinner and a few beers. With the sea flat calm there was the prospect of a good night's sleep. Our camera team Tim and Sean spent a great deal of time testing all their equipment to make sure it was ready for tomorrow. I was glad that all I needed was a notebook and pencils – pencils because I had been warned that ballpoints and ink might freeze up. The evening was getting slightly riotous as crew members tried to drown the tension. I decided a flat still bed was more inviting and had my best sleep for a week.

5

Dust-up at Dumont d'Urville

FRIDAY 6 JANUARY: Up at 7 am to prepare for the boat ride inshore and the first meeting with the French. I am happy that at last something is really happening. Tim and Sean as ever are slow to move. Tim seems to have become the last person on the ship to go to bed and is usually the last to get up. As it turned out Tim was not the last of the shore party to move this morning, that fell to Pete Wilkinson. In any other organisation there would be trouble if the expedition leader chose the night before a big meeting to have a skinful, but in Greenpeace there is no censure.

As it happened I was glad of the extra time. It was a stunning morning. There was not a cloud in the sky and the sun was quite high. I could feel it burning my face even though the air was very cold, probably below freezing. It was not until I got on deck that I remembered warnings that the hole in the ozone layer might lead to skin burning, and the brightness to possible snow blindness. I had to go back to the cabin and put some cream on and get my goggles. The air and sea in Antarctica were crystal clear, one benefit of the unpolluted environment which the *Gondwana* was there to try to protect.

The current was carrying small icebergs quite close to the ship. Further out to sea bigger icebergs, as much as a mile long, appeared to be stationary, like islands. I took a turn round the deck, and a few minutes later the scene had changed, although again nothing seemed to be moving – a bit like looking at the hands of a clock. On most pieces of ice near the ship Adélie penguins stood and stared at us without any sign of fear. Coming towards the ship on a piece of drift ice was a large seal, which appeared to be asleep. It was not until the piece of ice actually bumped into the ship that the seal looked up in surprise, then slid into the sea. I had not worn my gloves for this turn on deck but had taken the camera, and learned for the first time just how cold fingers could get in a few minutes in these temperatures. I returned to my cabin and put an extra sweater under my padded jacket, then my hat, goggles, cream and gloves.

Pete was finally up, and we set off in the two inflatables twenty minutes later than planned for the 10 am meeting. The ship was anchored about half a mile away from two islands which he knew the French were blowing up to make the airstrip, close enough for them to read the protest banners the crew had erected overnight. We could see the French base on top of a hill behind the islands but had no idea how to reach it.

Before long we ran straight into some pack ice. We had all been warned that if we tipped into the water it was cold enough to kill us in three minutes. As we turned round to go back we were surrounded by Adélie penguins leaping in and out of the water like dolphins. They were named after the wife of Dumont d'Urville who discovered and laid claim to the French Territory. Fat little birds only about two feet high, on land they actually look like little old gentlemen, but in the water they are extremely fast and agile – presumably to avoid ending up in the food chain of either the leopard seal or the killer whale. The Adélies seemed to be playing with us and leaping out of the water to have a look. They were only two or three feet away from the boat.

We worked our way back past the ship to try and find another route to the French base. There was a helicopter carrying supplies strung underneath on a cable, and we aimed for where it appeared to have landed. As we rounded a headland we saw it was hovering while men unloaded the sling beneath it. Nearby there was a large workboat on a hoist, and a small inflatable, like ours, drawn up on the shore. We had found somewhere to land. We scrambled ashore as quickly as possible, since we thought we were already late. In fact we discovered we were operating in a different time zone from the French. We finally arrived on shore at 10.30 am our time, but the French thought it was 9.30 am, so we were thirty minutes early.

There were two boatloads of us. Pete Wilkinson and Paul Bogart, the campaign leaders, and Liz Carr, the Greenpeace scientist, were the official party. Pierrette Paroz, our helicopter pilot, who came from the French-speaking part of Switzerland, was to act as interpreter if necessary. Tim and Sean, the film crew, Naoko Funahashi, the Japanese freelance, Mary-Ann Bendel, very American, and me, represented the world's press.

The French workmen who had been unloading the helicopter pointed us up towards some buildings on the top of the hill. They showed no surprise at our arrival, no interest in us whatsoever. This struck me as very strange because by any standards our arrival must have been an event in their lives. The French base was several hundred miles from any other human outpost and received only one supply ship a season.

We trudged up a steep rocky path that appeared to have been hacked out by heavy machinery. As in the sea the penguins were everywhere, on the rocks, standing on the patches of snow, struggling across the path in front of us making squawking sounds. Slightly further up the hill on both sides of the track were the breeding colonies of the penguins where we could see black chicks being sheltered by their parents. The helicopter flew overhead with another load, and some of the penguins, which until then had seemed unafraid, ran about in panic. As soon as its shadow and noise had passed they continued on their way.

A few minutes later a man of about thirty-five, in glasses, with the look of a civil servant, came to greet us. He had a broad smile and introduced himself as Jean François Houssin, the chief executive of French territory in Antarctica. He led us up to the canteen headquarters of the base and we were ushered in and told to take off our outer clothing. After struggling with our clobber we all sat round a long table. The French did not speak English, so Pierrette was immediately called on and introduced herself as the interpreter. Pete delivered formal Greenpeace greetings in his limited French, but then resorted to his native tongue for a long statement explaining why the *Gondwana* was there.

He was blunt. Greenpeace had come to stop the building of the airstrip, he said. The French were destroying the nesting sites of thousands of birds. This was contrary to the Antarctic Treaty. The use of explosives to level the site was also contrary to the treaty. The French government had not informed other governments of the destruction they were causing or the extent of their activities as required by the treaty. Greenpeace had come to intervene on behalf of its 2.2 million members worldwide. Nothing could justify this destruction.

There followed a tortuous two-hour meeting, Greenpeace making accusations through their interpreter and the French giving long and voluble answers. Pete accused them of building the airstrip to get access to the Antarctic for mineral extraction.

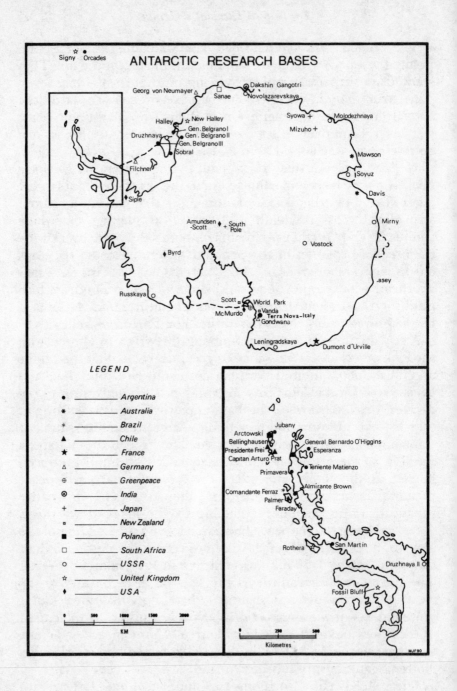

ANTARCTIC RESEARCH BASES

Signy ☆ Orcades ○

Georg von Neumayer △ □ Sanae ○ Dakshin Gangotri
Novolazarevskaya

Halley ☆ New Halley Syowa + ○ Molodezhnaya
Druzhnaya Gen. Belgrano I Mizuho +
Gen. Belgrano II
Gen. Belgrano III ✶ Mawson
Sobral ○ Soyuz
△ Filchner ✶ Davis

◆ Siple ○ Mirny

Amundsen ◆ + South
-Scott Pole ○ Vostock

◆ Byrd ..asey

Russkaya ○ Scott ○ World Park
McMurdo ◎ Vanda ■ Terra Nova - Italy
◆ Gondwana
Leningradskaya ○ ★ Dumont d'Urville

LEGEND

Symbol	Country
●	Argentina
✶	Australia
*	Brazil
▲	Chile
★	France
△	Germany
⊕	Greenpeace
◎	India
+	Japan
▫	New Zealand
■	Poland
□	South Africa
○	USSR
☆	United Kingdom
◆	USA

0 500 1000 1500 2000
KM

Jubany
Arctowski
Bellinghausen General Bernardo O'Higgins
Presidente Frei Esperanza
Capitan Arturo Prat
Primavera Teniente Matienzo
Comandante Ferraz Almirante Brown
Palmer
Faraday

Rothera San Martin
Druzhnaya II ○
Fossil Bluff

0 250 500
Kilometres

MJF90

International agreement did not yet permit such exploitation. M. Houssin said the purpose of the airstrip was to service the scientific base. There would be no mineral extraction.

At this point Michel Engler, the project manager for the airstrip, joined the proceedings. Here was a much tougher man, not a civil servant but an engineer. He announced that the French government had decided to build a new station, 620 miles inland from Dumont d'Urville. It would be called Dome C and was entirely for scientific purposes, studying the ozone layer and other atmospheric subjects. I chipped in, asking him why, if the airstrip was only for scientific purposes, a consortium of French manufacturing companies, some of them nationalised, backed the project. He gave a ten-minute answer in French. It boiled down to the fact that the French had no cold territories in the world outside the Antarctic and these businesses were supporting the project because they wanted to test their products in a cold and hostile environment. I found this hard to believe.

There was a great deal of argument about whether the nearby emperor penguin breeding colony would be affected. The penguins bred inshore from the airstrip. The French agreed that the penguins would have to cross the runway to feed. However, they claimed, it would now be easier for them because the islands in between which obstructed their path would have been flattened.

Liz Carr was not convinced, and said that the penguins, which breed in the winter in total darkness, would be disorientated. The colony might be badly affected.

The destruction of the Adélie penguin colonies by the explosions was regretted by the French – but they claimed it was necessary for the airstrip. They were trying to minimise the impact by replacing the fertile eggs with plastic ones and then taking the fertile eggs to other islands away from the runway and placing them under other birds in the hope that these would bring up two chicks. Their scientists, who were also at the meeting, conceded that they had no evidence yet that this was working.

After two hours of this it was clear that Pete wanted the meeting to end. He broke in to say that the French had originally set up the base at Dumont d'Urville to study the bird colonies but by building the airstrip they now seemed intent on destroying them. He repeated that Greenpeace would stop construction. M. Houssin was surprisingly mild about it all and shrugged his shoulders. Perhaps he realised Greenpeace had come to

demonstrate not negotiate: negotiation was for politicians if
pushed into it by the voting public.

It was a relief to get into the open air again. M. Houssin had
given the press permission to go anywhere on the base to gather
information. He was clearly aware of the value of good public
relations and was treating us carefully, inviting us to come and
see him at any time. My immediate need was to get back to the
ship and file a story. When I got halfway down to the boat I
realised I had left my life jacket behind, and had to toil all the
way back to the top of the hill to retrieve it. I felt really tired even
though it was only half a mile. It was my first experience of how
draining Antarctic conditions can be, even in good weather.

One boat had already left when I got down to the landing stage.
We took a leisurely ride back; the air and the sea were completely
still and only the penguins fishing for their staple diet, the
shrimp-like krill, broke the surface. Again the arrival of our boat
brought them leaping close to us. Ken Ballard, the first mate and
a hardened professional seaman, who was in charge of the boat,
surprised me when he said quietly: 'It's just like fairyland.'

On the way back to the ship a small iceberg, about fifty feet
across, was drifting in our path, but about a hundred yards away
it split in two and without warning began tumbling over in the
water. At first it did not seem dangerous and we stopped to watch
out of interest. Lumps of ice as big as our boat then came up from
the bottom of the berg as it rolled and began shooting four or
five feet above the surface then dropping back into the water. If
they had come up underneath us we would have capsized. In a
couple of minutes the broken ice spread over the water and all
was still again. We circled round it and went back to the ship.

Back on board, while the campaigners briefed a crew meeting,
I began bashing away on the ship's computer to file a story. When
I finally sent it the office were very encouraging – but they later
rang back and asked if I had a map of the base I could fax to
them. I patiently explained, not for the first time, that I had
already thought of that before leaving England and had de-
posited a folder of maps in a drawer in the news desk.

The following morning, Saturday 7 January, the film crew were
up at 7 am. They had to be on the first boat to the airstrip to film
the demonstration from the beginning. It was again a lovely
summer's day, but in accordance with the rules I carried my

survival bag with extra clothing and chocolate in case the weather turned. We had to keep the chocolate supply secret from Tim, who claimed to be addicted to it. He said he needed at least a bar a day to stop withdrawal symptoms.

When we arrived at the half-built airstrip, a wide flat finger of rubble sticking out into the sea, the trucks and diggers were working at full speed. We scrambled ashore and stood amid swirling dust as the lorries pounded past, ignoring us. The top of a large island had been partially blasted away, and mechanical diggers were piling up the rocks into dumper trucks. These were driving in continuous relays down to the end of the half-built runway and tipping the rock into the sea. The idea was to blast the tops off six islands and use the rubble to join them up, thus creating an airstrip long enough for Hercules aircraft to land on. In the way were the breeding colonies of 10,000 birds.

Waiting for a gap between the lorries we headed towards what appeared to be an empty bit of land where the airstrip was wider. To our amazement there was a group of about fifty penguins covered in dust sitting there. Many of them were guarding chicks. The trucks were rolling past only a few yards away, but the penguins were clearly not moving. I crept close to take some pictures and the penguins ignored me too. I later discovered that this area had once been a small island with a breeding colony on top. The top had been blasted away, but these penguins had come back and rebuilt their colony thirty feet below where it had once been. The French construction workers had taken pity on them and driven round them to give them a chance to rear their chicks.

By now the Greenpeace inflatables had gone back to the ship and returned with some crew members complete with banners. They stood where we had done at the edge of the runway and held them up: 'Hands off Antarctica', 'World Park Now', 'Non à la Piste', and – rather disconcertingly – 'Press Here'. Were we regarded as some kind of magic protection?

At first it was all very good-natured. Off-duty construction workers who were on the second shift came over to take pictures, and the lorry drivers continued their work. More of the ship's crew arrived, about twenty in all. At a signal they stood across the runway with a single heavy-duty cloth banner strung between them proclaiming the World Park. The lorries were halted, three of them trapped between the demonstrators and the sea.

The drivers sat in their cabs and watched, turning off their engines, perhaps in the belief that the demonstration would be over in a few minutes. I watched as the Greenpeace inflatables returned yet again from the *Gondwana*, this time carrying the prefabricated sections of a rounded Antarctic survival hut. Still the construction workers just stood and watched. Then Henk and the others unloaded the hut piece by piece on to the runway. Soon the construction workers realised that Greenpeace were erecting a building in the middle of their runway.

A man who must have been a foreman of some kind ran to the lorries and instructed them to drive forward. He clearly wanted them to run over the base of the hut which Henk was bolting together. This would have wrecked it. Seeing the danger, Paul Bogart and Ian Balmer, the radio operator, stood in front of the hut base as the trucks bore down on them. Despite the urging of the foreman the trucks stopped three feet away from the two men. From my observation post at the penguin colony, thirty yards from the line, it looked a lot closer.

Michel Engler, the site manager, whom we had met the previous day, emerged from the construction workers' accommodation block on the island and ordered all his men away. He was clearly angry, but he did nothing to prevent Greenpeace erecting their building. Henk had brought the generator and drill over from the ship and was attempting to drive stakes into the runway to anchor the hut, but the rock proved too hard. Instead rocks were rolled up and used as anchors to fix the steel guy ropes.

From the Greenpeace point of view everything had gone according to plan. Tim and Sean, who had not seen these green shock troops in action before, were impressed by the planning and the military precision. As had been my experience on previous voyages, there was more to the crew than first appearances suggested.

I wandered down the runway and looked at the trucks, now abandoned by their drivers. I was joined by dozens of penguins which came out of the sea and stood on the runway, some squawking and some rolling stones with their beaks, a sort of nest-building ritual. It looked as if they were reclaiming the construction site as their own. A couple of seals were playing in the water. Now the roar of the trucks had stopped and the dust had settled, the beauty of the place came flooding back, and I remembered Ken's remark about fairyland.

I took advantage of the absence of construction workers to walk up the hill which the French were in the process of demolishing. From the top of the hill I could see the complete line of the runway, with one small and two big islands as yet untouched in its path. In the clear air it was possible to see the thousands of penguins guarding their young and the skuas and Cape pigeons wheeling about. These islands were not due to be blown up until next season, so the colonies of all three birds had been left for one more year.

Around 2 pm, since nothing was happening and we were all hungry, relays of people were taken back to the ship, leaving some crew behind in touch with the bridge by radio. We sat in the lounge and debated what would happen next. Suddenly there was a message from the runway to say the French had asked them to move – and had warned them that if they refused they would be moved. The French wanted their vehicles back, they claimed, because they needed to work on them.

Pete went to the radio room to talk to M. Houssin at the main base. M. Houssin agreed that he wanted no violence and said he would meet Greenpeace the following day at 10 am to discuss the situation. At the same time the bridge received a second and more urgent call from the hut to say the construction workers were gathering. I did not realise at the time that the hut was out of sight of the main French base and M. Houssin would not be able to see what was happening.

The boats were already in the water, and together with the off-duty crew I had my Antarctic outer clothing on in two minutes. We raced across the narrow stretch of water to the hut, and the boat returned for the film crew and their gear.

Nothing seemed to have happened. Some of the French construction workers had arrived and seemed to be taking batteries out of the lorries and replacing them with new ones. It appeared to be a false alarm. But then, from the centre of the island, a giant caterpillar vehicle followed by a bulldozer was spotted heading towards us. The men who had been changing the batteries jumped into the trucks and started them up, revving the engines. At first I thought it was just an attempt at intimidation. But the caterpillar truck kept coming, with the bulldozer alongside. Together they swept slowly up the runway towards us. This is the point at which the luxury of being a journalist lets you stand on one side; on the other hand, the crew were now my friends and I feared for them. With the bulldozer a few feet away from the Greenpeace line, Werner Stachl, one of the deckhands, and at forty-eight surely too old for this sort of thing, threw himself on to the bulldozer blade. Pat King, the cook, joined him. Four others climbed on to the bucket of the caterpillar truck and hung there. Both vehicles kept coming. I thought someone would be killed.

I could only stand and watch. Suddenly about thirty construction workers, who had been hidden in the dust of the oncoming vehicles, rushed in and grabbed the protesters on the bulldozer and bucket, dragging them clear. Three Greenpeace crew dived into the hut and locked the door to prevent it being shifted. Werner, Pat, Henk, Bruno and the others, who had been dumped at the edge of the runway by the French, were back on their feet in an instant and threw themselves in front of the bulldozer to prevent it reaching the hut.

The lead truck drove forward. Henk and two others produced handcuffs and clamped themselves to the moving truck. It stopped and bolt cutters were brought up to dislodge them. They were again dragged away.

The air was now filled with choking dust, fumes and shouts of abuse in several languages. The trucks eased forward, only to be stopped until Greenpeace crew were again dragged aside. At one point Henk's arm was trapped under a lorry's front wheel and it had to back off for him to be pulled away. I expected the arm to be broken, but it was his thick clothing that had been caught and undeterred he threw himself back into the fray. Greenpeace was losing ground as the superior numbers of the French told. The bulldozer backed off and first one lorry and then the rest pushed through the gap it had made.

The French, having freed their trucks, fell back, and Greenpeace were left still in possession of their hut, now covered in a cloud of dust. Tempers were very frayed, and a rapid check was made to see that everyone was present and unhurt. Clothes were ripped and some faces were cut, but the heavy clothing and gloves that everyone wore had protected them from serious injury. The hut had been pushed on one side by the lorries to make enough space to get past and one of the panels was cracked. Pete, who believed he had been double-crossed by M. Houssin, with his talk of a meeting the next day, got straight into a boat with Paul Bogart to go to the base and demand an explanation.

I realised I was pretty shaken. With tons of heavy equipment on the move while people threw themselves in the way it was astonishing no one had been severely hurt. There was no hospital within a thousand miles. I realised for the first time what had been missing. There were no policemen in Antarctica. It was a land without law.

In a short time Pete and Paul returned, and to my surprise they brought M. Houssin with them. I asked the French commander for an explanation of the violence. He jumped out of the boat saying that first he would speak to his men, and walked quickly away. Paul explained to me meanwhile that they had met him running down the path towards them as they went up towards his office. He said he had known nothing about the action to free the trucks and had given instructions that nothing was to happen until after the meeting the following day. A plot had been hatched by the men on the second construction shift without his knowledge or consent.

M. Houssin was away about half an hour. When he came back I challenged him again. He said he had been shown a video taken by one of his own men. The whole thing had been very violent, and he said he was shocked. He had not sanctioned the move against Greenpeace, and although the men were due to work until midnight, he had ordered them to return to their quarters to cool off.

I asked about the project manager. I had seen M. Engler ordering the bulldozer forward into the demonstrators and urging the construction workers to clear a path for the trucks. Was disciplinary action to be taken against him? M. Houssin said it was a matter for Paris. Nothing could happen now until the whole matter was referred to Paris. He then said he wanted to come back to the Greenpeace ship. He assured us nothing more would happen to the hut. Six crew members had sleeping bags and elected to stay the night – it was, after all, a survival hut.

It took considerable courage for M. Houssin to face the crew in the lounge of the *Gondwana*. He explained again that the attack was against his wishes. I believed him, but many of the crew clearly did not. It was a painful half-hour. M. Houssin said no further action would be taken before he had heard from Paris, and we would then be informed. The crew said they had little faith in Paris. I felt sorry for M. Houssin, caught between Greenpeace, Paris and his construction workers. He said he would talk to me again tomorrow; perhaps he felt I might put his side of the case.

On Sunday 8 January, after the ructions of the day before, Pete had to spend most of the day on the ship dealing with calls from all over the world. I had to write a long piece and decided to stay aboard too, popping up to the bridge from time to time to see if there was any movement on the shore. The French were leaving the hut and its occupants alone as M. Houssin had promised, but they had started work again with the freed machinery at the other end of the runway. According to our map this northern end of the runway was more or less complete: what they really wanted was to make progress at the southern end, where the hut blocked the way. Perhaps they were just keeping the construction crews occupied.

Although it seemed to me that Greenpeace had already achieved a great deal, on the *Gondwana* there was general unease that the French were working at all. After the pressure of press calls had died down, therefore, Pete and the rest of the crew decided on another action. This time they were going to place themselves under the lorries as they tipped the stone out into the sea at the other end of the runway. The idea was to force the French to stop tipping, but the protesters risked getting crushed to death. The film crew, Steve Morgan and I went in one boat with Lilian Hansen, the nurse, and Maggie McCaw driving, while the people to be involved in the action travelled in the other boat. The plan was for us to stay in our inflatable about twenty yards offshore so the film crew could get shots of the lorries backing up to dump their loads. Meanwhile, the protesters, carrying banners, stood between the lorries and the sea.

As the back of the first lorry lifted up to unload its ten tons of rock, Henk was underneath and stood firm. The rocks were poised ready to crash down on top of him – surely he would be killed. But just as they dropped he was dragged away by other crew members. There was only a split second in it. It was terribly dangerous. I wanted to get ashore and tell them all to stop. On the next load Henk repeated his action, and by now the French had brought up workers to drag him away. I found this very hard to take. I was fond of Henk, and I was watching him deliberately getting close enough to each crashing load to be killed – about once every minute. One tiny mistake and he would be crushed under tons of rock. Tim was even more upset than me and kept repeating, 'This is madness.'

The French gradually began to lose their nerve. They started dumping the rocks further and further away from the edge. Because of this we could see less of what was going on, but just as we were deciding to land to get a better view, an urgent message came through on the radio to say that the hut at the other end of the runway was under attack. We put on full power and within a minute were whipping through the water to reach them. My heart was in my mouth as we narrowly missed some substantial pieces of pack ice floating by.

When we arrived, a group of French construction workers were close to the hut, and it was clear there was a mad scramble going on. There were people wrestling amid a cloud of dust. Michel Engler was again directing operations and was driving a digger which had been fastened by a chain to the hut. He was attempting to drive backwards up the runway towing the hut. At the same time the Greenpeace people were trying to throw themselves into the hut to weigh it down. The chain then broke, whipping through the air but fortunately missing everyone. The French began trying to refix it. We stayed in the boat filming. Unable to tie the broken chain, the French retreated. The hut had been dragged thirty yards. The panel that had been damaged in the rumpus the previous day was now broken off completely. Phil Doherty, who had been inside the hut, had been dragged through the damaged panel by the construction workers. There was a great deal of shouting at the retreating French, and gestures that transcended the language barrier. I was very wound up. I felt it was all getting out of hand. After a few minutes of aimless pacing up and down I spied Michel Engler sitting behind a rock, out of sight of the Greenpeace crew. Tim was nearby and we went to interview him.

I realised how angry I was because I wanted to shout at him. Instead I told him his behaviour was unforgivable. He shrugged and said he thought the Greenpeace people were trying deliberately to have an accident. I asked him if he meant commit suicide, and he said yes. I asked him if he was going to proceed with the building of the airstrip whatever happened, and he said yes. He was blaming Greenpeace for the level of violence. I told him that as far as I was concerned he was to blame, and that was what I would be telling the world through my newspaper.

After my conversation with M. Engler I was even more

unhappy about the situation. M. Houssin had seemed to me a
reasonable man, and I decided to go and see him. He had, after
all, invited me the previous day, and it was important from the
story's point of view to know if Paris was aware of the level of
violence and if they had sanctioned it. The memory of *Rainbow
Warrior* and the lengths the French had been prepared to go on
that occasion was in my mind. The camera crew decided they also
wanted to come to the meeting. Then I realised I would need to
go back to the *Gondwana* to collect Pierrette so that I could
communicate with M. Houssin.

Sean had been filming the crew pushing the hut back to its
original position. The French had used big wire cutters to break
the steel guys which were intended to anchor the hut down, but
they were still just long enough to serve their purpose. The panel
which had been smashed had a large piece missing. A search had
failed to find it, so presumably the French had carried it off.
Henk was trying to work out how to make the hut weatherproof
so that it could continue to be occupied. The hut had originally
been intended for use as a survival hut for Greenpeace field
expeditions at their base on the Ross Sea. It would now need
extensive repairs. Members of the crew walked up and down the
runway tidying away all the small bits of fibreglass and other litter,
including a torn lifejacket left over from the earlier struggles.

When I got back to the ship I saw Paul Bogart and told him I
believed things had gone too far. Then we returned, with
Pierrette, to the French base. M. Houssin met us at the top of the
hill as before. We sat round the table as at the first meeting, but
this time Sean could not film. His camera had fogged up because
of the extremes of temperature outside and inside the hut. I had
a long discussion with M. Houssin. I was calmer now and more
rational. I described my feelings about the French actions. He was
defensive. Standing at the top of his base about half a mile from
the runway, he had watched the Greenpeace crew throwing
themselves under the lorries that morning. He said people doing
that were not involved in peaceful protest. We moved on to what
would happen next. He said that 'minute by minute' he was
sending reports and pictures to France. This answered one of my
uncertainties; at least Paris knew what was going on. I told him
that if anyone was killed it would be at least partly his
responsibility. In the absence of a police force it was up to him to
keep the peace. For me it was a good interview. I was able to get

all the anger and frustration out of my system and load it on to poor M. Houssin, and journalistically I had established the chain of command.

In his turn he made me his intermediary by getting me to take a series of messages back to the ship. First he wanted a cooling-off period for both sides. Then he said: 'If Greenpeace is reasonable, then I am sure Paris will be reasonable.' As a gesture of his sincerity he would order that the Greenpeace hut at the northern end of the runway should be left alone. We shook hands and he then left to go and talk to Paris. It was now late in the evening, and the time difference meant it would be morning in Europe.

A French cameraman who had attended the meeting then offered to buy us a beer. There was a bar next to the meeting room, a sort of social centre for the scientists. It turned out that the cameraman was from *Paris Match* and, by coincidence, had been visiting the French base on assignment when the Greenpeace ship arrived. For him it must have been a real bonus professionally. He clearly regretted what had happened, and we all parted on good terms.

Pete and Paul Bogart were waiting up for us in the *Gondwana*'s lounge: we told them about the interviews and M. Houssin's comments. We decided to play Tim's tapes of the conversations in the morning to hear again precisely what M. Engler and M. Houssin had to say.

Pete was up early next morning and was already ashore having a meeting with the party at the hut as I ate my breakfast. The hut had been untroubled during the night. The crew kept a constant watch, but there were no stirrings from the French construction camp. Work had not resumed at the other end of the runway either. From the bridge it was possible to see the funnel of a French supply vessel that had arrived in the night. Earlier Pete had talked to a group of people who had been involved in yesterday's action, and between them they decided the level of violence was too great. Greenpeace would confine themselves to actions at the hut at the southern end of the airstrip and only offer passive resistance if the French again tried to dislodge them. This was good news.

I started writing a piece to catch up on yesterday's events and rang New Zealand, to find that there were reports on the news wires that a Boeing 737 going from Heathrow to Belfast had come down near the M1: thirty-five dead at the latest count and one hundred survivors. As a journalist I knew this meant that my story would come way down the news list at home.

Half way through filing I was told that M. Houssin had been on the telephone to Pete asking for a meeting. The French were having a 'maintenance day' (which meant not working on the airstrip) to allow a cooling-off period. Pete went straight to the meeting, so I filed a note at the end of my copy saying there might be more to come.

After some time Pete returned and there was a long meeting, held on the bridge so that everyone on the ship could take part, including those on anchor watch. In Greenpeace everyone in the crew has a right to a say, and a decision is reached based on a consensus. Votes are rarely if ever taken, and outsiders like me are encouraged to give a view. This was a critical meeting because it appeared that Paris had taken charge and seemed to be trying to resolve the situation. Pete had already been over to the hut and reported to the shore party on his meeting with M. Houssin.

Apparently Claude Corbier, senior administrator of Terres Australes et Antarctiques Françaises, had telexed to the effect that Greenpeace could not stay on the airstrip indefinitely, but he did not want to get back into the situation of trying to remove them by force. Therefore the hut crew would not be molested provided Greenpeace gave a satisfactory date by which they would dismantle the hut and move on. Pete was for staying until the 17th, another eight days. The people in the hut thought that too long and wanted to strike camp on the 15th. I argued strongly that the French would not tolerate too long a stay. Arne, with his captain's responsibility for the safety of the crew, was strongly against any more violence. While we still had the high moral ground, Greenpeace should be seen to be reasonable, he said. Eventually a decision was reached to tell the French we would remain in the hut until the 15th and then leave Dumont d'Urville altogether − two days before we originally planned to do so, according to the itinerary for the voyage published in New Zealand, which the French must have seen. Pete thought this concession would persuade the French to put up with Greenpeace interference until then.

Later the office told me my dispatch would be going inside because of the air crash, but my piece that morning was across the back page, with a six-column picture. This was very cheering both for me and for Steve Morgan, who was wondering whether his stuff was getting through.

Tuesday 10 January: I take my time having a shower and a good rest, and get to breakfast to find M. Houssin has already telephoned to say he has passed our message on to Paris. Their initial reaction was not favourable, but so far he has had no official reply. In the meantime, he said, he would respect the agreement not to attack the hut. Work would have to start again at the northern end of the airstrip, but that would not interfere with the Greenpeace protest.

I learn from the bridge that last night four Frenchmen approached the hut with great caution holding a gift of a bottle of whisky. The Greenpeace crew of eight had been provided with some ship's wine to keep out the cold. International relations improved, and Pat King, the ship's cook, who told me about it on the radio, said considering they were all jammed in a survival hut it was quite a party. Since I have been feeling a bit restless I decided to go ashore and visit the people in the front line.

The hut has been repaired with tarpaulin and tape and the occupants hope it is weatherproof. Most of the crew are sitting down or lying asleep in the sun. Most of them seem to have streaming colds. The temperature is about −5°C, but does not seem so because the sun is out and the air is still. According to the ship's Admiralty notes about climate we are supposed to get blizzards twenty-four days out of thirty in January, so we have used up our quota of good weather and been very lucky.

It is good to be able to walk up and down and observe the penguins. They look very forlorn. The birds are covered in dust. It amazes me that they stick to the task of bringing up their young in such circumstances. I walk further down the runway to where the French have started work again. The giant machines that were in use against Greenpeace a few days ago are carving out the side of the hillside where the rock has been blasted to loosen it. They are fascinating to watch, like great dinosaurs.

Back at the ship we still have not had a formal reply from the French. I check with the office that my earlier copy was OK. Everyone is very pleased and are all looking forward to the next instalment. This cheers me up and I have a celebration beer before retiring. This climate certainly tires me out.

Wednesday 11 January: Woke up with a sore throat − obviously I have got the ship's cold. Better news is that there is a telex from the French official in Paris, Claude Corbier, via Dumont d'Urville, making an offer.

If Greenpeace move off the runway on the 13th, two days earlier than the crew suggested, then the French will guarantee not to attack them. As a carrot the French also offer to place the whole of the base open to Greenpeace so their scientists can be visited at work. We have a meeting on the bridge. Again, for the purposes of this meeting, I was treated as a member of the crew. It is rather a strange position for a journalist to be in, but I believe the idea is not to compromise my position but to understand my point of view. At the last meeting I disagreed with Pete and afterwards he was irritated with me for interfering. On this occasion, because I agreed, it was OK. Perhaps it would have made no difference to his attitude had I been any other member of the crew.

In this case Pete is in favour of accepting the French offer because otherwise we risk further violence. He says that the crew has got the issue of the Dumont d'Urville airstrip with its associated destruction of the penguin nests on the front pages – now it is time to concentrate on wider environmental issues. At this point I put my oar in and say we should accept. Greenpeace has scored a victory. It is the first time that the French have ever recognised Greenpeace as a legitimate organisation. From the journalistic point of view this is a new angle which I can report.

Afterwards people said it was my speech which swung the meeting, but I am a little alarmed by this, still a little unsure about how involved I am getting in this whole venture. Looking on the bright side, it certainly makes a good story – a victory for Greenpeace. First Pete and Paul Bogart have to go ashore and talk to the people still occupying the hut. They are thought to be a little more hardline than the people on the ship. Working with two meetings it is that much harder to get a consensus, but eventually, after much reluctance, they agree to the same package.

While I have been waiting I have been doing my washing. It is amazing how it piles up. The dryer has bust: someone has turned it up to fifty minutes and the dial has stuck, frazzling their clothes to death.

Today is also my day for doing the dishes. This is undoubtedly the worst job on the ship. Some people are very good about washing, drying and putting away their own utensils, but others just dump them in the sink. With thirty people on board that is a lot of stuff. The worst bit is the pots and pans. All the leftovers have to be put away in the fridge or stored elsewhere. There is never enough room. We try to waste as little as possible.

Thusday 12 January: This was a quiet day. I decided that it was time I rediscovered reading and playing chess. Nearly everyone on the ship has a streaming cold now and I am no exception. I was feeling quite sorry for myself. Tim beat me at chess, which does not improve things.

The weather changed for the worse last night and it began to snow. I was glad to be on the ship and not on the runway. Everything was covered in snow when I woke up, but it was only a thin cover. By afternoon the sun was out again and quickly melted the snow. It does not melt and go slushy as in England, it sort of evaporates. There is no actual meltwater. It must be because the air is so dry.

Since it is light twenty-four hours, sleeping patterns are a bit awry. Sean and Tim habitually stay up later than me, and Tim is going to bed about 3 am and not getting up again until noon. This is lunch time on the ship, so Tim's meals are a bit askew as well. As a result he is often in the galley eating at around midnight.

Friday 13 January: Back to business today – and everyone is up early for a team picture at the airstrip. Arne, the captain, Davey, the chief engineer, and a couple of others stayed behind on anchor watch, but the rest assembled for a 9 am picture in front of the hut before it was dismantled. Someone has found a bottle of champagne and Pat has brought enough glasses for everyone to have a drop. Pete called it a celebration of victory.

At 10 am, as arranged, the French arrived and we began a tour of the airstrip. The French tell us they capture the penguins by hand when they are about to blow up a rookery, put them in a pen behind high wire, and release them again when their breeding colony has been destroyed. Fireworks are used to frighten away the other birds such as petrels that nest on the same islands and cannot be caught. Some birds use burrows, but what happens to them no one knows.

This was all very distressing, but was also very tedious because everything has to be translated, so I was delighted when 12 noon came and we decided to break for lunch and to resume at 3.30 pm. Even in the Antarctic the French clearly take lunch seriously.

Back at the ship lunch was over quickly and I accepted an invitation to go with the film crew on a tour of the icebergs. It was a stunning ride. The water was beautifully clear and it was possible to see the penguins swimming about underneath the boat. They are incredibly agile in the water. The icebergs were dazzling in the full sun, even viewed through the obligatory goggles.

At 3.30 pm I'm dropped off at the jetty to get to the meeting. The film crew have decided not to bother with this and continue sightseeing. I run up the now familiar hill to catch up with the rest of the party and am in time to get a tour of the labs. We meet biologists, meteorologists, seismologists and people who study the stratosphere. Again Greenpeace hammer on about the penguins, which the scientists are clearly uneasy *about. They agree they are causing loss of habitat and cutting numbers.*

The head biologist of the station, Vincent Bretagnolle, agreed that the base and the construction of the airstrip were having a serious effect on the wildlife. For example, the original base had been built directly on top of a giant petrel colony of eighty breeding pairs. Only two remained and twenty had moved to another island. He had no idea what had happened to the rest.

The emperor penguin colony, the only one for 437 miles, was 12,000 strong in 1958 and was now down to 7,200. Human impact and natural disasters were both contributory factors.

He admitted that the building of the airstrip would wipe out large breeding colonies of other birds. This was forbidden under the Antarctic Treaty along with using heavy machinery and helicopters near breeding colonies. As a result of the French activities there was a shortage of suitable habitats. They had no idea where the adult birds would go or whether they could establish colonies elsewhere.

The reason for the new airstrip was to service the new base called Dome C. The ice there was 2.6 miles thick, the deepest in Antarctica. Since less than a quarter of an inch of snow falls there in a year, the ice only a few feet down was hundreds of years old. By studying this ice it will be possible to understand what is happening to the world's atmosphere because of pollution.

This was a good-humoured visit where I felt the scientists were sympathetic to Greenpeace's fears. It was followed by a two-hour meeting of questions and answers with all the scientists and M. Houssin. It was far more relaxed than any previous encounter. Paul Bogart then gave a restatement of the Greenpeace position opposing the airstrip. The French were very patient and accepted a large part of what was said. They abdicated responsibility: the airstrip decision was one for the French government and essential for the servicing of the yet-to-be-built Dome C. Paul Bogart was not impressed by this buck-passing.

A French journalist who had arrived on the supply vessel a few days ago came back with us to the Gondwana. *He upset Pete by saying Pete looked like his father. Pete is forty-one, and the French journalist said his father was seventy-five. We laughed, but Pete seemed offended.*

We wandered off to see what everyone else was up to and found Pat King with Henk, Tim, Bruno and Phil Doherty intent on disposing of a bottle of whisky. Using ice chipped from an iceberg earlier in the day, I had two or more scotches on the rocks. The ice was probably several thousand years old and the purest ice in any drink in the world. The snow which formed it fell when the atmosphere of the world was not polluted as it is now. Iceberg ice has a peculiar quality of making entertaining pinging sounds all the time. This is caused by the sudden release of small air bubbles compressed and trapped in the snow centuries ago by the weight of the snow above. It is these tiny air bubbles that are so vital to the climatologists studying in the Antarctic. By analysing the contents of the air trapped in the snow it is possible to measure the pollutants in the atmosphere at the time. We contemplated all this while we diluted our whisky with iceberg – I also thought it would do my cold good.

Saturday 14 January: Got up feeling distinctly under the weather. Cold still bad but whisky also to blame. Pete told me the plan was to leave tonight rather than tomorrow. Liz has looked at the French rubbish dump and taken samples of their sewage to analyse back in New Zealand. The idea is to see whether the French are keeping to their treaty obligations and taking home all dangerous chemicals. With the thousands of penguins round here, I cannot see that ordinary human sewage will be a problem. The penguin rookeries smell even in this temperature. The French seem quite happy about letting her go anywhere, so it seems there cannot be anything to hide.

To our surprise we were visited by two of the French scientists late in the afternoon. We had issued a general invitation but had not expected any of them to come. They tell us that they have been informally discouraged from coming but they are not worried since they are on a fixed term of duty and it is a way of protesting about what their government is doing here. One of the scientists speaks excellent English. The pair were clearly very sympathetic to the Greenpeace actions but now a bit of an embarrassment because everyone seemed to want to be off immediately, which meant stowing all the equipment and battening down for the open sea. We saw the French pair off as politely as possible, although I think they had settled in for the evening. We sailed at 10 pm.

Because of the fine weather and events having moved so fast, we were two days ahead of the original schedule. On the bridge at midnight it was very beautiful. The sun dipped right to the horizon and sat on the icecap, making the sky pink, blue and green in different places. The icebergs came in all shapes and sizes. As we threaded our way through them I watched for growlers and thought about the last week. It had certainly been extraordinary, and thankfully we were all still in one piece. This was only the beginning of the voyage, and I wondered what else was in store. Then I noticed that the wind was beginning to rise, the sea had a slight swell and there were fewer icebergs. I remembered my previous seasickness and decided to go straight to bed.

6

Surviving the Pack Ice

THE FOLLOWING MORNING, 15 January, I woke up sneezing and lay in my bunk wondering whether it was worth getting up. After a while I realised that the sun was alternately shining in one porthole and then the other, which must mean the ship was steaming round in circles. Curiosity cured my cold and I was soon up on the bridge, to find the *Gondwana* had reached a place called Commonwealth Bay. Our plans were to make a landing for a bit of relaxation and tourism. This was one of the Antarctic's historic sites, once the base of Australian hero Sir Douglas Mawson. A contemporary of Scott and Shackleton, Mawson's first trip south was as a junior member of Shackleton's 1908 party which attempted unsuccessfully to reach the South Pole.

Back home in Australia Mawson decided to explore Antarctica again, and in 1911 it was to Commonwealth Bay, where we were now anchored, that this expedition found its way. The bay was previously unexplored, but Mawson settled on it because he could see the necessary bare rock on which to build his hut. From the *Gondwana*'s bridge it was still possible to see this building, just as he had left it, in a valley only a few yards from the shore.

Unknown to Mawson, however, he had the misfortune of building his hut at the windiest place on earth. His subsequent measurements registered gales on an average 254 days out of the 365 in a year. Here the wind reached over 200 miles an hour, and Mawson and his party were frequently unable to go outside at all for fear of being swept away. Even on better days they were roped to the hut as a precaution so their companions could pull them back in if they lost their footing on the ice. On one day, 14 May 1912, the average wind speed for a twenty-four-hour period was 110 miles an hour.

The cause of all the trouble is a long valley that extends hundreds of miles inland towards the South Pole. The land is

67

much higher inland, causing the cold wind at first to creep down the valley, gradually gathering speed, a bit like water down a smooth slope. These winds, called katabatics, occur in many places on the icecap, but nowhere quite as often and as violently as at Commonwealth Bay. Despite this handicap, the party persevered with the expedition.

On 9 November 1912, the beginning of the Antarctic summer, Mawson and two companions, Lieutenant Ninnis and Dr Mertz, set off on an exploration. Seventeen dogs pulled the sledges. On 14 December Dr Mertz was following his two companions and had with him the best team of dogs, and a sledge loaded with the expedition's tent and most of the food, when he suddenly plunged to his death down a crevasse, which had been hidden by a snow bridge which the two leaders had already passed over safely. The hole was only twelve feet across, but Dr Mertz had completely disappeared. His shocked companions were nearly four hundred miles from base. They had six dogs and ten days' food left.

Despite the impossible odds against them, Mawson and Ninnis made an improvised tent from spare canvas, with supports cut from a discarded sledge, and set off back. Three days later the last of their dogs died in harness from starvation. For another twenty-one days they struggled on before Ninnis became too weak to walk unaided; he died six days later, on 14 January.

Mawson was now alone; his skin was peeling, and the hardened soles were coming off his feet leaving raw flesh. He tied them back on, cut the remaining sledge in half and set off to walk the last 150 miles back to base. Despite incredible hardships he plodded for sixteen days and on 1 February, barely alive, managed to reach an outpost base he had established, five miles from the main base at Commonwealth Bay. A blizzard pinned him down at the hut for seven days, but when the wind finally dropped he struggled the last five miles – only to see that the expedition's vessel was not at its anchorage. At first he believed that his companions had sailed away leaving him for dead, but in fact a small party had been left behind in the hut in case he returned.

At first, when they saw him struggling across the snow, they did not recognise him. All his hair had fallen out, and his weight had dropped in three months from fourteen stone to seven. The ship was radioed to come back, but the wind against it was too strong and it had to give up the attempt and continue back to Australia.

When the ship returned the following summer Mawson had still not fully recovered, but he went on to complete the scientific programme of that expedition, and continued to lead others to the Antarctic until 1931.

All that morning the *Gondwana* had been going round in circles, afflicted by the same katabatic wind which had so troubled Mawson. It was a mild one by his standards, only force 7, one below gale force, but still not satisfactory for using the inflatable boats. A feature of these winds is the suddenness with which they spring up and just as quickly abate. Arne, who had had much experience of these matters, was confident that this wind would die away after lunch.

This suited me well enough because I had some copy to file. By the time I had finished I discovered that Arne's prediction had been right and the first two boatloads were already on their way ashore. I managed to get on the third. It was about a mile to the landing place, where we were given a short lecture about being careful not to harm the wildlife and plants. There was apparently a profusion, by Antarctic standards, of mosses and lichens in this area and we must avoid treading on them: moss can take ten years to grow a small clump an inch across, and a footprint in it can still be seen twenty years later. When we finally got ashore we found that all around there were tiny scraps of green moss and red, yellow and sometimes black lichen. I suppose it is black to absorb the maximum heat, the same colouring trick as the penguins and the seals use. A lot of the green moss turned out to be on skeletons of penguins and seals – presumably attracted by the nutrients.

Mawson's hut was across the valley from the chosen landing spot, about half a mile away. This valley was full of snow, the surface of which had melted and refrozen like glass. With great care we crept across. Superficially the hut itself looked almost as good as new. On closer inspection the grain of the wood had been etched out by the force of the wind, which had driven ice particles against the wood and worn away the softer parts. It was much more marked on the south side, the direction from which the katabatics come. The inside of the hut was full of snow, apparently forced through the cracks in the wood by the wind. Despite this disappointment there was plenty to see outside. There were piles of old Edwardian tin cans, boots, part of an old stove, the junk left over from two years of Mawson's occupation.

There were some huge beams of timber lying on the ground, similarly weathered to the timber on the hut. I realised these must be the radio masts which Mawson had erected in the hope of communicating direct with Australia. He did manage to get a signal through once at the beginning of the expedition, and so made history, but even such substantial poles were no match for the fierce gales and they were snapped within a few days of their erection. He put them up again but lost the battle with the wind before making another contact. It must have been a huge wind; the posts were twice the thickness of standard telegraph poles.

All the undecayed rubbish was rather depressing in such a beautiful place. I wandered off up the hill to look at the view and take pictures across the valley and out to sea, so taking in the Greenpeace ship. The rocks on the hill were very beautiful, and so exposed to the wind that they were devoid of any vegetation, even the black lichen. They had a polished appearance which made them shine in the light. Some of the boulders had splintered because of the cold and, against Greenpeace principles, I slipped two pieces of rock in my pocket, one black and a second one of white marble with gold specks.

Aware that I was also breaking the rules about always keeping in parties of three, I walked further off towards where the main ice sheet began. The wind had dropped away entirely now, and I was warm enough to take off my gloves and unzip my jacket. It was a wonderful feeling to be completely alone. I passed half a dozen penguins sunbathing. They were lying face down on the ice with their backs to the sun to get maximum warmth. I do not suppose they looked any dafter than holidaymakers on the beach in Spain or Greece. They did not move even though I was only a few feet away, merely swivelling their heads round to watch me walk past. In the distance someone spotted me and shouted, indicating it was time to go back to the ship. I waved back to show I was coming. I was unwilling to leave, but I knew Arne was nervous about the possible return of the wind as the day drew on. It was already getting colder as the sun dipped closer to the horizon, and I zipped up my coat and put my gloves back on for the journey across the water.

Back on the ship, during dinner, a member of the crew made several unfriendly remarks about Japs in a loud voice. Naoko, the Japanese journalist, was sitting at the next table near me, but the crew member concerned had not seen her because they were back to back. She said nothing but must have heard. After a game of chess with Tim, which was notable for me as the first I had managed to win against him, I was sitting down to write up my journal when Naoko approached me.

Her English had improved dramatically since the beginning of the trip, and she came straight to the point. Did I think Greenpeace people were racially prejudiced against the Japanese? She was asking me because I was a journalist and an outsider like her. I said I did not think so, but she was wound up and said it was all connected with Greenpeace's intended action against the Japanese whaling fleet later in the trip. She wondered whether Greenpeace was taking the right action, especially if the Japanese thought it was motivated by racial prejudice. Naoko said she felt this particularly strongly as the only Asian on board. I had never seen her so animated before, and tried to reassure her, but despite my best efforts I felt she was unconvinced. I suggested she talk to Pete about it, but she said, rather angrily, that he was always busy or drinking with his friends.

Later when I went back into the lounge and found Pete with Ken Ballard and Paul Bogart, indeed having a drink, I joined them and told them of Naoko's fears. It would be sad if Naoko gained the wrong impression of Greenpeace because of the stupidity of one member of the crew and her own inability to communicate with the rest. Pete took the problem seriously, and said he would try and make himself appear available, but hesitated to broach the subject himself. I told him I would keep an eye on the situation, a sort of veiled threat to hold him to his promise.

We sailed that night, heading for Leningradskaya, the Russian base in Oates Land, an extremely inaccessible place even by Antarctic standards. Because of the ocean currents the pack ice is not dispersed off this part of the coast even in high summer. This means that Greenpeace expeditions have not even been able to attempt to visit before. The base can only be brought within helicopter range by ploughing through the pack ice in a specially strengthened vessel like the *Gondwana*. The flights promised prolonged discomfort too, since we thought the closest we would get to the base would be about seventy miles.

Except at Auckland, where the weather and sea were warm, we had not used the helicopters. Now we had to practise putting on survival suits and getting in and out of them. Ditching in the

Antarctic would be a tricky proposition. Tim and Sean were practising putting their suits on in the hangar, but there was not room for all of us, so Pierrette and I arranged to go back the next day.

While the *Gondwana* ploughed on to our next destination, everyone attended to domestic chores and there was a queue at the washing machine. Back in our cabin there was a discussion about women overwintering. Most base crews were men only, but Greenpeace seemed to discriminate in favour of women at all levels. As a result, this year the overwintering team was two men and two women, the first time this had been achieved. The team was supposed to have all the skills that would allow the team to survive the winter, keep fit, and carry out a science programme. Thus Lilian Hansen, the Danish nurse, looked after the medical side but also assisted with the science. Bruno Klausbruckner, the Austrian base leader, whose first love was mountain climbing, knew about mechanics, and Phil Doherty, the New Zealand communications man, doubled as electrician. Liz Carr, the American base scientist, was also an athlete, keen to go on expeditions. All four had to cook in rotation and share the domestic chores. The two women were considerably younger than the men and all but Bruno were unmarried. Bruno, eighteen years older than Liz, the youngest of the overwinterers, had left a wife and two children behind in Austria.

Scientific studies of the behaviour of base-camp personnel during the long winter nights in Antarctica are said to have shown that women are a civilising influence but do not necessarily reduce tensions. The so-called Antarctic syndrome (in which the prolonged darkness, cramped conditions and hardship induce irrational behaviour in which lifelong friends can fall out and never speak again) seemed as prevalent when women were around. The current Greenpeace team, which we were due to pick up and return to civilisation, consisted of three men and a woman. Pete had taken the precaution of hiring a psychiatrist to be available to check on their mental health when we reached New Zealand.

There were six other women on board: Maggie McCaw, the deckhand; Pierrette, the Swiss helicopter pilot; Naoko, and Mary-Ann Bendel, the Japanese and American journalists; and unusually for Greenpeace both cooks were women. They were Pat King from New Zealand and Merriann Bell, an American.

Having interviewed some of the male members of the crew, I had decided they were natural loners, sort of rolling stones, but the motivations of the women as yet remained a mystery.

I finally got my washing done at close to midnight and then decided to ring the office, my parents and my wife, to keep them all up to date with progress and reassure them of our safety since there would be nothing in the paper for a few days. It was hard to have a proper conversation at ten dollars a minute with an echo on the line, but things seemed to be all right.

Next morning, 17 January, we were well away from the coast, having come north to get clear of the pack ice which we knew from the weather maps was hugging the coast between Commonwealth Bay and Leningradskaya. We turned east during the morning. The plan was to pick a point opposite the Russian base to turn south again, but our turn east proved premature. We immediately ran into pack ice and had to edge round it. It was five hours before we could turn east again.

Several people on the ship had begun to suffer from the cramped conditions and were going out on the helideck in the mornings to exercise. Lilian had a skipping rope and I borrowed it. In the galley a new list of jobs had gone up and I found it was my turn to clean the downstairs toilets. This was a pretty bad job, mainly because the ship was rolling so much, and the floors, including the showers, needed a scrub. Because the water sloshed about so much I had to wear wellingtons to finish the job.

The day was Bruno's and Liz's birthday. Bruno was forty-four and Liz twenty-six. Strange that two of the four overwinterers had the same birthday, but it was an excellent excuse for a party. Bruno produced two bottles of schnapps. Unfortunately for me I was due on watch that night. Since Dumont d'Urville, normal ship's duties had been resumed, and Sean, Tim and I had been asked to share a twelve till four watch, turn and turn about. This made us all feel we were making a contribution without diverting us too much from our other jobs.

When I got ready and went down to the galley for a pre-watch coffee the ship was rolling badly and the party was almost over. The main reason for this, as I fully appreciated when I reached the bridge, was the wind speed. It had reached an average force 6 and the sea was getting up. The barometer was falling and so were my spirits at the prospect of four hours of worsening weather. In the event the time passed quickly because there were icebergs to worry about. It was misty, with visibility less than three miles. Then it began to snow, further reducing visibility, and there was quite a bit of scattered pack ice on the water, which I was grateful for because it cut down the swell. But if there was ice there was always danger, and I was pleased when I got a pat on the back from Albert Kuiken, the Dutch third mate in charge of this watch, for being first to spot a growler.

I had developed a real liking for Albert. As third mate, he was in charge of the bridge eight hours out of the twenty-four, apart from when Arne came up and took charge. Like many seafarers from the Netherlands he had perfect command of English and was a willing teacher. He often laughed and made gentle fun of people, but he never minded answering serious questions about the sea, or the ship, and displayed enormous knowledge with the detail of his answers.

He was well over six foot and lean, and enjoyed his own athletic prowess. He startled me on this shift, when we were on the edge of the pack ice and the temperature had dropped well below freezing, by leaping over the safety rail on the front of the bridge. The wind was force 6 and the sea had been spraying the windscreen on the bridge, obscuring our vision, and the cold had frozen the water in the bridge screen washers, so that even with the windscreen heaters on we could not shift them. Albert had leapt out of the bridge to do something about this. He grabbed a rail running along the roof of the bridge and swung hand over hand along the front of the windows, hanging about thirty feet above the deck. He let go with one hand and, producing a scraper from his pocket, furiously polished the windows free of salt and ice.

Since we were alone on the bridge at the time and I had no idea what to do if Albert's stunt went wrong, I went and shouted at him from the bridge wing to come back in. He smiled and broke into what sounded like a Viking battle song, shouted into the teeth of the wind. After a couple of minutes, during which I was sure his bare fingers must freeze and he would lose his grip, he swung back and jumped to safety. He was amused by my anxiety and insisted it was all in the line of duty and it would be my turn next.

I persuaded him to let me pin him down to an interview in the lounge the following day. The first topic of our conversation was how old he was – forty. This was a surprise, he looked younger. He was married, but separated. This was clearly a sadness to him and he promptly produced a picture of his wife. He was still in love with her, he said, and he thought she was in love with him, but they lived very different lives. They remained great friends, however, even though they had decided that marriage in the traditional sense was not working, and he always sought her advice about important matters.

His grandfather had been a drifter fisherman in the North Sea. This was a coincidence since mine had been too, and we speculated that their small sailing boats had probably passed each other on the Dogger Bank. Albert's family fishing business was ended when the great dyke in Holland was constructed in 1932, cutting off the traditional fishing villages from the sea for the sake of the new land that could be reclaimed.

But the sea was in Albert's blood and he had thought of little else when he was at school. Although he did reasonably well at lessons, he left at sixteen and went straight into deep sea merchant navy service. He had no skills and worked in the galley and on deck, and was very happy. After a couple of years he came ashore and went to nautical college to get his mate's certificate, then went back to sea with the Blue Funnel Line, a famous British company.

After a few more years he felt restless again. He came ashore and worked in a children's home. The work was full of 'sorrow and sadness' with so many unhappy orphans, and children of broken marriages. The children were sometimes very strange and difficult to handle. He worked with boys aged between twelve and twenty, some of them very tough. He stayed there for two years and then found escape again on the sea. Increasingly he became alarmed about pollution, and started campaigns on his ships to stop dumping oil and rubbish over the side. He said he always met with cooperation from the seamen.

He was now earning enough money to work for only six months of the year, so he gave the rest of his time to efforts aimed at conservation. In May 1988 he wrote to Greenpeace offering his services as a seaman but heard nothing. He badgered Greenpeace and, discovering that ships' crews were chosen in London, travelled there and found the office. He was offered a job immediately on the *Sirius*, a ship operating in European campaigns, and then later on the *Gondwana*. He said that for the first time in many years he felt content. It was true he was only getting paid half what he would get in the Dutch merchant navy, but it was enough, and he felt he was doing something worthwhile. He wanted to stay with Greenpeace.

He found the atmosphere on the ship very good, and he particularly liked the mixed crew and the multinational flavour. He had been laughed at for suggesting mixed crews in the Dutch merchant navy, but Greenpeace had proved that they worked.

It was Albert's first visit to Antarctica, but he had lots of experience of ice in the Baltic. He laughed. 'There, in an emergency, you could call on an icebreaker to come and get you out, carve an escape channel. We had to do it more than once, and were so casual about it we played football on the ice while waiting for them to arrive. There is no such service here – we shall have to be more careful.'

Wednesday 18 January: Woke up to find the ship steady. The rhythmic note of the engine died suddenly and a few seconds later there was a crunch as we hit something. For a moment I was alarmed and then I realised we were in the pack ice. Excited, I went straight up to the bridge. There was ice as far as the eye could see. The broken lumps varied between a few feet and many yards across. They stuck up a foot or so above the water. Salt ice has about three-quarters of its thickness under water whereas denser freshwater icebergs float much lower in the water. The weather was dull and snowy, but we could see a long way. It required great concentration to weave the ship in and out of the ice, steering for the clearer bits of water but always looking ahead for a route to follow. When a collision with a piece of ice became inevitable the engines were cut so the ship drifted into it slowly. The Gondwana *was to push the ice out of the way, rather than smash it like an icebreaker. Once the ship had lodged against a piece of pack ice the engines were given heavy throttle and she bulldozed the ice out of the way. Now I understood why we had such enormous engines for such a small vessel. Provided the ice was not more than two metres thick we would be able to make headway. Progress was slow, however, about three or four knots, and as we went on the pack ice closed in behind us again, leaving no mark of our progress.*

When I finally got to breakfast I found the drinking water supply for the ship was brown again after the buffeting we had taken the previous night, so I had a big bowl of cereal with milk rather than tea. There was also fresh fruit salad still available, a tribute to the ship's stores.

During the day the ship's engines kept cutting out. Whatever you were doing you just paused and held your breath, waiting for the coming crunch. It was sometimes quite a jolt, tipping crockery over.

Arne was clearly the most experienced man in the ice, and whenever things got difficult he was called to the bridge. We had to avoid hitting the comparatively rare growlers because freshwater ice is much harder than salt pack ice and would make a nasty dent even at slow speed. I supposed all this must be second nature to Arne, who clearly enjoyed operating the ship in ice conditions.

Eventually he found what is known as a 'lead', a clearer stretch of water through the pack ice. If the ice-free water lasted it would treble our speed. Otherwise, at our previous pace it would take us at least three days to get within helicopter range of the Russian base.

Arne told me that the ice conditions were graded by the officer on watch and sent back to the New Zealand Met Office for records and to inform any other ships. If the ice covered half the surface of the sea it was called five-tenths pack.

After dinner there was a crew meeting to discuss progress. It was decided that we should be ready to set off for Leningradskaya any time after tomorrow, and that we would need two lots of trips with the helicopters. Bruno would take care of emergency food and sleeping bags; we would all take care of our own emergency clothing. The idea was that we could survive for up to a week on the pack ice if anything went wrong.

Thursday 19 January: I slept much better in the ice and decided to have a shower. No water. To everyone's consternation the water supply had frozen up. On a ship designed for ice conditions this seemed a bit ludicrous. I went to the bridge to see what was happening and found we were in eight-tenths pack ice. In these conditions progress was very slow. However, the ice seemed thinner and softer than the stuff we had encountered the day before, and we discovered that by pushing hard the big pieces split in two and we could make our own lead through the middle.

At times the ice reached nine-tenths, but we kept going on, although sometimes only at two knots. After working all day the engineers finally unfroze the pipes in the bowels of the ship. We had a celebration cup of tea and some people even washed.

The following morning Pete woke us early and said that good progress had been made and we were close enough to reach Leningradskaya. I was ready and checking through all the gear I would need when Tim came back and said the Russians had been contacted and reported only five kilometres of visibility at their base. This was too little for flying helicopters in the Antarctic. The ship was still moving through the ice towards the coast. After breakfast on the bridge I found that Arne had decided to park. I say park because the water was too deep to drop an anchor, about 500 fathoms or 1,000 yards. Instead the ship was attached to some pack ice. To the north, from where we had sailed, the ice was churned up, but ahead to the south the ice was solid as far as the eye could see – in the jargon ten-tenths pack ice. Arne put the ship facing the wind into a big ice floe, keeping the engines gently on thrust.

In the middle of the morning Pierrette took one of the helicopters up with Dave Walley, the chief pilot, as passenger. They flew for about half an hour round the ship checking that all the systems were working. The helicopters had suffered many jolts since we left Hobart, and despite the loving care lavished on them by Noel Caton, the helicopter mechanic, test flights were vital. All appeared to be well except that radio voice reception on the bridge was poor.

The wind was about ten knots and the cloud was thinner out to sea where we had come from, but south, where we wanted to go, was much darker. We were sixty-eight nautical miles from Leningradskaya, just over half an hour's flying time. We believed that the ice was nine-tenths to ten-tenths all the way to the coast, so it would be foolhardy to take the ship any closer.

At the start of my noon watch the second helicopter was tested and we contacted the Russians again because the weather round the ship seemed to have improved. But they said their visibility had worsened, down to less than a mile, and although at 4 pm they reported things had improved, with visibility eleven miles, Dave Walley decided that the weather was still too changeable over the land mass for comfort and we would have to wait until the next day.

The weather over the ship continued to improve, and by late afternoon we were bathed in sunlight. In the distance someone spotted a lone figure on the ice floe. Through the binoculars we could see a very fat Adélie penguin striding towards us across the ice. It took a full thirty minutes for it to reach the ship, even though it was going remarkably fast and at times lay on its stomach and used its stubby wings to push itself forward like a toboggan. Eventually the penguin came to a halt five yards from the hull and walked up and down while we took pictures. Then, taking advantage of the clear stretch of water the ship had created, the Adélie plunged in and spent a happy half-hour fishing for krill round the ship, before setting off back across the floe. It amazed me how creatures could survive and thrive in such conditions.

In the evening Arne decided that rather than waste fuel he would cut the engines, since the ice seemed quite stable. A twenty-four-hour full bridge watch would be maintained to make sure the ice did not move. If it did, the engines had to be started immediately, and the duty mate's instructions were to cut a piece out of the ice floe to give us a harbour space and stop us being crushed.

Today was my daughter Clara's twenty-first birthday. It was late when I rang her at her college digs in Portsmouth to wish her many happy returns. With the twelve-hour time delay it was still early for her. She told me she was having a champagne breakfast. It was wonderful to speak to her: normal life seemed to be far away, and I realised again how much I was missing my family. Paul Bogart produced a bottle of bourbon. Where did all this booze come from? Time for a celebration, he said. It was late when we got to bed.

7

Leningradskaya Cheer

WE WERE ROUSED early next morning by Pete and told to be ready to fly by 9.45 am. After last night I was feeling lethargic, but a shower and a shave cured this. As I was putting on the layers of underwear necessary for such a trip Sean, who had rather surprisingly stayed in bed, said he was not going to Leningradskaya. The risk of flying in a single-engined helicopter over so much ice was too great. He said there was also the problem that the helicopter pilots had had a couple of beers the night before. Tim got up and got dressed and they discussed the issue. It was a highly charged situation. I went to breakfast and mentioned the problem to Paul Bogart, who happened to be there. He said nothing for a few moments, then Tim appeared and sat down with us. Paul asked what the trouble was and Tim snapped at us both, saying it was none of our business. Pete came in and made the situation worse by complaining because no one was yet ready. 'We leave in ten minutes,' he said.

I decided to go ahead with the trip anyway, and went to put on the rest of my clothes and the survival suit. We had been warned that it would be much colder than we had so far experienced, so I crammed on everything I could. Sean was still in the cabin during my preparations, silent and upset. He went out and told the helicopter pilots of his decision, and then Pete. Because Tim was Sean's sound man there was no point in him going to Leningradskaya either. Tim had come back and told me (in Sean's absence) that Sean had friends in the film business who had been killed recently in helicopter crashes, hence his reservations. Exactly what Tim felt about Sean's decision was not clear, but he loyally made no comment.

Outside it was snowing again. Pete had decided that Sean's decision had simplified matters and we could now all fit into the two helicopters, with no need to make a second trip. He did not

comment further, but it must have been a blow not to get film of
the Soviet base for the television programme Greenpeace hoped
would be made about the expedition.

We were all ready on the helideck when Dave took another look
at the weather and decided to postpone the trip until midday. We
all trooped back to the lounge and took the top layers of clothing
off. It was all very frustrating.

Just as we were deciding that another day was wasted, there was
a message from the Soviet base to say all was clear there. We
scrambled back into all the gear, and then I was crammed into
the back of Dave Walley's helicopter. Pierrette took off first with
Naoko and Liz squeezed in the front, the three smallest of the
party, and Paul Bogart and Steve Morgan in the rear seats. Dave
Walley then took off, with Bruno next to him in the front as
spotter, and me and Pete in the back. We headed almost due
south towards the coast, and to our surprise, since it was all
supposed to be solid ice, we found we were over open water.

After twenty minutes' flying we could see a line of what seemed
to be coast in front, but it turned out to be the line of fast ice. It
was studded with old icebergs, and even from 1,500 feet up it was
easy to see the seal families gathered round their breathing and
fishing holes below. The Russians had turned on their radio
homing beacon for us to lock in on. All I could see in front was
a vista of varying whiteness like a giant iced cake, but Dave said
suddenly that he had spotted the Soviet base: it was on top of a
mountain about five miles in front. Craning over Bruno's
shoulder, I now saw a couple of black dots on top of a large hump.
What a tiny footprint in such huge and magnificent scenery.

As we came closer we could see several huts and some radio
masts. There were two red flags planted out in the snow, clearly
marked out for us to land between. Pierrette went in first slowly
and we followed behind. The base was on top of a cliff 1,200 feet
high, and the landing spot was only a few yards from the edge.
It was a relief when we were safely down.

The Russians came across the snow and greeted us warmly with
handshakes and broad smiles, but, apart from 'hello' and 'good
morning', communication was difficult. There had been a
blizzard on the mountain during the early hours, and after
wading through virgin snowdrifts we were shown into one of the
half-dozen or so low buildings on the base. Rather than dig new
paths for themselves, the Russians had spent all morning using a

small bulldozer to flatten an area large enough for us to land on.

In the commander's office cum dining room we took off our outer gear, a major preoccupation in this climate. One Russian showed me to his room, ceremoniously hung up my survival suit and jacket, and gave me a pair of soft cardboard-like wellingtons worn by the Russians as a sort of indoor slipper. They were very warm, but my host clearly had very big feet and walking was not easy.

Bruno had found a German speaker among the Russians and they were getting on famously. Pete handed the base commander leaflets in Russian explaining Greenpeace's mission. The commander read one and then Pete and Paul Bogart explained the purpose of our visit. They told him, via Bruno and his German speaker, that Greenpeace was undertaking an annual tour of bases to check that nations were adhering to the Antarctic Treaty, properly treating wastes, and not damaging the environment. The Russian commander, Alexander Pochernik, a small jolly man, listened patiently through the three-way translation. Despite the fact that he must have been nervous about our intentions, he then insisted that we stay for a few days, and said his men had already prepared rooms for us. It transpired that we were the first visitors to the base since the Russians had been landed there by their own supply ship eleven months before. We were obviously the best break from the grinding routine they had had in all that time.

While all this was going on I noticed a large cucumber plant growing in the window of the commandant's office, complete with a cucumber about seven inches long. He noticed me admiring it and came over, clearly proud of his gardening skill. Pete noted rather sourly that since there is no soil in Antarctica it must have been grown in soil which was illegally imported, contrary to the Antarctic Treaty. The importation is prohibited for fear of introducing pests. I noticed that Bruno refrained from translating these comments; he did not want to spoil the party atmosphere. Now we had to put all our outside clothes back on again to go about 400 yards across the snow to the mess hall.

Despite our differences, the French had apparently passed on to Bruno a lot of letters to be franked at the Soviet base and then posted on when we reached New Zealand. Philately was a big hobby in this part of the world. Bruno fell energetically into this activity, stamping all the letters on a small snooker table while I wandered around. There was a pre-Glasnost portrait of Gorbachev on the wall, without the birthmark on his balding head. The picture must have been there some time. Our hosts seemed to be living in another era.

There was a large table spread with a gleaming white tablecloth in our honour. We were told the cook had had his sixty-first birthday the day before. He must have been one of the oldest people in the Antarctic, which is very much a young man's continent. We had soup to start with, which was thick mixed vegetable, followed by big folded pancakes containing meat. These pancakes were a traditional dish, covered in melted butter, and incredibly heavy. What dominated the meal, however, was the vodka. We had managed to restrain our hosts from opening it until just before lunch. Highly decorated glasses, slightly larger than eggcups, were distributed to every one of us, filled to the brim, and the contents were drunk in a single gulp. We began by toasting each other's health, then the search began for other things. One of the Russians stood up and said 'Manchester United.' We remembered Moscow Dynamo. There was a lull while we tried conversing in halting English. Curiously Naoko and a young Russian meteorologist, both with very little English, could understand each other better than anyone else. She kept telling me what he was saying. When the Russians discovered during all this that Dave Walley came from Aberdeen, it started a new round of toasts to football clubs. Then there was a toast to Greenpeace's aim of Antarctica World Park, to please us guests. When I tried to slow down my alcohol intake by only drinking half a glass of vodka per toast, our hosts were clearly offended and enquired if I was sick. I said no and was left with no alternative but to propose yet another toast to show I was healthy and in good spirits.

Dave Walley went off to the base's radio room to tell the ship what was happening and explain we were getting on fine. After the problems of the morning with Sean, and despite fears of offending our Russian hosts, neither helicopter pilot was drinking vodka. They would shortly be the only sober ones amongst us.

When he returned Dave said he was amazed by the antique equipment used by the Russians. It was still powered by valves. He said it took a whole shedful to generate enough power to reach the ship. The Russians had been equally astonished by his hand-held radio, which he had not used for fear of running down the batteries in the cold. This kind of technology was new to them. The lunch continued for some time with the aid of a large Russian–English dictionary which contained English words I had never heard of and therefore its translations only added to the confusion.

Nevertheless I did discover that there were a total of sixteen Russians on the base, including a doctor and a dentist. There was an electrician, a mechanic and an engineer to help the meteorologist and the geophysical engineer, who did most of the scientific work. The main business of the base was observation of weather patterns in conjunction with four other Soviet bases in the Antarctic, all of them bigger. It involved releasing a balloon every day and taking pressure, temperature and other measurements as it rose.

Pete and Paul, listening to us ramble on, were anxious not to lose the purpose of the visit, and through the German speaker, who was also base doctor, they now reminded the commandant why we were there.

Obligingly the Soviet commander showed us round his camp. It was now a glorious day, the wind had died completely, the sky was blue, and it was possible to see mountains in the far distance. We were told these were fifty or sixty miles away. I found this hard to believe, but the clear air was very deceptive; also we were perched high above the surrounding ice.

We stood at the edge of the cliff on which the Russian base was built and looked down. Since the base was set up in 1971, each team had clearly copied the last and thrown their barrels and general waste, only partially incinerated, over the edge. Although some was half buried in the snow, large quantities could still be seen. Food waste was dumped down a crevasse near the cliff edge, which was standard practice and permitted by the Antarctic Treaty in inland sites, but mixed with it were plastics and glass, which Pete told the Soviet commander was contrary to the treaty's code of conduct. The commander explained this was an oversight. Since 1986, when new instructions were issued, the base personnel had been taking more care. Some plastics and glass were still dumped, but four months' worth of debris was taken back to the Soviet Union each year. The problem was that only once in six years on average could the supply ship get to within reasonable operating distance of the base. Last year the ship had only managed to reach a hundred miles away, an hour in the helicopter. It was very difficult to take out much rubbish in such circumstances because helicopter fuel was in short supply.

On the other side of the base there was a steep slope rather than a cliff. On it were oil tanks with a mess underneath from old oil spills. The commandant said that for three years they had been planning to build a proper reservoir to catch the spilled oil, but so far there was not enough money in the budget. The site was littered with empty fuel barrels and old trucks, some looking like museum pieces, which had succumbed to the cold and been abandoned on the slope. All the sewage was collected in barrels, according to the commander, and returned to Russia. Paul said plastic and glass should be a higher priority, but the Russians insisted it was correct. Through such convoluted interpretation and so much vodka I was not sure that proper understanding was possible. I was, however, convinced that all the sewage went into barrels. The Russian toilets consisted of a seat over a hole in the bottom of the hut going straight down into one of the empty barrels. The draught up the hole was alarming, with the temperature at −7°C, but at least it kept the smell down.

We all stopped to watch one of the Russians feed scraps of meat to a skua, a large brown bird rather like a seagull, only bigger. They can be very aggressive, especially near nesting sites, but this one clearly knew his friend and took the meat out of his hand. While Liz wandered round taking samples for analysis back in New Zealand, we all went back to the base leader's office. The meeting lasted for nearly an hour. Paul Bogart thanked the commander for his welcome and his openness. 'It makes our job so much easier,' he said. He insisted that waste glass and bottles should be returned to Russia. The commander picked up a bottle of mineral water and said: 'That would make this water as expensive as brandy by the time it had come from Leningrad to Leningradskaya and back.'

He then said he understood our position and he agreed in principle, but it was a question of money. Each man on the base produced a hundred pounds of waste a year. It would be very helpful if Greenpeace made some recommendation on how to get rid of it. Business then came to an end by mutual agreement, and our hosts produced some beautiful china cups for coffee, and another round of drinks. This time it was neat whisky, which Paul had brought. Again there were toasts – and then straight down the hatch. At least I had the satisfaction of seeing the Russians blink as this more unfamiliar spirit hit the back of their throats. Pete produced Greenpeace T-shirts, badges and stickers for the men on the base. We in return were given enamel badges of Lenin and other small gifts. Bruno and the doctor were already in a different league, swapping their hats and then, with a great deal of laughing and back-slapping, their boots. To the delight of the base commander Pete then swapped his Greenpeace baseball hat with the commander, and Paul did the same with another of the Russian party.

Despite repeated invitations to stay and make a real party of it, we made our way unsteadily back to the helicopters. We were already more than an hour behind our original scheduled departure time, but everyone wanted to take pictures. All the Russians wanted to be photographed with the women of the party, particularly Liz with her red hair. Everyone linked arms for a party picture in front of the helicopters in the snow. Eventually we were allowed to climb into the helicopters and depart, amid promises that Greenpeace would make the visit an annual event to cheer up the Russians in their isolation.

The view was absolutely stunning. We flew on, this time in front of Pierrette, keeping in radio contact. Suddenly the radio cut out. There was a minute or so of static and broken words, and then silence. It was a heart-stopping moment. We craned our heads round but could see no trace of her.

Dave slowed our helicopter right down. Pierrette's helicopter was equipped with floats, which made it a slower machine than ours. Dave was listening closely to the radio and thought that it was just a radio fault and she had merely fallen behind. To our relief Bruno and I soon spotted her coming up on our right, and after that we kept her in sight all the way back to the ship. Again we realised how vulnerable we were, despite all the technology; in this vast and unforgiving landscape we were mere ants. We were glad to be back in one piece.

Arne started the ship's engines as soon as we were safely down, and the *Gondwana* began the long trek north and back to open water. I still felt very exhilarated by our trip to see the Russians, and sat down to write a piece for the paper while it was all fresh in my mind. It was quite late now, and I stopped writing to take a picture of the midnight sun across the ice floes. I did not finish writing until 1.30 am, but I was very pleased with my 'colour' piece on the Soviet base and hoped the news desk would like it.

On the bridge the night was stunningly beautiful. There was a layer of mist over the ice, pink with the sun, which was just on the horizon. There was not even a breath of breeze, and the lead through the pack ice we were following was freezing over. The ship carved through it at two knots, hardly making a sound – the new ice being so thin. It was the perfect end to a splendid day.

I discovered later that while I was writing my piece in the office in the bowels of the ship, Sean had gone up in the helicopter to film the *Gondwana* in the ice. He had not told Tim he was going to do this and left Tim asleep in his bunk. This had led to a terrible row when Sean returned, which many had heard, but, two decks below writing my copy in the office, I had fortunately missed it.

There was a crew meeting the following afternoon, designed to keep everyone up to date with what was happening, including a stream of telexes from Greenpeace offices round the world. Pete and Paul Bogart filled the crew in on the events of the previous day and gave a fairly critical assessment of the Soviet environment record.

The official Greenpeace record of the trip published months later said in part: 'The language barrier between Greenpeace personnel and base staff made it difficult to determine exactly what waste disposal practices are in place.' Greenpeace suggested 'a return of plastics and a halt to open burning of wastes. The return of discarded vehicles and other large items required the use of a larger helicopter than normally used at the station – one should be made available for the purpose. Containment facilities for fuel stores should be made available. The feasibility of cleaning up the hundreds of barrels at the foot of the cliff should be investigated. Overall a comprehensive clean-up and plan for the future is necessary at Leningradskaya. It should be noted that the base personnel seemed both interested and supportive of such a clean-up.' There was no mention of the great time we had.

Having dealt with Leningradskaya, the crew meeting moved on to the next place on the itinerary, the Italian base at Terra Nova on the Ross Sea. Pete said the Italians were reported to be blowing a hole in the ground to put in a seismic station. They had not prepared an environmental impact assessment of the project, and Greenpeace was filing a formal protest from the ship before the visit. Pete added that relations with the Italians were always excellent, but Greenpeace should not let that stand in the way of legitimate protest.

Harking back to Dumont d'Urville, Pete said that in France the debate started by the Greenpeace actions was still reverberating in the papers and political circles. Reminding the crew of a less successful moment, Pete reported that the adverse publicity Greenpeace had received in Hobart from the oil spill had at last died down, but there might still be a prosecution.

Bruno had taken a video of our visit to the Soviet base and he showed it on the lounge television. Rather strange to see pictures of myself wandering around in the snowy wastes. It was clear to me that no camera could make up for the thrill of seeing things with the naked eye. It made me realise how lucky I had been.

We then had the long business of filing copy and press releases and selecting pictures to send. At the end of several hours of effort the office had finally received and read my effort – and they liked it – so I was able to retire to the lounge for a nightcap. It was 2 am: what a strange lifestyle this had become. I was pleased with myself all the same, for I had finally persuaded Maggie McCaw, the quiet American deckhand, to submit to an interview. Several times I had tried talking to her about herself, but without success. She was one of the most experienced and longest-serving Greenpeace 'persons' and to me typified the quiet, unspoken dedication of the crew. We had made an appointment to meet the following day after lunch.

The interview was a long one. Maggie had had an unusual life since leaving her home in the Hudson Valley in New York State. I tried to pin down what it was that marked her out as different from other people, and eventually she said, with a hint of pride: 'When I was a child my mother confided to a friend that she was worried about me because "my daughter thinks too much".'

I discovered that she had two sisters and a brother, all of whom were married and had conventional jobs. Maggie on the other hand had dropped out of college at the age of nineteen, during a degree course in environmental studies. She said at first that she left because she was tired of being at school, but then she said that was not the real reason at all. She had been thinking of what lay ahead in her career. 'With a degree in environmental studies you could only get a government job, monitoring work or office work. Even if you advised what should be done to be best for the environment, it was unlikely to happen, industry would always

win out. It would be a constant compromise. I did not want to
spend my life compromising.'

She travelled for two and a half months through the United
States and Canada, then, attracted by the publicity surrounding
a new environmental group's protest against Soviet whaling in
1978, she joined Greenpeace in Boston. The organisation was in
its infancy and in those days everyone was a volunteer. Maggie
worked in a vegetarian restaurant from 7 am to 2 pm to earn
enough money to survive, and then for Greenpeace until 7 pm.
She had been on the campaign trail ever since.

One of her first ventures was to take part in a 2,500-mile walk
from South Dakota to Seattle to raise money for the organisation.
Then she worked to stop the clubbing to death of seals in Canada,
and on the way back got involved in an anti-nuclear organisation
in Toronto. It led to her first prison cell. She had parachuted into
a partly constructed nuclear power plant site as part of the
protest, and was arrested for trespass and breaching federal
aeronautical regulations. After a few days in jail she was bailed,
and was fined at her later trial.

Other campaigns in the United States followed, including an
attack on uranium mining and a campaign for native rights. It
was then that the real travelling began. She worked on the
original restoration of the *Rainbow Warrior,* the old trawler
Greenpeace had bought for its flagship, the same ship that was
finally sunk by the French in New Zealand. It was the days of
working for nothing but her keep and a berth on the ship.

An invitation then came to join Greenpeace's European fleet.
Maggie always worked as a deckhand, although qualified as a first
mate. She was very keen on the idea of mixed crews, and maybe
she was proving a point by always taking on the worst jobs. She
said it was worth it for her because of the companionship, being
with like-minded people working towards the same end.

During her European tour she was jailed in Norway for
chaining herself to the crow's nest of a whaler, and was hit by stun
grenades and arrested by French paratroopers while trying to
prevent the export of plutonium from Cherbourg. She returned
to the United States to see her family and was drawn into more
causes. First she trespassed in a nuclear weapons factory in
California and was briefly sent to prison. Then she joined the
peace walk to Florida against Poseidon and Trident missiles and
spent two weeks in prison. On her release she helped organise

(*Previous page*) A lone Emperor penguin joins the demonstration against the airstrip at Dumont d'Urville. (*Above*) French construction vehicles trapped behind the Greenpeace survival hut on the runway.
(*Right*) Celebrating the success of the demonstration: Pete Wilkinson and Liz Carr (in front); (2nd row, left to right) Merriann Bell, Pat King, Bruno Klausbruckner, Pierrette Paroz and Maggie McCaw; (3rd row, from left) Paul Bogard, Dave Walley, Naoko Funahashi, Mary-Ann Bendel; (at the back) Henk Haazan (holding a cup) and the author (in white).

(*Top*) Transferring supplies for the winter from the *Gondwana*'s helideck to the World Park base and (*above*) Capt. Arne Sørensen on the *Gondwana*'s bridge.

(*Top*) The Russian
meteorologist Vladimir
Bystrov, expedition
photographer Steve Morgan,
and the author over lunch
at Leningradskaya.
(*Right*) Capt. Scott's stores,
preserved in his hut.
(*Above*) An albatross with a
newly-hatched chick in the
Campbell Islands.

the community of resistance till every last protester was released. 'I confess after all that I was mentally and physically exhausted.'

Through Pete Wilcox, a longtime friend and the captain of the *Rainbow Warrior*, she was called back to Greenpeace and offered a job on the Antarctic campaign. 'I had my reservations because Greenpeace had built a base in the Antarctic, so we, as campaigners, were having an impact on the environment we were trying to protect. However hard we tried, we were bound to spill a bit of oil and lose some rubbish. Things can still go wrong. Any organisation also likes to go on building, falling into the dangerous game of bigger is better.' Despite this she decided ultimately to come because the creation of the base also had its positive side. It demonstrated by example how things should be done in the Antarctic, how little adverse impact need be made. It also proved that Greenpeace was capable of operating at a professional level. The aim was to get Greenpeace observer status at the Antarctic Treaty negotiations, and if it worked it would be worth having used these resources.

Getting back to Maggie and her future, I said that surely it was a young person's life with Greenpeace, and what would she do when she got older? She rejected my conventional assumptions. At thirty she was still one of the younger members of the crew. The oldest person she had sailed with was sixty-seven. She said none of the people who sailed on Greenpeace ships lived conventional lives. It was impossible to have a normal family and a commitment to a campaign.

This brought her to the vexed question of pay. She had started to work for nothing, but as the organisation had become more affluent her pay had taken a 'big leap' to US $100 a month, about £75. This was still well below a competitive salary, but she wanted to do the job so she did not protest. She claimed Greenpeace was 'not a people-orientated organisation' – in fact it treated its loyal servants rather badly. Furthermore, as the Greenpeace organisation grew to seventeen national offices worldwide with 2.2 million members she said there were now some 'armchair campaigners' who treated the organisation as a stepping stone in their careers. She wondered whether they had any real personal commitment to what they were doing. These people asked for and got a competitive salary when working for the organisation. Her pay had now been raised to £250 a month, but this was less than a quarter of the pay of an 'armchair campaigner'.

(Later I asked Pete about the problem of pay and the need to employ professional people. Pete admitted that pay varied wildly, depending 'sometimes on how little they could get away with'. He said that Greenpeace had thousands of volunteers and had a policy of employing the best. Sometimes with specialist jobs this often meant having to pay a near commercial rate. 'Helicopter pilots and captains who are going to operate in these conditions have to get paid a decent rate for the job, but let there be no mistake, everyone works just as hard, and Maggie harder than most.')

Back to Maggie. I asked her again about the future. 'I'm not sure I could settle down in the traditional sense of the word. I have no strong desire to get married; my basic belief is that I don't think I am suitable.' She said instead she had a network of friends all over the world whom she was very close to, male and female. Relationships with men which had seemed 'promising' had up to now always broken down in the end because campaigns had been given priority. She shrugged when I asked her whether this was a matter of regret.

What about the world's future? 'I am not terribly optimistic about the future. I would like to think the human race could pull itself together and improve things, but at the moment I do not see much encouragement in that line. I am not optimistic about my own chances of surviving to old age, let alone any children, certainly not without seeing major environmental disasters which will wipe out large sections of the human race.' She said she was still holding on to hope and trying to have a positive attitude, 'otherwise I would go and find a nice island somewhere and live out my life and let the rest of you get on with it.'

Maggie laughed. She said she was laughing at her own impotence. How could a 5 foot 4 inch deckhand save the world? All she knew was that she had to try. After the voyage she was going to take a long holiday and visit some of her long-lost friends and her family. She was godmother to two children in London, there were nephews and nieces to see in New York and Mum and Dad to visit . . .

I was very happy with the interview. People like Maggie were the backbone of what journalists sometimes described as 'the alternative movement'. She was not the long-haired layabout stereotype so frequently portrayed by my colleagues on the British popular press. Maggie had clearly worked hard but not unquestioningly for the causes she believed in. It was also clear that she was always ready to evaluate and question her own aims and the motives of those around her in a way that most people would find very discomforting. I admired her commitment and her courage.

I just had time to be beaten at chess by Tim before dinner. We had been making steady progress through the ice. The wind had got up and it was snowing heavily. I had hoped to go to bed after dinner and get some sleep before my watch at midnight, but Sean was having a Spanish lesson in the cabin with Merriann the cook. Both had decided to use this voyage to learn a language and so were helping each other. I finally got to bed, to be woken at 11.40 pm, in time to get my warm gear on and go for a cup of tea before the watch.

We were at last out of the pack ice, and the ship had its familiar Southern Ocean roll back. Albert stationed me by the port side window to look for ice. Visibility was poor, about half a mile, and the sea, driven by a force 7 wind, was quite choppy. Albert was nervous about the possibility of growlers and other ice so close to the pack we had just left.

Several times we had to change course to avoid larger pieces of ice which were being thrown about by the waves, and we came within a couple of hundred yards of a small iceberg. The wind slackened at about 3 am and the ice seemed to flatten the waves a little. The snow reduced too, and it got lighter in time for the 4 am crowd. I had enjoyed my four hours, plenty was happening, and we celebrated our successful watch with eggs and bacon in the galley before going to bed. I could see what Albert had meant when he said the *Gondwana* was a happy ship.

8

The Chase

ON TUESDAY 25 JANUARY, Albert came in just as I was off for an afternoon snooze, and said there was high excitement on the bridge because the watch thought they had spotted a ship on the radar. In these waters it was an important event. The area south of the Antarctic Circle is so remote from shipping lanes that the ship could only be a whaler or one of the rare Antarctic supply vessels. If it was a whaler – and Greenpeace desperately wanted to find the Japanese whaling fleet – it would be a remarkable coincidence in 150,000 square miles of ocean.

I went straight to the bridge. The *Gondwana* was closing in on something that we had yet to confirm was a ship. On the radar, ships produced the same echo as a medium-size iceberg. They were only distinguishable from icebergs because they did not move at the same pace. This particular blob on the screen had been noticed twenty miles away because it was moving differently from the rest. It could be a ship.

Now everyone was having a look, and as we got closer we believed we had identified two suspicious blobs. Confidence was growing that this really was the Japanese fleet, and someone had been dispatched below to hunt through the filing cabinets in the office for pictures taken of the whaling fleet in port. Soon through the binoculars it was possible to make out an outline and there were claims of a positive identification. A large black vessel looked like the Japanese whaling factory ship *Nisshin Maru No. 3*, last seen leaving Tokyo for the Antarctic. Soon the watch had concluded that there were three additional smaller ships – three whalers to service the factory ship.

Naoko was in the radio room scanning through the radio frequencies and soon tuned in to the waveband used by the four Japanese captains. They were already aware of the stranger heading straight for them. She started laughing. They were

worrying in case their visitor was a Greenpeace ship. They too
were prepared and had pictures of the *Gondwana*. They decided
to send one of their catcher boats forward for a positive
identification. First he confirmed the red bow of the ship.
Eventually we heard the captain spelling out G-O-N-D-W-A-N-A.
Clearly our arrival was regarded as extremely bad news by the
Japanese. Immediate orders were given for all ships to stop
operations and return to the mother ship. Presumably they had
been hunting whales when we showed up on their radar screens.

Everyone on board the *Gondwana* marvelled at our luck. Several
times we had discussed the unlikelihood of finding the whalers
in such a vast ocean. We had set aside a week later in the voyage
for trying to locate them, but now we had come across them just
by chance, right at the farthest edge of the area in which they
were expected to be. Everything on the trip had gone so well for
Greenpeace so far that Ken suggested I might be their lucky
charm.

Now I had a story to write, and while I was putting it together
Pete had contacted the *Nisshin Maru No. 3* on the radio. Originally
Naoko was to have been used as an interpreter, but Ian thought
it would be to our advantage to keep her as a secret weapon. As
long as they did not think we had a Japanese on board, we could
monitor their radio frequency without them realising. In war,
intelligence of this quality wins battles.

The Japanese had English speakers and were honest over the
radio about their activities. They told Pete they had already killed
forty whales but now all whaling had stopped because of the
Greenpeace presence until they heard back from their government. Pete decided on a crew meeting to discuss the situation.

His view was that we should stick to the factory ship and do
nothing until whaling resumed. Then there were a number of
alternatives for Greenpeace. The traditional intervention method
was to place the inflatables between the harpoon guns and the
whales. Greenpeace also had a number of smoke canisters on
board. These had not been tried before, but the idea was to
obscure the harpoonist's view. Then there was a range of options
involving the helicopters. We had a banner to be trailed which
would make a visual point for the cameras and obscure the view
from the ship of the target whales. One of our problems was that
the *Gondwana* could do a maximum of twelve to thirteen knots
and the Japanese whalers sixteen to seventeen. We did not know

the capabilities of the factory ship, but perhaps they could simply outrun us. Even so, they would not be killing whales in the meantime.

The meeting was adjourned to await events. With all the excitement and running up and down stairs to write up events on the ship's computer, I was feeling pretty seasick. Perhaps the computer was feeling sick too; it was not until the fourth try that it connected to London.

Before the confrontation with the whaling fleet is described it is necessary to tell the extraordinary story of mankind's exploitation of Antarctic wildlife. The Japanese in fact were merely following a long tradition begun by European traders.

One of the striking features of Antarctic wildlife is that only a few species have adapted to survive in such difficult conditions, but those that have done so have used the enormous space and plentiful food supply to breed in huge numbers. This phenomenon was recorded by Captain James Cook, the brilliant seaman and explorer. In his tiny 460-ton wooden vessel Cook braved the icebergs and pack ice to discover the islands now known as South Georgia, which are outside the Antarctic Circle but still extremely bleak. He described them as 'A country doomed by nature, never once to feel the warmth of the sun's rays, but to lie buried under everlasting snow and ice, whose horrible and savage aspect I have not words to describe.'

But Cook also recorded the staggering quantities of wildlife on the islands – the millions of penguins and hundreds of thousands of seals. In the sea there were countless whales, so unafraid of men that they nudged the ship in curiosity. The mention of seals quickly alerted the merchants in Europe, and by 1800 there were seventeen sealing ships operating in the islands, mainly British and American, and in four months they killed 122,000 animals. By 1822, when Captain James Weddell, a member of the Royal Geographical Society, visited South Georgia, the fur seal was virtually extinct. He estimated that 1,200,000 seals had been killed in the previous twenty-five years.

This appalling destruction continued, following in the wake of the explorers as they discovered more scattered islands, the South Shetlands, and then the Antarctic Peninsula. Competition remained fierce, and sometimes sealers even went ahead of the explorers, finding new islands the existence of which they kept

secret so they could go back and plunder them unhindered the
following year. Logs of ships and records of voyages were
destroyed rather than reveal the whereabouts of seal colonies to
rivals.

As the fur seal was wiped out, the merchants turned their
attention to other species, including the docile sea elephant and
penguins. None of these creatures had any fear of man, so they
were easy hunting. The sea elephants, weighing up to a ton each,
were put in huge pots and boiled down for their oil, about half a
ton an animal. Smaller penguins with their feathers and plentiful
fat were used as fuel, while the larger king penguins were also
boiled, yielding a pint of oil each. In the interests of faster
production not all these birds were killed first; instead they were
driven like sheep into runs which ended in giant pots where they
were boiled alive. Only the seabirds that could fly escaped this
terrible carnage, and when the sealers departed the bloodstained
and empty beaches they left a dire legacy – rats. The sealers' ships
were infested with them and they escaped on to the islands to
feast on the eggs of the ground-nesting seabirds. Populations
were severely reduced on many islands as a result.

Once the seals had been pushed to the edge of extinction men
turned their lethal attention to the whales. For a long time whales
had been protected by man's lack of technology. The size and
mobility of the great whales made it impossible for men in open
boats with traditional harpoons to catch and kill them in any
quantity. But in 1868 a Norwegian whaler called Svend Foyn
transformed the whaling industry by inventing the harpoon gun
mounted on the front of the ship. This was further refined by the
use of a barbed harpoon which literally exploded inside the
whale. The great whales were doomed. Already by the 1890s the
Arctic whaling industry was suffering because stocks were
running low. As had happened with seals, it was the whale studies
of the scientific explorers that alerted businessmen to potential
new profits in the Southern Ocean. Early whaling ventures
proved difficult because of the weather and the ice, but in 1901
another Norwegian, Carl Anton Larson, backed by Argentine
businessmen, set up the first Antarctic whaling station in South
Georgia. The British leased the new whaling company 500 acres
on the island for £250 a year. It was ironic that on the very stretch
of beach where the first whaling station was built, there remained
the giant iron pots abandoned by the sealers a hundred years

before. Clearly it did not cross the whalers' minds that their predecessors had wiped out their industry by their own greed.

The whales, like the seals before them, had no fear of man, and Larson had no need even to leave the inlet on which his station was based during the first season – he just shot them as they swam in. The right whales and the humpback whales, which swim close inshore, took the brunt of the initial slaughter. (The right whale was so called because it was the 'right' whale to kill, since it came into shallow sheltered water to breed and did not sink for some time when dead. This unique creature, with its distinctive double spout, was therefore the first to be driven to near extinction.) After ten years of easy harvests these whales had become scarce, and no longer commercially viable, so whalers turned their attention to the giants of the sea, the blue and fin whales. This entailed hunting in the open ocean but must still have remained very profitable, because by 1914 licences for a further seven whaling stations on South Georgia had been granted by the British government.

In the First World War oil from the baleen whales, which include the blue and fin whale species, was used for the production of glycerin – which was a vital ingredient of explosives. As Edwin Mickleburgh says in his book *Beyond the Frozen Sea*, 'Thus a macabre circle of death was joined in which men slaughtered whales in order that they could slaughter each other.'

By 1924 the first realisation of what was the likely outcome of this indiscriminate slaughter had dawned on the whaling industry. It funded a British Colonial Office ship to research the effects of whaling on Antarctic stocks. By 1930 a laboratory had been established opposite Larson's old whaling station at South Georgia, but the whalers failed to heed warnings issued by the scientists they had appointed and continued the relentless 'harvest'.

When factory ships were developed South Georgia was abandoned as a base for shore stations. Such ships could follow the whales as they were hunted. The ships were fitted with rear slipways (like the Japanese whaling ship Greenpeace was following) for dragging up the carcasses of the newly-killed whales so they could be processed by teams of workers. Each factory ship was supplied by a team of smaller catchers. This allowed the whaling fleets to follow the giant herds of whales south in the summer as they went to their feeding grounds on the edge of the ice. The slaughter continued and increased, so that in the summer season of 1937/8 31 factory ships serviced by 256 catchers were able to kill a total of 55,000 whales.

This level of 'harvest' could not go on. The reason was that the biggest and most productive animals, the blue whales, were being wiped out. The smaller whales were now taking the brunt of the attack, and as a result the increasing catches no longer produced more oil, but less. In 1931 1,000 blue whales were destroyed near South Georgia alone, but by 1965, despite the most up-to-date tracking equipment, including helicopters, the industry only saw 4 in an entire season.

In 1946 the United Nations had set up the International Whaling Commission, with its headquarters in Cambridge, England. The aim was to regulate stocks so that only sustainable harvests were taken. But the quotas set for the industry were far too high: the scientists' objections were always being overruled by an industry guided by short-term profits. The plunder continued almost unabated. Species of whales previously thought too small to be worth hunting were now the main target as the larger ones had simply disappeared. Protection for the blue whales was brought in during the 1963/4 season. Only a handful have been seen each season since, and the world population has slumped from 250,000 at the beginning of the century to an estimated 500 to 1,000. The future of the species remains in doubt.

Even though the quotas set by the IWC were fatally over-generous, the big whaling nations – then the Soviet Union and Japan – ignored them. In 1978 scientists leaked the information, and also accused them of hunting young animals and nursing mothers, totally contrary to IWC regulations. Such violations, combined with advances in technology made in the mid-1970s which enabled all whale products to be replaced by man-made or plant-derived alternatives, gave impetus to the growing conservation movement. While the World Wildlife Fund (now called the World Wide Fund for Nature), Friends of the Earth, and the International Union for the Conservation of Nature lobbied hard for change, it was Greenpeace which really caught the public's attention by taking on the whaling fleets on the high seas. Television pictures of the slaughter and of the Greenpeace volunteers in their small boats trying to stop it brought this issue to the world's television screens. The IWC was forced to place more and more of the larger species on the protected list. By the 1980s the minke, the smallest of the ten hunted species and less than one-tenth the size of the biggest, the 120-ton blue, had become the whalers' main target. Finally, in 1982, the Commission voted to suspend all commercial whaling from the season beginning in 1986. In the last open season, 1985/86, a total of 5,569 whales, mostly minkes, were killed.

But despite the high hopes of conservationists the killing did not stop. Several nations, including Norway, Iceland and Japan, exploited loopholes in the Commission's rules. The 1946 convention allowed the taking of protected whales for scientific purposes. These permits were issued by the government of the whaling nations and not by the Commission itself. Japan, Iceland and Norway therefore devised 'scientific' programmes. The Japanese, for example, claimed that only by killing whales could they establish their age, sex and condition and so construct population models. Conveniently the convention allowed that whales killed for scientific purposes should not be wasted and that the meat should be sold commercially to offset the cost of the research programme.

Greenpeace said this was commercial whaling under another name, but since the convention said 'scientific' whaling was in the hands of individual governments, only diplomatic pressure could be brought to bear on the countries concerned. And meanwhile the row over scientific whaling went on.

In 1987 the Japanese proposed to take 825 minke whales and 50 sperm whales annually in a twelve-year programme. There were many doubts cast on the Japanese programme by non-Japanese Commission scientists, and Britain led an international outcry against the scheme. A postal vote among IWC members condemned the programme. The Japanese then substituted a kill of 300 minke whales as part of a feasibility study for the larger research programme which they still planned to go ahead with at some future time. After the killing was over for that season it was again condemned by the international community at the 1988 annual meeting of the Commission.

It seems to me that the whole issue of whaling in Japan is about national pride and a refusal to be browbeaten by foreigners as much as anything else. Clearly the country is prepared to pay an increasingly heavy economic penalty for preserving the whaling industry. The losses on the fleet's activities for just one season were budgeted at £9 million. The government provided a £2 million subsidy and the rest came from corporate and public subscriptions. Over the years the number of people employed in the industry had fallen dramatically. Season after season the factory ships were never fully employed. All but one factory ship, the *Nisshin Maru No. 3*, were mothballed in Japan. Feelings on the issue were running high, and a bill was passed by the Japanese Diet, or parliament, enabling the government to resign from the International Whaling Commission if there was further pressure on Tokyo to stop whaling. Meanwhile the scarcity of whalemeat in Japan meant it had become a culinary rarity and its price was rising. Once, immediately after the war, it had been the cheapest meat, but in 1988 it cost twice as much as beef and ten times as much as chicken. It was sold in only the most exclusive shops and was eaten mostly by the over-sixties for special occasions.

In 1989, therefore, it was widely hoped that the Japanese would abandon their plans to continue with an annual 'scientific' programme. After several months of silence, however, the Japanese government issued a permit for the killing of 300 whales for the new season. The whaling fleet sailed almost immediately, making for the edge of the Antarctic ice sheet. It was this fleet that Greenpeace had just bumped into. Pete was not going to miss the opportunity to take them on.

The night of 25 January was rough. The ship was hove to in the middle of the ocean; I slid from side to side in my bunk, rolling with the movement. When Pete came along with a press release at 9 am I discovered we were on the move, following the Japanese mother ship, which had steamed off and then stopped again. We were now two miles away and closing because Pete had decided to try to reason with the scientists on board the *Nisshin Maru No. 3*.

Pete spoke to a Japanese with impeccable English who described himself as the chief scientist on board the mother ship. Pete told him of the international disapproval of their action. He warned the Japanese that Greenpeace would take nonviolent direct action if they started whaling again. The scientist said he had understood all that Pete had said. At the moment because of the weather (it was foggy) they were only doing scientific observation. He asked Greenpeace to give the mother ship 'sea room'. Pete said he would do so. For an hour or so Greenpeace circled the Japanese ship. The huge sides, painted black, towered above us. According to our notes the ship was 23,000 tons, compared with the *Gondwana*'s 1,200 tons.

Suddenly the *Nisshin Maru No. 3* radioed us and said it was moving ten miles south. Arne replied 'OK' and we followed. At lunch another call came through from the Japanese to say they were stopping again. Clearly they wanted to avoid any misunderstandings.

Naoko, now busy with a paintbrush up on deck, was very worried about the Greenpeace posters, which said 'Stop the Bloody Whaling'. She said the word 'bloody' was very offensive in Japanese and translated as 'barbaric', which would give gross offence. As a result she was painting out the word 'bloody' on the posters and instead making her own poster in foot-high Japanese characters to tow behind the helicopter. It said, she assured me, 'Stop Scientific Whaling'. We took her word for it and bowed to her advice.

At about five in the afternoon there was a sudden change in Japanese tactics. The factory ship set off at speed in an easterly direction. We were forced to pile on as much power as possible to keep up. There had been no communication before this sudden charge, and we could only assume they were acting on orders from Tokyo. The whalers had not attempted to follow their mother ship, and opinion on the bridge was that she was trying to outrun the *Gondwana*. The race went on for a long time. For some hours the *Nisshin Maru No. 3* kept in a straight line and then, again without any explanation, turned southeast, and we altered course to keep on her track.

At first it seemed the Japanese were succeeding in making their escape. After five hours we were eight miles behind, according to the radar screen. In the clear air we could still see the stern of the factory ship, but it did look smaller. After some consultation with the engineers, Davey Edwards, the chief, came up to the bridge and said we could put on more revs. We were making just over ten knots and losing ground, but he said we could in theory make twelve. Gradually over half an hour we began to gain on the *Nisshin Maru No. 3*.

On the chart was a large rectangular area which marked the old official whale-hunting grounds. The Japanese were committed to sticking to these for their scientific whaling. As they crossed this notional line on the chart they suddenly turned north. The *Gondwana* immediately cut the corner, bringing the two ships back to within four miles of each other.

As the pursuit continued through the night, the weather

worsened and there were fears on the *Gondwana*'s bridge that the bigger ship would be able to pull away: it carved through the sea, while we had to climb up and down the giant rollers. Davey resolutely kept up the revs despite the cost in fuel. We ploughed on.

To our surprise the *Gondwana* continued to hold her own. Through the binoculars it became clear that the high-sided factory ship was being caught by the wind and it was they and not we who were being slowed by the weather. I was on watch from midday to 4 pm, and by then we were only half a mile behind and were even able to reduce speed slightly.

Our problems were by no means over, however. It was now very windy, and shortly after 12 noon the porthole in the galley started leaking. Then things got worse: water was reported pouring through the galley ventilation system, which had not been properly battened down. A few moments later all the lights went out temporarily. Fortunately this did not affect any of the ship's controls, and Albert, who was in charge of our watch, put the ship to port to protect the damaged side from the weather. Orders were given that all portholes on the lower decks were to have their deadlights closed. Henk was dispatched to make the ventilator system weatherproof. The ship was now sideways to the waves and rolling wildly. At the same time the crew were mustered and told to take down all the banners on the upper decks and hangar in case the wind, now gale force, ripped them to pieces. By the time everything had been stowed and battened down we had lost a lot of ground.

Arne had now assumed command and, satisfied that the ship was now watertight, put on maximum revs, aiming to make up the lost ground. We looked up, expecting to see the receding lights of the factory ship still heading north, but suddenly in the gloom we could not locate them. The Japanese were trying to elude us. With our sudden change in pace they must have realised we were in some difficulty and had sailed in among a group of icebergs. Albert studied the radar screen for some time and then fixed on a blob which was moving differently from the rest. Within a few minutes it was clear that he had made the right choice.

Our troubles with the storm seemed to have inspired Albert. His blood was up, and he entertained us by singing what I took to be Viking battle songs. Between verses he sprang out on to the freezing bridge wings and waved his fist in the direction of the factory ship, shouting his imitation of Japanese threats. Hanging on grimly to my lookout chair, I wished that I felt half as well as he did.

Just before four in the afternoon the Japanese vessel suddenly started to slow down. They must have realised that they were not fast enough to escape, so they made themselves more comfortable by turning into the wind and reducing speed to six knots. The race was over, at least for now, and it made life much easier on both ships.

The wind was now blowing at forty knots and the seas were beginning to get very big. I dreaded writing anything in these conditions, but duty called and I went below. Just as I got to the end of the first draft we went over what must have been a particularly big wave. My chair was chained to the floor and I had my hands on the keyboard, but my body lifted off as the ship plunged downwards into the trough. My stomach had finally had enough too, and I had to get rapidly off the floor and stagger up the stairs to the toilet. I felt better after a few appalling minutes. With my stomach empty I was able to tidy up my copy ready to go two decks up to the radio room to file. The ship was pitching and rolling a good deal. In the doorway of the radio room I was lifted off my feet again and hit my head on the lintel. I was not a happy man. Ian Balmer, the radio operator, was not at his usual post. Phil Doherty, who looked pretty pale himself, was standing in for him, and offered to send the story for me. Gratefully, I staggered off to bed.

At 10.30 pm I got up to check that Phil had managed to get the stuff across and remembered that I was on the rota for washing the dishes. I had not eaten or been anywhere near the galley for hours and had no idea what had been happening down there. I knew that scraping food off plates would finish me off completely but felt compelled to go down. I was amazed and relieved to find that someone had already done it. The place had been completely cleaned up. It was a relief to get back to bed.

On Friday morning, 27 January, the sea seemed a little quieter, but our clothes, which, until the storm, had been neatly stacked in a chest Greenpeace had provided, were now all over the floor. The drawers had all come out in the night with the roll of the ship. Unwilling to sort out the tangle – Tim and Sean were still asleep – I stepped over the debris and got washed and shaved to prove to myself that I was ready for the day. Up on the bridge I learned that the factory ship had turned from north to southwest in the night and had steamed for an hour before turning head to wind and drifting.

I decided to tackle some fruit salad for lunch, the first food for more than twenty-four hours. It tasted good and stayed down. There was little to do but wait for developments, so I read for a couple of hours and then played Tim at chess. At least Greenpeace were achieving their object and had stopped the whaling so far. Just then the factory ship set off again, heading west. I went to the bridge, where Albert calculated that the current course would take us back to where we had first spotted the whaling fleet. The *Gondwana*, making ten knots, tucked in behind the factory ship. It seemed the *Nisshin Maru No. 3* was no longer trying to escape, so we settled in for several hours' steaming. I wrote and filed a holding piece without being sick, and concluded that I must be on the mend.

The office told me that Timothy Eggar, the Foreign Office minister in charge of Antarctic affairs, had been questioned in the House of Commons about the penguin killing at Dumont d'Urville. He promised a full investigation. I was interested that an MP had been concerned enough to ask a question – it was good news for the campaign.

I did a notice for the crew information board in the galley. Out in these thousands of miles of ocean it would cheer up the crew to know that their actions were having some effect.

9

Harrying the Harpooners

PETE CAME IN at 5.30 next morning to tell us we were back among the whaling fleet. I turned over to give this some thought. It was going to be a very long day. At eight I was woken by Paul Bogart, to be told that we were about to lower the boats. This meant we were going to try and interfere with the whale hunt. This time I was quickly up and on the bridge to watch events.

Greenpeace had two types of small boat: inflatables with big outboard engines on the back, and workboats which were slightly bigger, more rigid and heavier. An inflatable and the one workboat on board had been lowered into the sea and had set off for the nearest catcher boat, more than two miles away. The weather was much better, and the sea relatively calm. This was partly because there were a large number of icebergs around which were breaking up the waves.

Pete was grumpy with me because I had not got up when he first called me, so I went to see Naoko in the radio room to find out what had been happening. She had been monitoring the Japanese radio. She said that at 7 am the factory ship had told the fleet they should resume whaling, and instructions were given to the crews on what to do if their operations were interfered with. If Greenpeace tried to board any of their vessels they were to resist with fire hoses and clubs. She said that catcher boat no. 3 had already killed a whale.

Back on the bridge I saw that the inflatable and the workboat had caught up with catcher no. 1. The inflatable was between the harpoon and any possible target. The Japanese turned their fire hoses on, but the Greenpeace boats kept on the edge of their water's range and continued to harass them. Everyone on the *Gondwana* was pleased the fire hoses were on; it indicated a degree of panic on the part of the Japanese. It also would make a better picture for Steve Morgan, who was out there in the workboat. I

was very happy I could observe all this from the safe distance of
the bridge.

We were now between the factory ship and the catcher boats.
The catcher we were chasing went in a wide arc across our bow
about two miles ahead. We cut a corner to get closer and she
dodged behind a large iceberg.

At this point I decided there was enough happening to warrant
an update of my story, and there was still time to do a piece for
the third edition at home. I rang Duncan Campbell, who was on
night desk duty, and Foreign took eight new paragraphs. I used
the line about the Japanese being told to use fire hoses and clubs.
Pete, who was still not in a happy mood, told me off for this
because it came from an intercepted radio transmission. He said
it was a criminal offence to make use of information from such a
source. It was not just me who could get into trouble, it was Arne,
who as captain was responsible. I tried to make light of it and told
Pete it was my version of nonviolent direct action against people
killing whales. He was not amused. This was not like him.

While I had been sending copy the workboat had returned to
the ship so that Steve could go up in a helicopter with the film
crew. He wanted to take some more pictures of the inflatable and
the workboat in action against the Japanese. The action went well
at first, but then the workboat engine suddenly cut out and would
not restart. This was a difficult situation: we could not allow Henk
and the workboat to drift away in an ice-strewn sea, they would
be miles away in a short time. Over the two-way radio Arne
ordered Ken Ballard in the inflatable to give up the harassment
and turn back to escort the workboat. He wanted a line thrown
on board to stop them drifting further while we turned the ship
round to pick them all up.

The difficult job of getting everything and everyone back on
board safely now took precedence over the anti-whaling operations. The workboat was brought alongside by the inflatable. The
swell was still about eight to ten feet and the *Gondwana* was rolling.
This meant the boats were rising and falling wildly, very close to
the ship's rail. The boats were made ready for hauling up. They
each had four ropes, one in each corner of the boat, fixed to a
steel ring. Marc de Fourneaux, the ship's carpenter, who was with
Henk in the workboat, positioned himself to jump from the boat,
waiting until the swell brought him level with the rope ladder on
the side of the ship. We watched with some trepidation, unable

to help. Fortunately his timing was perfect.

With Marc safely on board, we lowered the crane hook, and after several attempts Henk managed to attach it to the workboat. He too scrambled out up the rope ladder. The slack on the hauling rope of the crane was taken up, and as the rope became taught the workboat was lifted out of the water. There were a few tense moments as the workboat crashed about the deck, but Pete, who was working the crane, kept his head, and as the boat swung over the rail he managed to drop it hard on to the deck. It was now Ken's turn to come on board. The inflatable weighed only a tiny amount compared with the workboat, and we were able, despite the swell, to bring it in quite easily.

The weather was now deteriorating again, so Pete decided to have a break for lunch, and to discuss what to do next. By the time we had got the boats in, the *Gondwana* was miles away from the catcher boats, and those on watch decided to head straight back towards the factory ship. Two of the catchers had gone back there too, and as we approached the three ships we could see two freshly killed whales being hauled up the slipway at the back of the *Nisshin Maru No. 3*.

Once a whale was harpooned and died it was towed back to the factory ship, where a hawser was let down from the stern, picked up by the catcher boat and tied to the tail of the whale. The carcass was then hauled up the ramp of the factory ship to be cut up by the teams of men waiting on deck. Within a couple of hours the whale would be divided up into neat whale steaks and packed away in the freezing plant of the ship. The scientists were supposed to study each whale as it was brought on board, finding sex, age, sexual maturity, genetic make-up and other features. Some organs were collected for testing. The catcher boats turned away from the factory ship once they had unhitched their catches, and we presumed they were going back to try for some more. Pete decided we should follow them.

The catcher boats each had two men who presumably were the experienced whale spotters at the top of their masts. There was one man on the bow with the harpoon, which was loaded with explosive grenades. Rather surprisingly, the catcher boats were not using their superior speed to get away from us, and we were able to shadow them while they searched for their prey. The first pod (group) of whales they spotted happened to be closer to us than to them. Both catchers headed for the whales, but so did we

– at top speed. We could see the whales clearly, about four in the group. With twin screws and rudders the *Gondwana* was far more manoeuvrable that the whalers, and with a head start and deft handling Albert was able to put us between the catcher ships and the whales.

Three times, just at the point where the harpoonist was about to fire, Albert was successful in getting our ship between him and the whales. Once the whale was less than thirty yards from the gun as Albert thrust the *Gondwana* bow between the two. The Japanese gunner threw up his arms in anger. We cheered – but it was all a little too close for comfort.

Inevitably, however, with the *Gondwana* alone against two catcher boats, it became an impossible task. Liz spotted whales to starboard already being hotly pursued by a catcher boat. We moved as fast as we could, blasting on the ship's klaxon. The catcher was going very fast towards the whales. The gunner moved forward, fired, we held our breath – he had missed.

The Japanese hauled the harpoon back in and reset it as the men in the crow's nest kept track of the pod of whales. The catcher set off again towards the whales, easily outpacing us. Even though they had to slow down to take aim, the *Gondwana* was just too far away. We ran close alongside the whaler in an attempt to make it shy away, but the captain and the harpoonist kept their nerve. The harpoonist fired, and after a few sickening moments it was clear that this time he had not missed.

There was total silence on the crowded bridge. The whale dived as the harpoon hit home, and we cut engines and waited only yards from the catcher boat to see what happened next. The whale broke the surface, streaming blood. It was still very much alive, but with every heartbeat the blood was pumping out of the wound made by the harpoon. The Japanese began winching it in. The whale flapped its tail, but there was no escape. The Greenpeace crew stood on the bridge, appalled by the scene. Some started taking pictures. Liz, so elated a few minutes before, had tears streaming down her face.

The whale was pulled to the bow of the catcher ship. It turned on its side, still flapping wildly, blood spurting. The whaler crew, undeterred by our presence and doing what to them must be a routine job, lowered further lines to the whale. Someone said they might be electrodes used to stun the animal and stop its pain. The whale continued to writhe and flap and pour blood. It was hard to know whether it was stunned or not.

The Japanese kept working and secured it further, lashing the now feebly flapping tail to the side of the ship and eventually pulling out the harpoon. The whale gave a final shudder which shook its whole frame. I hoped that this meant it was finally dead and its misery finished. I felt emotionally exhausted. So much for being a tough old hack.

The catcher crew set off back to the *Nisshin Maru No. 3*. The *Gondwana* followed. The whale was still streaming blood in the water. It was an appalling spectacle. We went in close as the hawser from the factory ship was lowered into the water, picked up by the catcher ship and attached to the kill. The whale was then released from the catcher and dragged up the slipway at the back of the factory ship to be carved up.

Tim and Sean had been filming the whole thing from the beginning, and to round off they got Pete to do a piece to camera. He was still upset and angry and said (waving towards the disappearing carcass) that it was a charade to call this science, it was plain and simple slaughter. The Japanese were killing any whale they could in order to supply the expensive restaurants in Tokyo. He pledged that Greenpeace would continue to hamper the whalers as much as possible.

Because of the swell it remained dangerous to put the boats back in the water. Someone came up with the idea of using the *Gondwana's* fire hoses to obsure the harpoonist's view. Pete decided this was an action which could be interpreted as aggressive rather than passive. A policy decision was required, so Pete decided to telephone Campbell Plowden, Greenpeace's whale campaign coordinator in the United States. It was 10 pm in Washington. Campbell was against using the hose at first, but after ten minutes Pete managed to persuade him that it would be all right to put a water screen in front of the harpoonist. Some water would be bound to blow on him so he would get very wet and uncomfortable, but the full force of the jet would not hit him. Campbell said that on no account should any attempt be made to knock a harpoonist off his boat.

Meanwhile Naoko was still listening to the radio to monitor events. She said that catcher boat no. 3 had just taken another whale. There did not seem to be any pattern to the whale kills that could justify the claim that this was selective killing for the sake of science. The Japanese seemed from our observations to be killing the first minke whale that came within range. Naoko said, in their defence, that the catcher boats had reported spotting other whales, notably sperm whales, and had not hunted them.

Earlier, on the bridge, I had been reading the proposed Japanese research programme for 1988/89 which had been submitted to the International Whaling Commission to justify the current hunt. This suggested that the catcher boats would make a careful study of each whale pod before a kill was made. This was clearly not happening with the harassment we were giving the fleet. Notes on the size of the pod and whether there were any calves would be impossible at the speeds at which we were forcing them to operate.

After watching catcher no. 3 take its whale back to the ship, we followed as two catchers set off together again. We could not hope to interfere with both ships, so Albert decided to stick to one. We cruised along together, the Japanese and us, both spotting for whales, but with different motives. We saw nothing positive, and despite occasional shouts from their crow's nest they did not seem to either. The *Gondwana* kept within twenty yards of the whaler, running them very close, testing their nerve. They must have known they would certainly come off worst if there was a collision, but Albert had no intention of letting it come to that. We were certainly close enough for some rude gestures, but Arne ordered them to cease immediately. After a hour or so the catcher boat turned back towards the factory ship. It seemed they had given up hunting for the evening. By then our crew was tired and I supposed the Japanese must be too. Also, although there was no darkness at this latitude in January, we were far enough away from the pole to be subject to a kind of twilight.

We had dinner, and back in the warmth of the lounge I risked a beer after three days of abstinence because of seasickness. It went down OK but still did not taste very good. A check on the bridge before bed revealed that the factory ship was still hove to and the catchers were without anyone on the crow's nests.

Next morning passed peacefully and allowed me to catch up with my chores. Sadly, the heating switch on the communal dryer had gone wrong, and my favourite brown Shetland sweater, a mainstay of my wardrobe, got overheated and came out about half its previous size. It was a serious loss. I went down to lunch and was told that Naoko had heard that the Japanese planned to start whaling again at 1 pm. Two whales had been brought in during the morning from the third catcher, which so far we had not had any contact with. It seemed to hunt on its own.

A new tactic had been planned while I had been worrying about my washing. The crew had been thinking round the fact that we could harass only one or two whalers at a time. However, if we crept up close behind the factory ship then we would effectively block the loading. This would mean the catcher boats could not get rid of their cargoes and thus we would have prevented them going back for more. And since the weather was much improved, it was also decided that we could, if necessary, put the inflatables in the water to further harass the catcher boats. The crew had decided, because of our last experience, that the workboat would be left on the deck.

In order to try out the new tactic the *Gondwana* needed to be close to the factory ship, so this time the Greenpeace crew simply watched as the whalers disappeared over the horizon. After a while I went downstairs to the computer to write up the previous day's events for the paper.

In the middle of the afternoon Dave Walley came down from the bridge to tell us that the catchers were returning with whales. He was going to take the helicopter up, but he said nothing would happen for another half an hour because the whalers were still a long way from the factory ship.

I watched from the bridge as the *Gondwana* closed on the *Nisshin Maru No. 3*. The atmosphere was tense because the catchers had understood our ploy and were going at top speed to get to their mother ship before us. Then Naoko, who was still glued to the radio, told us one of the catcher boats was being deployed to cut us off. Arne, who took over the controls, was unmoved by the catcher boat, which was heading directly towards us, hooting as it came. He steered directly for the stern of the factory ship, which was wallowing in the swell about half a mile away. Travelling at about seventeen knots, the catcher was suddenly very close, close enough to see the grim faces of the Japanese on the bridge, and for a moment I wondered if they really meant to ram us. At what seemed to me to be the last possible moment the whaler swung away in a tight turn, causing a powerful wash, and the *Gondwana* ploughed on towards its target.

Arne only slackened pace when he had made it to our intended position barely fifty metres behind the stern of the factory ship, which towered above us, making us appreciate for the first time how enormous it was. Realising his operations had been halted, the *Nisshin Maru No. 3*'s captain put on speed and began twisting and turning to try and shake us off, but our smaller ship, with its twin engines and rudders, was more than a match for him.

The stern of the *Nisshin Maru No. 3* was now crammed with Japanese, some taking pictures, some laughing. But an older man in red, who seemed to be in charge, was so angry he was literally jumping up and down in rage – the first time I had ever seen anyone in such a state.

He calmed down after a while and started issuing orders. Then our ship-to-ship radio, silent for a few days, suddenly began to crackle. The Japanese captain, who had been maintaining radio silence since he started his attempt to outrun us on the second day, came on and, without any of the preliminary politeness so characteristic of his people, demanded we give him sea room and leave the area. Arne acknowledged the message, but said nothing more. The factory ship, after waiting a few minutes, again began to twist and turn with the *Gondwana* close behind. One of the catcher boats, with a whale alongside, was now very close.

Pete had been rummaging around below to find a megaphone, with the idea that Naoko should address the assembled Japanese workers through it. I wondered about the wisdom of this, since the Japanese, seeing Naoko, would probably realise we could intercept their radio transmissions and so we would lose our intelligence advantage, but Pete was intent on getting the Greenpeace message across. During a lull Naoko, accompanied by Pete, went out on the bridge wing and tried shouting across the twenty yards between the two ships. Even with the megaphone, our ship's two engines and the helicopter, which was still hovering above, must have drowned her voice completely. The Japanese certainly showed no signs of having heard; perhaps they were just being inscrutable. We had now been locked in battle behind the factory ship for more than an hour. Two of the catcher boats were now close to us, looking for a way through, one with two dead whales slung alongside and the other with one.

Arne, who had been at the wheel the whole time, was increasingly nervous about an accidental collision with four ships moving fast so close together. He suddenly said that he felt that Greenpeace had made their point. The *Gondwana* had prevented the unloading and had severely disrupted the Japanese whaling operation. Such close manoeuvres carried high risks, and he told Pete 'Enough is enough.'

Pete bowed immediately to the captain's word on matters of ship safety. He suggested instead that we drew alongside the factory ship. From there, where there would be less noise, Naoko could address the Japanese captain on his bridge.

As we drew alongside, a man stepped out on the *Nisshin Maru No. 3*'s bridge wing and listened patiently while Naoko gravely addressed him. She told me later she had explained to him Greenpeace's viewpoint and that world opinion was against him. In the message she had added that the International Whaling Commission had condemned the so-called scientific whaling. She asked the Japanese to stop and go home. The man remained inscrutable. We had no idea if he had heard our message or if he was even the captain.

The weather forecast came through, and with a sinking heart I heard it was bad. It made Pete spring into action. He decided to have a quick dinner and put up another helicopter with a trailing banner saying 'Stop the Bloody Whaling'. The idea was to have a publicity picture that could be sent out the following day to keep up international interest if nothing happened or the weather was too bad. A professional manager of the news.

I had no time to watch this stunt or to wonder what the Japanese would make of it because I had to go below to finish writing and filing to London. After I had filed, Mike Ellison on the news desk was pleased with the piece and said AP had Steve's pictures on the way. Steve was revving up to file another picture but he was not quite ready, so I seized the opportunity to ring home. Just when I was giving up, Maureen answered. She was cross with me because I had not rung before, I told her she was never in, and so the conversation went on. At least she was alive and full of spirit. The good news was that I had had a tax rebate; the bad news was that Maureen had spent it already. She also told me the crocuses were out in the garden, and for some reason this made me feel very homesick. As she got less cross she said she had been worried about my safety because of the gales. She had been reading my reports in *The Guardian*. She was not as worried as I had been, I wanted to say, but instead I assured her there was no danger.

During the night I became aware that the wind had got up as forecast, but in the morning we were still just behind the factory ship and watching the catchers on the horizon. Nothing much happened until after lunch, when Paul Bogart told me the civil servants who represent Australia at the International Whaling Commission had telephoned the ship. One Rhys Puddicomb was very supportive of Greenpeace actions and wanted information on the Japanese operations. The Australian Environment Minister, Graham Richardson, was currently on a visit to Tokyo and wanted to make a formal protest about the whaling. The Australians would also support a British resolution condemning the so-called scientific programme at the International Whaling Commission annual meeting in the spring. This resolution was news to me and looked like the story for the day.

While I was on the bridge the conditions were not ideal for spotting whales and the Japanese were not having much luck. During the evening they did finally kill one. I was not on the bridge, but it seemed the watch did not notice what was happening until it was too late. When the *Gondwana* moved to block the ramp the catcher boat managed to sneak in first.

Although at first there seemed no discernible pattern to the whaling fleet's movements, it became clear from the plotting of our position that the Japanese factory ship had been gradually steaming north over the previous couple of days. Even at an average of about four or five knots we were a long way north, and it was noticeable that twilight was lasting four or five hours. The Japanese presumably knew that the *Gondwana*'s itinerary was to have taken us due south and we were now well behind schedule. I doubted whether their gradual move north was a coincidence.

London Greenpeace had faxed a copy of that day's front page of *The Guardian* showing two of Steve Morgan's dramatic pictures of Ken Ballard in the inflatable taking on the whalers. Everyone on board was delighted except me. I knew it was silly, but I was upset because they had cut my copy. The pictures told the story more graphically than I could have done.

The following morning I was sitting in my cabin sorting out all my papers when Pete came in and said there was a catcher approaching. I got up to glance out of the porthole and was astonished to see the catcher only yards away. It had a whale streaming blood tied to its side. This was the closest we had been to one of the whalers. In half a minute I was out of the cabin, up the stairs and standing on the bridge rail. Both the *Gondwana* and the catcher were heading towards the stern of the factory ship. I felt I could almost reach out and touch the whaler. The Japanese crew stood opposite looking at us with blank faces. The whale between the two ships looked as if it might be squashed. There was now hardly any water between the three ships – we were on a collision course.

Someone's nerve had to go and it was the whaler captain's. His ship was put hard to starboard, but he had left it a little late. As his bow turned away his stern swung across towards us and hit the *Gondwana* amidships. The bump was hardly noticeable, but it caused great excitement on both ships. We stuck to our station behind the *Nisshin Maru No. 3* while people ran about to see if they could spot any damage. We could not find any at all. The catcher ship, still with the whale attached, had stood off about half a mile away, and through the binoculars we could see members of the crew inspecting a badly bent rail at the rear of the ship. There did not appear to be any other damage, and what we could see was not serious.

For the next hour there was a series of exchanges between Arne and the captain of the *Nisshin Maru No. 3*. From time to time the Japanese fleet commander conferred with the captain of the whaler with whom we had just collided. There was a lot of argument about rules of overtaking at sea, and from Arne's exchanges, and Naoko's understanding of what the two Japanese captains were saying, it was clear they felt in some difficulty. They feared that the *Gondwana*'s owners could take them to court for breaking No. 13 of the International Rules of the Sea, about overtaking vessels. It was apparently the responsibility of the overtaking vessel to leave enough room to avoid a collision. According to Arne in this case the whaler was overtaking us and came too close to avoid hitting us when turning to starboard.

At first during the exchanges the Japanese had adopted an angry tone, saying Arne was responsible; then, presumably, having consulted the rule books like us, they confined themselves to claiming we were in their working area and should be careful.

Arne responded by saying Greenpeace would undertake not to collide with the factory ship, but warned them not to allow the catchers to collide with us. 'We are a very strong ship.' At another point Arne said: 'We realise it is very frustrating for you. It is very frustrating for us to see you killing the whales, pulling them on your ship and cutting them up. We do not like you killing the whales.' There was no reply to this, but the Japanese finally asked the *Gondwana* to keep 200 yards away. This was refused.

After a period of stalemate with the three ships hardly moving, the Japanese factory ship captain suddenly threw his ship into reverse. This new tactic seemed to have come straight from his study of the rule book. According to the rules, if a collision occurred the *Gondwana*, as the following ship, would be in the wrong.

Fortunately, reversing a ship the size of the *Nisshin Maru No. 3* takes some time, and Albert, quick as ever, was able to take evasive action – although the gap between the two ships was as narrow as ten yards at one point. This ploy having failed, the factory ship began to cruise slowly forward again, heading still further north. The *Gondwana* followed close behind.

One of the other catcher ships was also in sight. This joined the one carrying the dead whale and they appeared to resume hunting. Pete decided it was time to step up the action again as the water was calm enough for the inflatables to be put back over the side. The *Gondwana* left her post and set off towards the catcher ships. After a while it was clear they were not hunting but waiting for an opportunity to double back and get the dead whale on board the factory ship. But when catcher no. 1 did a rapid U-turn and tried to get back to the factory ship, Albert was too quick for it and cut off the route. No. 1 turned away again, not anxious for a repeat of the earlier duel.

Pete decided to risk launching the workboat and the inflatables. But the workboat got stuck halfway through the launch and crashed into the side of the *Gondwana* in a repeat of the mess we had got into before. Catcher No. 1 realised we were in trouble and made another dash for the factory ship. Valuable minutes were lost getting the workboat free and into the water. Arne turned the *Gondwana* to try and cut off the whaler, but it was clear our ship had lost this race. Henk and Pat King, up from the galley and proving Greenpeace sexual equality by crewing the workboat, had other ideas. They were faster than either ship. Despite being thrown about terribly in the swell, they streaked across the gap to the factory ship and managed to get between the stern of the *Nisshin Maru No. 3* and the catcher. The Japanese were clearly enraged by this latest intervention and turned on fire hoses, pouring thousands of gallons of near-freezing sea water into the workboat. Fortunately it was buoyant and unsinkable, and Henk and Pat remained on station. We launched a second boat, an inflatable crewed by Ken Ballard and Ian Balmer.

As we got closer we could see the Japanese were hanging over the side of the catcher with grappling hooks, and Pat told me later that they were apparently trying to tip the boat over. From the bridge we could see, through the jets of water, the workboat tipped right on its side and Henk and Pat hanging on to avoid being thrown into the sea. They were perilously close to the wake of the factory ship and, realising perhaps the possible consequences of what they were doing, the Japanese let go and the workboat fell back on an even keel. By now its engines had cut out.

Half drowned under the force of water from the fire hoses, Henk was unable to restart the engines and the workboat began to drift away. By this time Ken Ballard had reached the area. Realising that the workboat was no longer a threat, the Japanese turned the full force of their fire hoses on the newly arrived inflatable. In the ensuing confusion the Japanese managed to hook up the dead whale and were ready to haul it in.

The *Gondwana* had lost that round. As we turned to pick up Henk before the workboat drifted too far away, he unexpectedly got the engine of the workboat going again and set off to harass the catcher boat. Pierrette took Steve Morgan up in a helicopter to take more pictures, and they hovered close to the bridge of the catcher ship, a form of intimidation on its own.

Naoko, still listening to the radio traffic, had heard the chief scientist telling the crew of the factory ship to prevent Greenpeace getting pictures of them cutting up whales. Fascinating though all this was, time was getting on and I had to go below and start recording the day's events.

By the time I had written up a piece Pat King, still soaking wet from the fire hoses, was being helped back on board by a dozen willing hands. She had a deep cut on her nose and two broken front teeth. Surprisingly this was not caused by the Japanese boathooks but by the workboat flying up in the air on a wave and causing her to tip forward and hit her head on the dashboard. The incident with the grappling hooks had frightened her more, however. She summed up simply: 'I thought I was a goner.'

News of the collision and other events of the day had reached the outside world via one of Pete's press releases, and the pressure of calls from radio stations and newspapers wanting interviews with members of the crew had grown so great I had considerable difficulty getting my own copy out. I wondered how long the story could maintain this level of international interest.

Every night the Japanese captains had a 'radio meeting'. They all got on their ships' radios together and had a four-way discussion. Naoko, who spent at least fourteen hours a day by the radio keeping track of events, was at her post as always on this particular night.

The captain of catcher no. 1, with whom we collided earlier, complained that Greenpeace were always picking on him. He said, according to Naoko: 'I have lost my nerve, I cannot go on much longer.' Instead of being sharp, as we would have expected, the captain of *Nisshin Maru No. 3* was very sympathetic and understanding. He suggested that they all stop whaling for four days and only take part in a whale stock survey. This was readily agreed all round by the three catcher boat captains as a way of avoiding further confrontations with Greenpeace.

Delighted as he was with this information, Pete was at a loss to know what to do next. If nothing was happening there were no new stories for the press. On the other hand everyone was tired and the expedition was way behind schedule. Unless other projects were to be abandoned the *Gondwana* would have to be on its way soon anyway, visiting the Italian and German bases on Antarctica, and relieving Greenpeace's own base. What was needed was a way of ending the campaign against the *Nisshin Maru No. 3* with honour. Pete's first thought was to try to arrange some kind of meeting or interview with the Japanese. He decided to sleep on this and discuss it with the crew the next day.

10

The Battle Is Won But the War Goes On

ON THE FOLLOWING day, 1 February, news came through of a resolution presented by Britain, backed by Australia and New Zealand, to the International Whaling Commission condemning the current Japanese whaling programme. This was going to be resolved by a postal vote rather than waiting for the IWC's meeting in June. Countries had until 31 March to vote. If the resolution was supported in the ballot by seventeen countries, a simple majority of states belonging to the IWC, then it would be passed.

This was very cheering news to take to the crew meeting at one o'clock, where there was a wide measure of disagreement on what to do next. Personally I had had enough of whaling, but there were many among the crew who were not prepared to leave. One tactic that Greenpeace had prepared for this trip but never used was discussed for the first time. Below in the stores were several drums of molasses. The idea, dreamed up in the summer, was to warm the molasses, carry the drums up in the helicopter, and pour them out on to the person manning the harpoon gun as he prepared to fire on the whales. The crew had a considerable debate about this. First there was the question of whether it adhered strictly to the Greenpeace code of nonviolent direct action. Then there was the question of what happened to molasses in this climate. No one knew at what temperature treacle froze, but it would soon go pretty solid. Everyone was nervous about possibly injuring someone at this stage in the protest, having so far had such a good reaction worldwide.

Ton Kocken, the second engineer, diverted us from this difficult debate by suggesting we use the helicopters to drop a message about the IWC resolution to the factory ship in case they did not know about it. I suggested that Naoko translate it into Japanese and Greenpeace drop it on all four ships in the fleet. The meeting liked this idea, and Pete, obviously not happy with using the molasses, suggested that we do this as a final action before we left to go south again. There remained a little reluctance among some about leaving, but eventually we reached a consensus in true Greenpeace style, and a decision that we should try and leave within twenty-four hours.

One other matter was raised at the meeting. Dave Walley, the chief helicopter pilot, said a dent had appeared in the rear of one of the helicopters. He was very concerned about how it had got there but also worried that no one had reported it. He gave us all a lecture.

The notice board in the galley was now covered in congratulatory messages from all over the world from people admiring the *Gondwana*'s actions on the whaling. It was clearly time to get our feet back on the ground.

At the end of the action, in terms of whales saved, Greenpeace could claim that it had stopped the Japanese fleet from killing for six of the ten days it had harried the *Nisshin Maru No. 3*. Far more important, however, was drawing world attention to the continued hunting in the face of condemnation by the scientists of the International Whaling Commission. The level of public support for the *Gondwana*'s actions was enormous. In the week after my stories first appeared Greenpeace UK alone gained 3,000 extra members.

On 2 February Merriann Bell, one of our two cooks, whose speciality was pastries and cakes, had been up since the early hours making whale-shaped gingerbreads for delivery to the Japanese fleet, along with the message about the whaling resolution currently being transcribed by Naoko. The message was an attempt to tread the narrow line between preaching and attacking Japanese personal and national pride. Naoko and Pete were very anxious to avoid making the Japanese feel they had 'lost face'. Finally we contacted the Japanese and told them our plans, and that after the delivery we would be leaving the area. It must have been a tremendous relief to them. The captain was even moved to say 'roger' himself to acknowledge the message rather than leave it to the interpreter. The factory ship, which had been steadily cruising ever northwards, slowed to a crawl to facilitate the dropping of our present and message.

(*Previous page*) First mate, Ken Ballard, places himself between a Japanese whaler's harpoon-gun and the whales, in an attempt to stop the slaughter.

(*Right*) A minke whale is hauled into the Japanese fleet's factory ship.
(*Below*) The factory-ship crew butcher a newly-dead whale.

(*Left*) Ken Ballard and Pete Wilkinson check for 'growlers' from the *Gondwana*'s bridge wing.

(*Below*) The overwinterers outside World Park base: (left to right) Sabine Schmidt, Keith Swenson, Wojtek Moskal and Sjoerd Jongens.

(*Below*) The Greenpeace base at the foot of Mount Erebus on Ross Island.

(*Top*) Old fuel-oil barrels await disposal at the US McMurdo base and (*above*) collecting cadmium-contaminated water from McMurdo wastepipes for a demonstration against pollution.

The whole thing was delayed for an hour by a snowstorm which cut visibility to a few yards, making it impossible to fly the helicopters. Eventually Dave Walley went off with Maggie McCaw as his 'dropper' to the furthest catcher, which was thirteen miles away on the radar. Tim and Sean, and Steve Morgan, were flown by Pierrette to record the drop at the second and third catchers. The helicopters then returned to the factory ship, which we had continued to escort. Because of the aerials slung from the masts and other rigging it was impossible for the helicopters to get close enough to lower the canisters on to the deck as had been done on the other ships. They had to be dropped, which I expect damaged Merriann's carefully made biscuits.

The captain of catcher no. 1, the man who had said a couple of days previously that he felt victimised and his nerve was going, actually came on the radio to say thank you for his present. Naoko then overheard him remark in Japanese to the captain of the factory ship that he would probably have stomach ache the following day.

The helicopters were loaded back on board, and with a blast on the whistle and a cheer from everyone on the bridge we turned 180 degrees, due south. The whaling fleet had taken us so far out of our way that it was around 1,000 miles back to the Antarctic mainland and our next port of call, the Italian base.

Just as I was finishing off my farewell-to-whaling piece Pete came storming in. Not a man to get angry easily, he was clearly furious. He had ordered the ship to turn back. The messages in Japanese that had been so carefully prepared, had for some unaccountable reason been left out of the canisters which had been dropped on to the whalers and factory ship. They had just been found lying in the radio room. All the Japanese had received was the whale biscuits with a message saying 'Eat whaleshapes not whalemeat'. No wonder they had been so jolly.

Pete had already sent out his press release about the message, and for a while as we headed north at full speed it seemed we would have to put out an embarrassing correction because we could not find the fleet. Then suddenly, to Pete's great relief, the factory ship acknowledged our signals and gave a position. We continued north until the helicopter was ready to be relaunched. Arne then drifted until Dave Walley radioed back that he had managed to deliver the messages safely. We then turned back south knowing Dave would soon catch us up. Pete took a long time to calm down – it had cost us four hours' sailing, and it had been our turn to lose face.

I took the evening off, happy to be going south. I watched *Apocalypse Now*, the updated film version of the Conrad story 'Heart of Darkness', on the crew's video. Pure escapism and no icebergs in it. Lots of hot steamy jungle instead.

The British postal resolution condemning the Japanese whaling programme failed by one vote to get adopted. Sixteen countries voted in favour and none against, but under the IWC rules such resolutions require that a majority of the thirty-three paid-up members respond positively. In effect abstentions count as no-votes.

The Japanese whaling fleet returned to Tokyo at the end of the 1988 Antarctic summer with only 214 minke whales on board, instead of the expected haul of about 300. The official Japanese explanation for this was bad weather and the intervention of Greenpeace 'terrorists'. Greenpeace claimed that the fleet's failure was simply because there were not enough whales left to kill.

The political battle over whaling continued at the 1989 IWC meeting in San Diego. Here the debate over whale stocks dominated the proceedings. There was shock among the conservationists when Professor Doug Butterworth reported on the findings of the survey of the whale stocks of the four largest species which had been carried out by the IWC scientific committee. Numbers were well down on even the worst previous estimates. The professor said that since 1983 a total of 22 blue whales had been sighted in the Southern Ocean. He believed that meant there could be a maximum total stock of this species of 1,100 left in existence. In 1890, before killing began on a large scale, the stock of this whale, the largest mammal, was estimated to be 250,000. Professor Butterworth said the scientific committee was uncertain whether there were enough blue whales left to ensure the survival of the species.

Turning to the three other surveys of great whales in the same period, he said 27 fin whales had been sighted. He thought there were about 2,000 of these left out of an original population of 100,000. Eighty-seven sperm whales (the same species as Moby Dick) had been seen. There used to be one million of these in 1890; now he believed there were around 10,000 still alive. The largest numbers of the four species seen were of the humpback, a total of 179. These sometimes congregate in shallow water and are easier to count. The current estimate for the population of the species was 4,000 from an original stock of 200,000. There were no estimates of whale numbers yet available for the North Atlantic or other oceans.

The low numbers in this count led to renewed calls for an extension of the worldwide moratorium on whale hunting. The Japanese, Norwegians and Icelanders were unrepentant. The Japanese claimed that the stock of minke whales which they were hunting was between 400,000 and 700,000, although this figure was disputed by the conservation lobby. The Japanese still had a plan to take 825 minke whales and 50 sperm whales as part of their next season's 'scientific' programme. The meeting broke up with the moratorium intact and a general agreement that more scientific evidence was necessary from all sides before any decisions could be made on a continued ban or limited harvesting.

The United States meanwhile attempted to put diplomatic pressure on Japan to stop its whaling programme. Japanese fishing fleets were banned from US territorial waters, but this was only a token gesture since they rarely used them anyway. President Bush did not impose the second and far more serious action of banning imports of Japanese fish for fear of starting a much more far-reaching trade war.

Greenpeace was putting pressure on the Icelandic government to discontinue the scientific killing of whales, by organising an international boycott of the country's biggest export – fish. The Icelandic fishing ministry said that there was competition between whales and man for the fish stocks, and whale numbers had to be kept under control. They refused to budge for many months and denied the boycott was working, but subsequently suspended their scientific whaling programme. Norway cut the number to be taken for research to seventeen.

For several months there was uncertainty about whether the Japanese would press ahead with their extended scientific programme during 1990. It was not until mid-November 1989, when the fleet was due to sail, that the Japanese government said it was going to issue scientific permits for that season. Again they cut the number they proposed to take from 825 minkes and 50 sperm whales to the more limited programme of 300 minkes. On 8 December the fleet made its first kills. Greenpeace, again on a resupply voyage, attempted to find the fleet and do battle a second year running, but this time they were unsuccessful. By the end of the season the Japanese had killed 330 minkes. Ten per cent extra 'for error' is allowed under the research programme. The whalemeat can fetch as much as £70 a pound in Japan, and with a minke weighing 12,000 pounds that gives the industry quite a lot of potential and explains why Norway and Iceland are anxious to exploit their own local stocks and export them to Japan.

The Japanese insist that the clash over whaling is cultural. Western ideas about whales are mere sentiment which the Japanese do not share. To prove the point the Japanese are allowing their fishermen to increase their catches of bottlenose whales and dolphins, which are outside the IWC convention. They claim this is to meet an unfulfilled market demand for the meat of great whales. Their opponents claim it is blackmail: in effect the Japanese government is saying it will allow its fishermen to endanger these species too if they are not allowed to hunt whales.

Norway put in an application to the July 1990 meeting of the International Whaling Commission at Noordwijk in the Nether-lands to have the North Atlantic minke whale taken off the protected species list. They based their application on the fact that stocks of the whale had been estimated by them at 77,000. They said the IWC estimate of 20,000 for the same stock was wrong. The Norwegian argument by Ministry of Fisheries spokesman Jon Lauritzen echoed that of the Japanese. The IWC was a whaling commission not a whale commission – in other words, to supervise harvesting, not to protect. He said that unless the IWC worked on that basis the Norwegian government might have to reconsider its membership. Japan had already passed a bill through its parliament giving the government power to leave the IWC, but so far it has stopped short of going its own way.

The IWC scientific committee is still putting together a scheme for monitoring and calculating the stocks of whales. Ultimately they claim that if they get the methodology right, and if stocks can be shown to be recovering, then they will be able to fix sustainable harvesting numbers at some time in the future. The conservation lobby remains sceptical and against any form of harvesting, saying that there are alternative products that could replace everything taken from the whales.

Meanwhile the moratorium on commercial hunting will remain in place until at least the 1991 meeting of the IWC in Iceland.

The Norwegian government reduced its scientific catch to five in 1990. The Japanese said they would continue scientific whaling until the IWC made up its mind about harvesting quotas – in other words, they intended to keep their whaling industry alive despite the moratorium.

11

Tourists on the Rocks

ALL THE RECENT talk on board the *Gondwana* had been of an Argentine supply vessel carrying some tourists which had gone aground at Palmer Station, on the Antarctic Peninsula, on the opposite side of the icecap to us, roughly 1,000 miles away. There were 250 people on board the *Bahia Paraiso*: they all escaped injury and had been rescued. The details were very sketchy, but we were told that the ship appeared to have been abandoned by the crew. It was stuck on the rocks and in danger of breaking up. Because there could be as many as 250,000 gallons of diesel on board, the wreck posed a serious threat to Antarctic wildlife. This was because some oils do not disperse easily in the cold, and because the food chain was heavily dependent on the shrimp-like krill. These creatures, up to two inches long, live just under the surface and would surely be killed by any concentration of oil.

When I filed a piece about whaling later I mentioned the sinking of the *Bahia Paraiso* in passing as a major disaster for the Antarctic. The office had only had a couple of paragraphs from Reuter on this and was anxious for a fuller story. I told them that I was almost as far away as they were, but the truth was they were anxious to use my by-line, datelined Antarctica, so I had no alternative but to have a go at writing a piece. Fortunately Paul Bogart had a satellite telephone number for Palmer Station and had already spoken to them. It turned out too that Bob Graham had been to Palmer Station with last year's expedition and had made a special study of the area. We had the charts on board that he had used, and he was able to show me what must have happened to the *Bahia Paraiso*. It seemed the ship had turned up a wrong channel, straight on to the rocks.

The *Gondwana* also had a number of reference books on board that gave details of the wildlife around Palmer Station, including the sites of special scientific interest which would be damaged by the escaping oil. With all this wealth of information I was able to put together a substantial piece.

In the piece I quoted Ted Delaca, the US National Science Foundation official who ran Palmer Station. His staff had looked after the survivors from the wreck until they could be ferried out to South America. Mr Delaca said that oil had been pumped overboard by the crew of the *Bahia Paraiso* in an unsuccessful attempt to stop the ship sinking. His men had set up oil booms to try and prevent the oil spreading but had only been partially successful. I then included a quote: 'The krill are literally jumping out of the water to try and escape the oil. The birds in the area are going crazy seeing this food and are diving to get them, getting oiled up as a result.' Later, when American newspapers followed up my story, Paul Bogart got a lot of flack from the National Science Foundation in Washington because I had quoted one of their officials saying that the krill were 'jumping out of the water'. The Foundation scientists in Washington claimed that krill were not capable of jumping. Paul Bogart was upset by this criticism because Greenpeace prides itself on not making unsubstantiated claims, but I told him I stood by my story. To me an eyewitness report is as reliable as a scientific theorist 10,000 miles away.

Without a doubt the *Bahia Paraiso* sinking was the worst environmental disaster that had so far hit the Antarctic. It was immediately adopted by the conservation lobby as one of their most potent arguments warning against the Minerals Convention, showing what must inevitably happen if the oil industry was allowed to move into the area. The disaster also had the important function of focusing the Antarctic Treaty nations' minds on the increasing problems of controlling tourism on the continent.

The Argentine ship had been used to supply that country's bases, and at the same time to carry groups of tourists. This was important to the Argentines, because it virtually paid for the cost of supplies. Increasing numbers of cruise ships were showing an interest in visiting Antarctica. Although the total number of visitors during a summer season was minute compared with the crowd at a single international football match, the industry was – and still is – steadily growing. The small scale of the industry may seem to make the problem insignificant, but the tourists have a potential for damaging the fragile wildlife that is out of all proportion to their numbers. As I have already said in an earlier chapter, a footprint in the moss can still be seen twenty years later.

Also, more than a year after the *Bahia Paraiso* was wrecked, no attempt to salvage it would have been made, despite promises from the Argentine government. Only a small part of the superstructure was visible above the surface in April 1990. By then much of the oil was believed to have solidified in the fuel tanks because of the intense cold, but in the summer, when the temperature was above freezing, for a time an oil slick was visible seeping from the wreck.

Both Argentina and Chile see a potentially increasing income from Antarctic tourism. Chile has built a hotel which can cater for eighty at its Teniente Marsh base on the Fildes Peninsula. They have an airstrip next to the hotel and fly groups of tourists in. Plans by the treaty nations to designate part of the peninsula a Specially Protected Area (SPA) were abandoned once the Chilean base was built (an SPA is an area so precious that no one may go there without a special licence, and then only for scientific purposes) because there would be no way of controlling the tourists.

Currently about 3,500 people a year visit the Antarctic Peninsula purely as tourists; these are mostly Americans paying between £3,000 and £12,000 for a visit, which usually lasts less than a week. Most are ship-borne at the moment, living on the ships and making landfalls to visit penguin, seal and wildlife colonies, mostly to take pictures at close quarters. This can disrupt both the breeding patterns and the work of the scientists, especially since all the scientists, tourists and wildlife tend to be crowded into the same small areas. Tourists sometimes leave film wrappers, water bottles and cigarette butts in their wake. Elephant Island even has tourist graffiti. There are also an increasing number of 'adventure' holidays, including hiking, mountain climbing, dogsledding, camping and skiing. These involve aircraft with skis dropping people deep into the interior.

In the season of 1987/8 the officer in charge of the Russian base at Bellingshausen on the Peninsula commented: 'Tourists are not official guests and therefore we cannot control them like our own staff. Some tourist ships educate their passengers, others do not do so at all. There are hardly ever tourists on Soviet ships, but if there are, they are told to behave like base personnel. Outside the stations the tourists generally behaved reasonably well, but on the base itself they were often disruptive, disturbed work and went into buildings without being invited. Sometimes the staff felt like animals in a zoo.'

On the other side of the continent in the Australian territory, which is next to Dumont d'Urville, a Sydney company, Helmut Rohde, planned in 1989 to spend £100 million on a conference centre, hotel, hospital, and runway capable of taking jumbo jets. This would open up the continent to large-scale business and tourism, and it was opposed by the Australian Tourist Industry Federation and by environment groups. The Australian House of Representatives started an inquiry into tourism in the Antarctic, and the vast majority of witnesses were opposed to the development since it would have to be on hard rock and would use up even more of the diminishing area of land free for wildlife.

At present the Australian government has no power to prevent the development going ahead, but the government has made it clear that it is against exploitation of the continent, and because of this antagonism the Sydney company's project remains a fairly distant threat.

For once, there is a wide measure of agreement between the conservationists, the scientists and governments. No one is in favour of a ban on tourism, which would in any case be impossible to impose since there is no police force, but some sort of discipline is needed. The better tour operators have come up with a code of conduct that forbids visitors to harass animals, enter research stations unless invited, or take souvenirs, but this does not seem to be enough. It will also be difficult to exercise control over the increasing number of amateur yachtsmen visiting the area: the popular bays in some northern Peninsula islands look like holiday marinas, according to some scientists.

The Antarctic Treaty nations are now taking the problem seriously and are trying to evolve rules which will put certain areas completely out of bounds except for viewing from ships. Limiting the size of parties and the possibility of civil and criminal penalties for infringements of the rules are being considered. Liabilities may have to be imposed on tour operators to make the rules work.

The treaty nations agree that unless tourism is controlled, much painstaking scientific study of the wildlife could be spoilt. The view of the treaty nations is that they can and will solve the problem by mutual agreement. As one Norwegian diplomat put it: 'If we can contain the strains of the Minerals Convention

without the treaty system falling apart, then we can cope with
tourists. The fact is, we have to cope with both if we are to fulfil
our responsibilities as custodians of the Antarctic.'

12

Landfall at Last

IT HAD BEEN very stormy in the night of 2 February, and I thought about getting up several times, before finally putting it off until after lunch. Eventually I went downstairs and found the lounge was like a morgue, with people lying flat out on the seats, not even bothering to grunt a greeting.

In the galley, where those less affected were sitting, I decided I was well enough to eat something. It looked likely to be a dead day, so I retired back to bed to read and wait for better things. A couple of hours later the wind suddenly slackened, the sea assumed its more leisurely swell, and the ship came back to life. More than half of us turned up for dinner.

It was Steve Morgan's thirty-third birthday, and despite the weather the cooks had managed a birthday cake large enough for the entire crew. Steve was given a large home-made card. I wished I had a present to give him, but they were hard to come by six weeks into the voyage. By coincidence Carol Stewart, the campaigner in charge of the Auckland office, had sent him an offer of work in Patagonia when he had finished in Antarctica.

He came from Cottingham, Hull, and went to Leeds University, getting an honours degree in zoology. He started his career as a cleaner at Butlins and then became a management development trainee in the supermarket business. After two years he was working in Bromley in Kent and desperate to find a different job. By chance he saw an advertisement for a photographer on a new free weekly in his home town of Hull. At the time his parents ran a small graphic artists' shop in the town with its own darkroom. With a portfolio of the pictures he had taken for a hobby he got the job – and took it, even though it halved his salary. His career was slow to take off, but a turning point came when he was employed by Greenpeace to photograph one of their actions against a company on the Humber that produced whitening agents – a story I covered myself for *The Guardian* without managing to meet him. Steve went to Iceland with Greenpeace, and distinguished himself by getting pictures inside a whaling station by posing as a tourist. Work with Greenpeace grew, and in the previous year he had been down to the Antarctic Peninsula and had photographed the pollution at a number of bases. It was a bonus for me as a reporter, and for Greenpeace, to have such a high-quality professional on board.

4 February: Felt really refreshed this morning after sleeping better than for a long time. Started work on a long piece commissioned for an Australian paper. Since the washing machine was only just down the corridor from the office, I managed to fit in my washng at the same time. It was after dinner before I finished work, and I was long overdue for a visit to the bridge. We were entering the Ross Sea, which divides east and west Antarctica. I noticed that the barometer was plunging again but was told that this might not matter because we were heading for more sheltered waters. It had been snowing for some hours, and some of the crew were having a snowball fight on the boat deck. Lack of exercise and so long at sea were making people a little wild. I kept indoors in the safety of the bridge.

I decided to interview Ian Balmer, the radio operator, for the Australian piece because he was the only Ozzie crew member on board. At twenty-three he was the youngest member of the crew, but already a Greenpeace veteran. His home was in Hobart in Tasmania, where he had a small boat which he lived on a lot of the time while he 'improved' it. Ian had wanted to go to sea but was rejected by the merchant navy for the rather strange reason that his mathematics was not good enough. Instead he became a radio engineer. He had been on the first Greenpeace trip three years previously and had been due to overwinter as the base radio operator. He would have been very young for such a responsibility, but the ship never made it through to set up the base camp because of the conditions, so he missed the opportunity.

The following year he had a steady girlfriend who was opposed to him overwintering, so he settled for being a member of the ship's crew. He was commendably philosophical about the fact that she had ditched him before he returned home.

Ian had had one of the key roles during the whaling campaign. He was in the inflatable Ken Ballard drove, crouching down out of the wind holding the radio to his ear. As the *Gondwana* fell further and further behind and the catcher boat dodged behind the icebergs, Ian was keeping Arne informed on the bridge. The link was vital: without it Arne would not have been able to keep track of what was happening, and Ian had roped himself down to the bottom of the boat to prevent himself being tossed overboard.

At 11 pm we were about four hours' sailing from Cape Adare, the peninsula that sticks out from the northern edge of the main Antarctic continent at the entrance to the Ross Sea. We were so far south that the sun was still well up, and no period was so dark that we could call it night. The air was so clear in this part of the world that, even though the glaciers and cliffs of the mainland were more than fifty miles away, I could see them clearly. I was quite excited by the sight of land.

Back in the lounge, as Liz Carr got close to the base camp where she would spend a year of her life, she was feeling reflective. Quite unexpectedly she told me she had once been a professional tennis player, having only given it up after several years on the circuit. She had started playing seriously at nine, and people had high hopes of her championship potential, but at seventeen things started to go wrong. Suddenly she was out of favour, younger better talent was coming along. It must have been a terrible blow to the self-esteem of someone of that age. She had become a marine biologist, a job she enjoyed, but she was still not settled in herself. She hoped that a year in the base camp would give her time to resolve inner conflicts.

Pete and Naoko interrupted our discussion with an acrimonious argument about smoking. Naoko was strongly against smoking and had started a campaign against the smokers which involved stealing their cigarettes whenever they put them down. As Pete, Ken and others smoked a lot, this was causing tension. As someone who had given up smoking ten years previously I was reasonably tolerant of their addiction. It had, however, always surprised me that environmentalists seemed to smoke more than other people.

5 February: We are well into the Ross Sea now and the weather is good. Quite a lot of pack ice about which has to be carefully negotiated.

Bob Graham, the second mate, told me a lot of stories about the dangers of the Antarctic for a 'Young Guardian' piece. Although in my experience the wildlife was very friendly, Bob said it was not quite as it seemed. The leopard seals were the top carnivores in this part of the world, eating penguins and other smaller seals, especially the crab-eater.

Bob told me about an incident a couple of seasons previously when a photographer had got too close to a leopard seal. The seal grabbed him round the ankle and began dragging him to the edge of the ice. These seals are bigger than a man and weigh twice as much. The photographer, desperately clawing at the ice but losing ground, beat the seal over the head with his camera bag, full of heavy gear, but it refused to loosen its grip. Another member of the party was fortunately near enough to help. He held on to the photographer but could not prevent him being dragged towards the water. As the two got to the edge of the ice and were about to be pulled into the sea, the second man was forced to use the ice axe in his belt to hit the seal over the head. He had to deal it several hard blows before it would let go. The two men fell back on the ice, relieved to be safe, but the seal came back at them, this time grabbing the second man's leg. Only the combined assault of both men made the seal give up and swim away. Neither man was badly hurt, saved by their thick clothing, but they had been dragged to within a few feet of the water.

In his time Bob had been a lighthouse keeper, and he had also been in charge of the New Zealand base on the sub-Antarctic Campbell Island, which we hoped to visit later. This was inhabited by a wide variety of wildlife which was being studied by New Zealand scientists. Among the species was the normally docile sea elephant, a giant seal, which had been much misused by the hunters, who boiled it down for the oil. In the breeding season each male dominates a small patch of their island, keeping a harem of the females. In the centre of the territory there is usually a mud wallow, a favourite place of rest and recreation, and stoutly defended against all comers. Occasionally, if one of the females becomes troublesome, the male deals with it by using his bulk: males grow to as much as five times the size of the females. Sea elephants simply sit on their wives until they submit. During Bob's stay on Campbell Island the scientists had become so used to the sea elephants being docile that they just walked among them without giving it a second thought. In the breeding season this casual approach was inadvisable. As one of the biologists passed near a wallow, the male sea elephant, with surprising agility, sprang up and knocked him over into the mud. Before he could get up and escape, the sea elephant had sat on him, using its weight, in excess of a ton, to pin him down. Other members of the party who had been a few yards behind were both very amused and worried about their companion's plight. When they approached tentatively to see if they could pull him clear, the sea elephant leaned harder on the biologist until he was almost unable to breath. When they stepped back the pressure was relieved, but not enough for the biologist to slide out of the mud. From his prone position the biologist pleaded with his friends not to come near again but to wait and see what happened next. The sea elephant remained impassive and finely balanced so that every time the biologist struggled or tried to ease himself out from underneath, the sea elephant leaned harder. Eventually, realising that the sea elephant had the upper hand, the biologist, now utterly miserable, and thoroughly humiliated, decided to wait it out. Two hours later the sea elephant rolled over in his wallow and let the biologist go. He had made his point effectively. The biologist never went within twenty yards of a sea elephant's wallow again.

We had a crew meeting late in the afternoon to discuss the impending visit to the Italian and German bases. Pack ice permitting, we should be arriving the following day. Pete said everyone should have the opportunity to go ashore after so long cooped up in the ship. Late in the evening I spent some time watching the seals and the penguins out of the portholes. I rather liked the twenty-four-hour daylight, which at the time was twenty-four-hour sunshine.

6 February: Was called early by the watch because we have made good progress in the night and are now at Terra Nova Bay on the west side of the Ross Sea. We have an appointment with the Italians at 10 am their time, 9 am ship's time. We do not seem to be able to get these things to synchronise. It is snowing but there is no wind, and the water looks like glass. Sheer cliffs about half a mile away come straight out of the sea and disappear into the low snow clouds, a very dramatic landscape.

Running from the base of the cliffs there was solid sea ice for several hundred yards. Anchored alongside the ice shelf, using it as if it was solid land, was the Italian supply vessel, used as a dormitory for a group of twenty geophysicists for whom there was not enough room at the base camp. We could see the Italian base itself on a small hill on the edge of the bay about half a mile away. We set off in the inflatables. One of the Italian base team appeared on the shore and guided us to the landing stage.

It was clear from the start that this was a base with a different philosophy from the others we had been to. At the top of the landing ramp there were four litter bins, each one labelled for different sorts of rubbish – glass, paper, plastic and metal. The paper was burnt and the resultant ash packed and taken back home with the supply ship; the glass and metal was packaged for recycling in Italy; and the plastic was packaged for dumping, also in its country of origin.

We were greeted at the jetty by Mario Zucchelli, the officer in charge, who was very friendly. He opted to have a private meeting with Pete Wilkinson and Paul Bogart, and a press conference afterwards. This suited me because it meant I could go for a walk. I asked permission to climb the hill behind the base. The Italians said I could go where I liked.

It was great to be on dry land again. Just walking up the slope to the base had been a pleasure, but now I set off on a much steeper climb. The rock shapes were terrific. Lava was mixed in with granite and there were rocks of all colours, shapes and sizes which I could not identify. No wonder geologists got so excited. The going got a bit tough up the hill because the snow was coming down hard and it was quite a steep slope. My trusty Greenpeace issue boots kept me from slipping and I finally made it, puffing hard, to the top. It was probably only 300 yards high, but it seemed a great achievement.

It was more than an hour before I got back to the camp, and as I approached there was a loudspeaker announcement in English calling us to a meeting. Mary-Ann, Naoko, the film crew and Steve had all been wandering around like me and now converged on the main building, a two-storey prefabricated affair, all metal and glass, looking very modern.

Signor Zucchelli was sitting with Pete, Paul, Liz Carr and a number of his colleagues in a big room with a large table down the middle. It looked rather like the boardroom of a bank in a modern office block. To my surprise there were some members of the Italian press present. I later discovered there were 6 women and 130 men living on the base, plus the 20 geophysicists sleeping on the supply boat. There was also the ship's crew and some construction workers living in a different camp, making 200 people altogether.

There was a lot of shuffling to get all the press in, and an interlude for coffee. Signor Zucchelli then gave us a rundown on the base. As it was only a summer camp, the team arrived on 12 December and was scheduled to leave on 28 February. Terra Nova had been built in the last three years and was designed to have minimum environmental impact. There was little wildlife in the vicinity, apart from skuas. No penguin colonies were nearby, and only a few Weddell seals on the ice in the bay, which continued breeding undisturbed.

Signor Zucchelli talked about a deal signed with New Zealand for cooperation between all the nations with bases located on the Ross Sea: the United States, Italy, West Germany and New Zealand. This would include logistics support, a rescue service, ice and weather reports, and conference facilities to be shared by all the nations in Christchurch, New Zealand. These would be used before and after the season to discuss scientific discoveries and cooperation.

The Italians were questioned about their plans for expansion and how they would keep up their environmental standards with a bigger base, but they were adamant that the base would get no larger, and would remain a summer-only base.

The press conference over, we were taken on a tour of the base. One of the projects that the scientists were involved in turned out to be a cave blasted in the intensely hard rock for a seismic station. It was really quite a small opening into the rock – indeed, I contrived to hit my head on the roof on the way in. There was no wildlife living in the area, and work had been carried out with a series of small gelignite explosions. The cave went thirty feet deep and had the most wonderful ice crystals which sparkled in the lights like diamonds. The seismograph was embedded in a very old and stable rock formation and would be able to detect earth tremors anywhere in the world – including those caused by underground nuclear tests.

This was one of the most advanced of a series of stations round the world. It would be set to function all the year round, and when scientists came back the following summer they would be able to evaluate the data collected. They were clearly very excited by the prospect.

My mind was taken off my painful head by the aquarium building. Some of the fish looked like those little fresh-water fish sometimes called miller's thumb, which I remember catching when I was a child. There are also Antarctic scallops and some weird-looking fish with long, trailing, fleshy feelers. The extreme cold means that fish have had to adapt to survive. One has no lung and blood circulation system, and as a result no red blood cells to carry the oxygen round the body. Instead it absorbs oxygen through the skin. This is possible because very cold water is oxygen-rich, but even so the fish can only move very slowly. If it gets too excited it simply runs out of oxygen and cannot function. Another adaptation was even stranger. In order to combat the cold the fish had developed an antifreeze to stop their blood turning to ice. The Italians were taking blood samples every day to see how the antifreeze worked and to try and isolate its components. They were trying hard to damage the fish as little as possible and returned them to the sea alive within a few days.

By now a lot of the rest of the Greenpeace crew had arrived on shore and it was time for lunch. We went to the main canteen area. It was very embarrassing because the Italians were overwhelmed. They had only invited those at the press conference to lunch but, not understanding this, the whole crew had arrived. Our hosts, too polite to say anything, produced crates of wine to entertain everyone while large quantities of new food were prepared. We had no wine on board the *Gondwana* and soon some of the crew were plastered. I sat down with Signor Zucchelli and Pete, and we were joined by Roberto Cervellati, a physicist, who was also scientist in charge. He spoke perfect English and said rather ruefully that he spent so much time on administration that he did not do any research himself.

We were served a wonderful Italian meal with excellent wine, a marvel in such circumstances. Dr Cervellati was a very amiable man. He told me about nearby Mount Melbourne, an active volcano, whose summit was lost in the clouds about fifteen miles away across the bay from the base. The mountain had only been properly explored in the last few years and scientists were astonished to discover life up there. Where gases from deep inside the volcano reach the atmosphere the soil is hot for quite large areas. There are beds of moss on the mountain which are warm to the touch even though the air temperature may be $-20°C$.

The moss is a type normally found on tree trunks in South

Australia, and it was not thought possible for it to exist in Antarctica. Even more surprising is a type of bacteria in the soil which survives elsewhere only in hot climates at temperatures over 30°C. Scientists are baffled as to how it has reached Mount Melbourne across the icy wastes of Antarctica.

Other scientists who came to talk to us included Professor Silvano Onofri, who took us on a tour of the impressive laboratories, and Michela Maione, who was responsible for the air-sampling programme. She was trying to discover what pollutants were reaching the Antarctic from industrial regions, and also if man's activities at the bases in the continent were damaging the atmosphere.

She came from Urbino, which she said I must visit. Since she was a very attractive woman I asked her if she experienced any difficulties living on a base with so many young men. She said she found it very difficult to keep them at arm's length without appearing to be unfriendly.

In the midst of all this Pete received a message via the radio from the ship to say the weather was closing in and the crew must start back immediately. Being inside, we had not noticed that the wind had got up a bit, driving the snow and making the sea choppy. The Italians used New Zealand pilots to fly their scientists inland, and one of them said the cloud ceiling was high enough to allow the use of one of their helicopters.

Signor Zucchelli, who was paying us a return visit, and Pete, were flown out to the ship to save them getting wet and cold in an inflatable. The pilot was kind enough to make a second trip with five more of us, and some cases of Italian wine which the officer in charge insisted we take with us. He seemed rather shocked that we had none on board. They had been extraordinarily generous to us.

13

Minerals and Mixed Motives

IT HAD BEEN a long day, and I was writing up my journal and thinking of having a doze when I was told that we were off to visit the German base. They were only about five miles from the Italian base, but it was across a frozen arm of the sea and accessible only by helicopter. The base was, like our ship, called Gondwana, appropriately in their case since they were all geologists. Gondwana was the super-continent that had once included the whole of South America, Africa, India, Australia and Antarctica, before it split up and drifted apart, forming the existing land masses.

All but two of the fifty-four German scientists stationed at Gondwana were out in the field. These two greeted us in the middle of a large flat plain strewn with small rocks. The wind was quite strong, and the frozen snow blowing across the area had stuck to their beards while they waited for us. The helicopter blades kicked up tremendous clouds of snow, making the weather seem a lot worse than it was.

I was amazed to find that the Germans insisted on sleeping in tents the whole time. Dr Michael Schmidt-Thome, the senior geolosgist in charge of the base, said tents were fine down to around −20°C but it got a bit chilly below that. He said it was a wonderful feeling, sleeping in a tent in the Antarctic. When the wind stopped, you were in total silence. There was no machinery, animals, birds or insects to spoil the absolute silence. The air was wonderfully pure. I was not sure I would share his enthusiasm, but it did strike me that the Italians, living in comparative luxury, and the Germans, being so spartan, had imported their national characteristics to the Antarctic. The Germans claimed to take away absolutely everything they had brought with them. Out in the plain were the fuel drums emptied of their original contents but refilled with sorted rubbish and labelled ready for the return

145

home. There was also a regimented line of rubbish bags weighed down with stones.

The German were building a small station, but only for use as a laboratory, and for cooking and eating indoors. We had a look round the new building and Pete discussed the rubbish disposal system and how it would work. We were told that after ten years of occupation the site had been assessed for environmental impact and there had been none. Dr Schmidt-Thome was justifiably proud of this.

The wind was strong now and the snow crystals made talking outside difficult, so we all retired to a small wooden hut on the other side of the plain which was used for storage but also contained a couple of bunks and a table. We had a very interesting discussion about the geology of the region. Every year the doctor compiled a new and up-to-date map on the rock formations based on the past season's surveying. Every year, he said, his assumptions from the previous year had been challenged. His men had found fossils which showed that Antarctica was once ice-free, and they had proved that the continent once had plant and reptile life typical of temperate climes. The same reptile fossils had been found in Antarctica as in southern India, showing that the two continents were once joined. He said that Antarctica had not drifted south; it was just that the whole world was once much warmer.

We were having tea and chocolate biscuits, a serious luxury, when we had a call from the *Gondwana*. Ken was on the radio saying that Greenpeace in Italy were desperate because they had a press conference planned in an hour to give news of the Italian base and had not received any information from Pete. Could Pete return immediately and fax them a press release? Pete promised to return, but a glance out of the window showed that the weather had closed in. After about half an hour Dave Walley said he would give it a go. A helicopter load including Pete trooped off into the snow while we watched through the window. I was quite happy to stay out of the wind in the comparative comfort of the hut, eating more chocolate biscuits.

We listened rather nervously on the radio to the progress of Pete's party and were happy to hear that they had made it. The weather had worsened even as they landed and it was judged too dangerous to make the return journey. Since I had a world-renowned geologist to interview I did not lose the opportunity. I wanted to know from him what he thought were the prospects for the commercial exploitation of minerals in the Antarctic. Even sitting in a hut cut off by a blizzard the subject had to be discussed in undertones, with the genial doctor leaning forward and saying: 'I think this is the real reason that Britain fought the Falklands war.' Theoretically, he explained, the mineral riches of South Africa, India and Australia would be mirrored in the rocks of Antarctica since they all come from the same original super-continent, but no one who had been to Antarctica thought that mining on the mainland was a serious option. Offshore, however, and on the Antarctic Peninsula reaching up to South America, South Georgia and the Falklands, it was a different matter. The summer was longer, much of the area was ice-free, and the sea shallow enough to present few problems for modern oil platforms developed in the North Sea by Britain and Norway.

I told him that the official policy of the British Foreign Office was to deny any interest in or intent to exploit this area for minerals, even though Timothy Eggar, then the Foreign Office minister responsible for the Antarctic, had gone a little further. In an interview just before I left, Mr Eggar had said that exploitation was unlikely in the near future, but if it did prove possible, then Britain, which claims the Peninsula as part of its Antarctic territory, 'is entitled to its share'.

Also, despite the protestations of lack of interest or knowledge about minerals in the region, it is known that between 1972 and 1975 British Petroleum, with the backing of successive Conservative and Labour governments, surveyed the area south of the Falklands for oil. British Petroleum found large areas of potentially rich oil reserves on the relatively shallow Burdwood Bank one hundred miles south of the Falklands in 1975. Further survey work was discontinued when the price of oil went down after the 1973 crisis and the attraction of exploitation diminished. The same reasons for not continuing with exploration could be put forward now: the low price of oil, the distance from markets, the technological challenges, but mostly the complex politics involved.

One of the most promising areas to have been surveyed is still the Burdwood Bank. Although outside the Antarctic Treaty area, it is close enough to be politically sensitive as far as treaty states are concerned, and if things went wrong during exploitation it would be a potential pollutant of the Antarctic area. Burdwood Bank is claimed both by Argentina and Britain, and sharing it

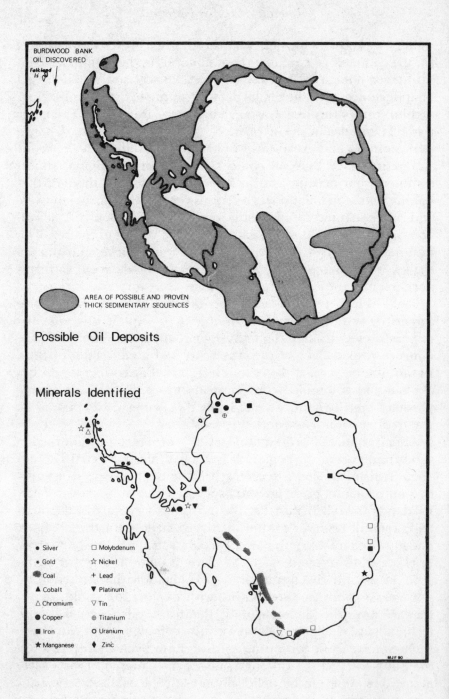

BURDWOOD BANK
OIL DISCOVERED

Falkland
Is

AREA OF POSSIBLE AND PROVEN
THICK SEDIMENTARY SEQUENCES

Possible Oil Deposits

Minerals Identified

- • Silver
- * Gold
- 🌫 Coal
- ▲ Cobalt
- △ Chromium
- ● Copper
- ■ Iron
- ★ Manganese

- ☐ Molybdenum
- ☆ Nickel
- + Lead
- ▼ Platinum
- ▽ Tin
- ⊕ Titanium
- O Uranium
- ◆ Zinc

MJF 90

would take an enormous breakthrough in relations.

Dr Schmidt-Thome knew a lot about politics, science and the art of getting research grants out of governments. He said that politicians who had never been to the Antarctic had a different idea of what was possible in these regions from the people who actually travelled there. Politicians asked scientists whether it was possible that there were minerals in large quantities. The answer was yes but that a lot more work was needed. It was important not to discourage them if the flow of money to enable further research was to be maintained. This year he had got a good grant and gathered a great deal of information. He leaned forward again with a little smile: 'So far we have found that there are no minerals worth exploiting. Let's hope everyone keeps on discovering the same thing.' But I got the feeling that he and his fellow scientists would not be telling anyone back home quite how pessimistic the picture was, in case they were not allowed back the following year.

This fascinating discussion was interrupted by the bridge of the *Gondwana* calling us on the radio. They could see another window in the weather. We must be ready on the field to be picked up. We scrambled into our clothes and, despite repeated invitations to stay, we bade our hosts goodbye. The good doctor insisted on pressing a whole box of chocolate bars into my survival bag. These things were like gold dust on the ship.

The helicopter arrived, whipping up a dense cloud of ice particles, and we piled in, shaking the snow off as best we could and strapping ourselves in. The wind was driving the snow across the plain and it was very difficult to distinguish between ground and sky. For a minute or two we discussed whether it was safe enough to set off, but Dave Walley decided it was worth a try. He took off and we headed towards the ship, or where we thought it was. All we knew was that below us was solid pack ice on which we could make a landing if necessary. Dave continued slowly on, searching for the ship in the white glare, anxious not to overshoot and end up over the open sea. Just when we were beginning to feel alarmed we spotted a mast sticking out of the driving snow. We soon identified it as the *Gondwana*, rather than the Italian supply vessel. Ken Ballard, at his post on the helideck to guide us down, signalled carefully, and Dave made a perfect landing on the rear deck, even though the painted markings were partially obscured by the snow.

The ship was very quiet when we finally struggled from the helideck down into the living quarters. Most people had already gone to bed. My stomach reminded me that I had eaten nothing except chocolate biscuits since lunch time – eleven hours before. I found some chicken in the oven, left over from dinner, that the cooks had thoughtfully saved for us. Then I made the fatal mistake of ringing the office and asking them if they wanted a story. They did. It was 4 am when I finally went to bed, the longest day of the trip so far.

Since my talk with Dr Schmidt-Thome the controversy over the Minerals Convention has dominated Antarctic affairs. Even while the *Gondwana* was still at sea there were developments in several capitals round the world. Events seemed to be at least beginning to move the way of those opposed to exploitation in the Antarctic. Even French attitudes to the Antarctic were radically changing, mostly due to the intervention of veteran oceanographer and explorer Jacques-Yves Cousteau. The extraordinary influence of this seventy-nine-year-old man on French public opinion is hard to understand for an outsider, but when he decided to raise a petition against the Minerals Convention it was an event of major significance. Within a few months his Cousteau Foundation had collected 1.5 million signatures in favour of an Antarctic wilderness preserve.

While this was happening in France, the same cause was making great strides in Australia, and by May 1989 the opposition parties in Canberra had declared their unwillingness to sign the Minerals Convention. The Australian upper house, the Senate, passed a motion saying that signing the convention was incompatible with the protection of the Antarctic, and a similar motion was passed in the Victoria Legislative Council.

On 22 May, after a long debate in cabinet, the Prime Minister, Bob Hawke, announced that Australia was opposed to mining in Antarctica and would not sign the convention. Instead it would work towards the development of a comprehensive environment protection convention at the 15th Antarctic Treaty Consultative Meeting due to take place in Paris in October 1989. Mr Hawke talked about the establishment of an 'Antarctic Wilderness Park', which was so close to the 'World Park' aim of Greenpeace that it caused jubilation in the organisation.

This declaration changed the whole situation, since the basis of the treaty organisation is consensus. If Australia stuck to its decision not to sign and ratify the Minerals Convention then the consensus was broken. Also, Mr Hawke's decision promised continuous lobbying for the wilderness park idea within the treaty system, and diplomatic attempts to win over other countries.

When Mr Hawke visited France in June he found the Cousteau campaign had already gained enormous publicity and great public support. The new French Prime Minister, Michel Rocard, was receptive to his views, and when he paid a return visit to Australia in August 1989 the two prime ministers in a joint declaration said they saw mining in Antarctica as incompatible with the protection of the environment.

Mr Hawke followed his visit to France in June by calling on Mrs Margaret Thatcher at 10 Downing Street and insisted on putting the Antarctic on their agenda. Mrs Thatcher brushed him aside, saying that Britain wanted to keep its options open as far as minerals were concerned. By then Mrs Thatcher had already decided to ignore Australian dissent. On 22 March Britain had formally signed the Minerals Convention, and on the same day ordered the early promotion of legislation to allow ratification of the agreement, and a Minerals Bill enabling the British government to grant licences for prospecting activities in the Antarctic. But after Mr Hawke's visit there were second thoughts in Britain too. In July when the bill reached the House of Commons the Labour Party, having originally supported the legislation in the Lords, changed its mind. The government met some opposition in the debate, and the differences of opinion were summed up by Mr Donald Anderson, Labour MP for Swansea East. He said that both sides wanted to protect the environment but were not sure how best to do it. But, quoting Lord Glenarthur's earlier statement for the government in the House of Lords, Mr Anderson reminded members that his lordship had in fact set out the government's motives for the bill with brutal frankness. 'It has been our objective throughout the negotiation of the convention to make sure that the UK, as a claimant state in Antarctica, should have the largest possible share of any benefits from minerals activity within the British Antarctic territory.' Mr Anderson said that this admission clearly showed the government's motives. It showed that environmental considerations came a long way down the government's list of priorities: it betrayed a narrow, national commercial interest, a determination that when the carve-up came, Britain would have a big piece of the cake.

Replying to the debate Mr Tim Eggar, said the Antarctic Treaty system had been committed to the protection of the Antarctic environment for nearly thirty years. The government did not believe that sticking a wilderness park label on the Antarctic would ensure its future. It was not right to rule out the possibility that Britain might want to extract minerals at some time in the remote future. The convention provided the best practical environmental protection.

The second reading was passed by 217 votes to 121, and the bill became law in the summer of 1989. But although Britain then became the first country in a position to ratify the convention, perhaps significantly it has not yet done so.

Under the provisions of the Antarctic Treaty conference the nations concerned meet every two years. The 15th Antarctic Consultative Meeting was held in Paris from 9 to 19 October 1989, and although I had been warned repeatedly that the treaty system was the most secretive of all international organisations the reality still came as a shock. As a reporter anxious to attend the conference I discovered that provisions for the press were virtually nil. We were allowed only into an area outside the conference hall where delegates could have coffee, and into the hall itself only during the opening address of the host Prime Minister, Michel Rocard. His speech emphasised that the agenda was taken up with items improving the protection of the environment in the Antarctic including new rules on air safety and rubbish disposal, but he lost no time in coming to the contentious issue – the Minerals Convention. He said the current meeting had a special significance: the Antarctic Treaty system was entering a new era, and he believed it would be enhanced and consolidated by declaring the continent and the surrounding seas a nature reserve.

He said: 'The time has come for politicians to face up to their responsibilities. The message from the scientific community is clear: the build-up of gases giving rise to the greenhouse effect; the reduction of the ozone layer; the far-reaching changes in the conditions prevailing on earth, are not irrational grounds for anxiety. The findings are the outcome of measurements and scientific studies. The fact that these have been particularly precise in Antarctica is not due to chance, but stems from that continent having remained virtually unblemished. Its purity is such that it is an irreplaceable site for observing the ozone layer and the changes taking place in the atmosphere.' He said it was imperative to safeguard the purity of the region, and it was a prime requirement for all the world's political leaders. 'All due account has to be taken of the right of future generations to inherit from us a planet that is still fit to live in.'

As well as pushing his point of view M. Rocard emphasised the importance of keeping the treaty nations together. It was clear that none of the parties wanted so damaging a split on the minerals issue as to place the treaty itself in danger. This had been reflected in pre-conference negotiations between individual countries. Even in his opening address M. Rocard was able to say that he hoped the conference would agree to an extra meeting in Chile in 1990, at which the idea of a nature reserve would be the main item on the agenda. In a supporting position paper put in by Australia this additional conference was also recommended as a constructive way forward.

Britain and the United States, however, were still anxious to push on with the Minerals Convention. The United States official, Bob Skully, was particularly sore at the sudden resistance of a few countries to signing the agreement. He was, however, aware that some politicians in Washington, notably the influential Senator Albert Gore, had been successfully canvassed by environmental groups to resist ratification of the convention in the United States. As a result he did not have the backing of legislation similar to Britain's which would allow Washington to ratify the convention.

Other countries previously in favour of the convention were wavering and moving towards the wilderness reserve idea. The Belgian parliament had passed a law banning any of its nationals from taking part in minerals activity in the Antarctic, and the Italian government had indicated that it felt the continent should be saved for science. Chile had put forward a very long document which seemed to be a compromise between the two. One of Chile's delegates summed up to me the dilemma of his country's position on the convention: 'Everyone is suddenly for the environment, like everyone is for peace, but that does not stop them having atom bombs and chemical weapons.'

Eventually everyone agreed to put off a decision in the interests of the treaty as a whole. Even so, the French and Australian proposal for another conference at the end of 1990 to discuss the wilderness park idea alone was not acceptable to Britain and the

United States. If they agreed to just that one item on the agenda
it would rather suggest that they were prepared to consider the
wilderness park idea as an alternative to the Minerals Convention,
which they were not. Instead they extracted their own price for
putting off the decision. They insisted on discussing, at the
proposed conference in Chile, one of the Minerals Convention's
unresolved issues, a protocol on the subject of liability for damage
as a result of mining or drilling activities in Antarctica. Neither
France nor Australia wanted it on the agenda, but Britain and the
United States insisted that if they were to discuss the possibility
of a world wilderness reserve then the liability protocol must also
be discussed. This compromise was finally agreed and any
diplomatic rift was avoided.

On 19 January 1990, the environmentalists' campaigning
appeared to pay off in an unexpected quarter. An English
translation of part of a speech Mr Gorbachev gave to the Global
Forum Meeting on Environment and Development for Survival
read: 'The Soviet Union shares the concern of many scientists and
public figures over the exploitation of the Antarctic's natural
resources. Our grandchildren will never forgive us if we fail to
preserve the phenomenal ecological system. The U S S R is ready
to join the programme for creating a life-support system for the
Antarctic – a natural reserve which belongs to the world and
which is our common laboratory.'

Admittedly the jubilation of the Green movement was later
tempered by Soviet officials who said this encouraging statement
had not resulted in any policy changes and they had received no
instructions. But the environmentalists were not dismayed,
reasoning that, as with many things in the Soviet Union, the
bureaucracy took a long time to react to pressure from the top.

At the beginning of March 1990 a conference on the central
issue of minerals in the Antarctic was held in London at the Sir
Robert Menzies Centre for Australian Studies. Its title, 'Antarctica: An exploitable resource or too valuable to develop?' drew
key officials from London and Canberra to the debate.

Dr Richard Laws, Master of St Edmund's College, Cambridge,
and until 1987 director of the British Antarctic Survey, gave a
résumé of the scientific significance of the continent and the
surrounding seas. His outline was followed by talks by Dr Robert
Willan, a geologist, and Dr David Macdonald, a sedimentologist,
on the prospects of oil and mineral exploitation in the Antarctic

– political considerations aside. They concluded that not enough was known to make a proper commercial assessment because only rudimentary exploration and surveying had taken place.

For the British Foreign Office, Dr John Heap, head of the polar regions section, said that the facts of whether exploitable minerals existed or not in the Antarctic were secondary to the realities of politics. Dr Heap said the advocates of a ban on mining in the Antarctic argued that the Minerals Convention was the thin end of a dangerous wedge: once prospecting had started then exploration and exploitation inevitably followed. He did not accept that. For example, it might be found that there were no deposits worth mining. In any case, because there was no ban on scientific research, knowledge about exploitable deposits would accrue anyway. Stopping the convention would not stop the research. Indeed, he feared that, without the convention, as knowledge built up about possible exploitable reserves, suspicion between treaty parties would tend to grow. Each would wonder what the other had discovered. This could lead to tension between states which had conflicting claims to territory.

He said the ban was based on the Calvinistic ideal of leaving one place in the world not despoiled by man. It was ethically rather than objectively based. He said it was not enough to ask whether a ban was morally right, it also had to work. Therefore a bridge must be built between the two sides on the minerals issue. Neither side should claim moral superiority, just as neither side could get all that they wanted.

Mr John Burgess, assistant secretary of the environment and Antarctic branch of the Australian Department of Foreign Affairs and Trade, pointed out that the question of Australia signing the Minerals Convention no longer arose, because the deadline for nations under the agreement had passed on 25 November 1989. Australia and France had let the date pass. However, Australia did not claim to have the monopoly of all wisdom. He could see it might not be possible for other countries to accept the Australian idea of a total ban on mining in the Antarctic. He therefore outlined what he saw as a new, all-embracing regime for the Antarctic, intended to safeguard the environment. This would include outside inspection, coupled with some way of enforcing the rules. Any agreement would need greater integration and coordination than the current system. He did not believe that the lack of an agreement on mining would lead to arguments between states and a breakdown in the treaty consensus.

Dr Heap replied that it would be very difficult to reach a compromise, but since the alternative was a possible breakdown of the treaty he was sure all states would work towards some sort of middle ground.

The search for agreement is continuing, although the two sides seem as far apart as ever. Constant lobbying by the conservationists seemed to be strengthening the hand of the Australian and French governments. On 17 August 1990 Gareth Evans, the Australian Minister for Foreign Affairs and Trade, and Ros Kelly, the Environment Minister, jointly announced that the Australian government would introduce legislation to ban all mining in Antarctica to the extent of Australia's legal capacity to apply such a ban. This would prohibit mining by everyone in the Australian Antarctic Territory and on the adjacent continental shelf. The legislation would also ban Australians from mining anywhere else in the Antarctic region. Mining for the purposes of the legislation would include oil drilling and the related steps of prospecting and exploration. In a statement the ministers said: 'We are determined to secure through the Antarctic Treaty System a comprehensive system to environmental protection. Our message is that while we want to keep Australia green, the Antarctic must stay white.'

New Zealand had originally proposed the World Park idea back in the 1970s, but the idealism was rejected by the other nations. Then through their polar expert, John Beeby, New Zealand had been instrumental in negotiating the Minerals Convention in the early 1980s in order to safeguard as much of the continent as possible when mining took place. Once the hard-won agreement was reached in 1988, New Zealand was unwilling to put it on one side and proposed instead a moratorium on mining until well into the next century. Then on 24 August 1990, with elections approaching, New Zealand Prime Minister Geoffrey Palmer went on television to announce that his government had 'abandoned' the Minerals Convention. 'We are for permanent bans on mining in Antarctica. Now I just don't know how we can be more in favour of environmental protection of Antarctica than we are.' He said his country now had an identical position to that of Australia.

The Greenpeace campaigners preparing for the next voyage of the *Gondwana* had a party on board that night, but it was only a single battle won in a long campaign. In London, Environment Minister David Trippier was reiterating his government's opposition to the World Park idea. He did not believe that mining in one part of the Antarctic would irrevocably damage the Antarctic environment as a whole. 'Whilst such a ban may have a certain symbolism we do not believe it will stand up in a scenario of an increasing world population pressing on a finite resource base.' Clearly there was still little chance of a compromise.

14

Ghosts from the Past

7 FEBRUARY: THERE was a crew meeting called immediately after lunch to discuss the next stage of the trip. We had to make arrangements for our long-waited arrival at the Greenpeace base to pick up the overwintering party and begin the resupply. We had hoped to arrive at 6 pm today, but had run into some heavy pack ice in the night which had slowed us down to a couple of knots for several hours. The earliest we could get there now would be 3 am. Although it was still light then, it would mess up everyone's routine to arrive at that time, so it was decided we would take it steady through the night and arrive mid-morning after a sightseeing tour of the Ross Ice Shelf and the Ross Island mountains. After the meeting I filed some copy and caught up with this journal while enjoying a glass of Italian wine. It was a real treat.

As we approached Ross Island, which was still forty miles away, we could see the summit of Mount Erebus, rising to 12,000 feet, poking through a layer of cloud which hung over the island. Through the binoculars at first, and then with the naked eye, it was possible to see a thin plume of smoke rising from the crater. The clouds gradually shifted, revealing a second mountain slightly lower than Erebus called Mount Terror. This was a rugged and beautiful snow-covered mountain, another volcano, but believed to be extinct.

While we were watching this scene, in the still, early morning, as the *Gondwana* was gliding at half power through the water, we were distracted by whales. There were dozens of them. We saw solitary sperm whales, then pods of different whales, probably minkes, then there was an enormous blow from an unknown whale. It was three times the size of anything else I had seen, but it was too far away to make an identification.

As we approached the mountains the clouds dispersed completely and the view was perfect. We were approaching the furthest south a ship could travel. On the horizon we spotted a thin white line, the Ross Ice Shelf, one of the wonders of nature, a giant sheet of ice spreading hundreds of miles over the sea. It has a giant cliff and extends many feet below the water line, often grinding on the ocean bed. The tide gently moves it up and down, and occasionally this motion causes huge chunks to snap off and float away, forming the tabular icebergs we saw hundreds of miles to the north in the Southern Ocean.

The sun had not dipped even close to the horizon during the night watch, but the temperature on the bridge wing was down to −9°C at 2 am. This was the Antarctic at its most beautiful. In such cold, however, it all looked pretty terrifying. I tried to ring my wife to tell her about what we had seen, but there was no reply. It was not until I got to bed that I realised I had spent too long on the bridge wing: my hands and feet were freezing.

Tim and Sean were woken at 9 am with the news that they were missing a great filming opportunity. Tim, unusually, bounced out of bed and rattled on in great good humour. I recalled the beauty of the previous night and decided that it was worth giving up the rest of my sleep to have another look.

We were now sailing round the coast of Ross Island, at the foot of Mount Terror where it plunged into the sea. Disappointingly, cloud had formed at a couple of thousand feet and it was impossible to see the top. After breakfast the cloud began to lift, and we were told we would soon be close to Mount Erebus. The volcano must have been steaming away gently in the crater because there was a plume of sulphurous yellow smoke coming steadily out of the top. It was being flattened by the wind and carried towards the South Pole, like a child's crayon mark across the blue sky.

At lunch Pete was tense and began nagging me to be ready on time for the helicopter taking some of us on ahead to the Greenpeace base. The idea was that the film crew and the press should fly to Cape Evans in advance of the *Gondwana* arriving so we could record the arrival of the ship and the old overwinterers greeting the new. It was hard for me to see how I could make a story out of this and I told Pete so, but he insisted I should go anyway. I had a go at him about being a dictator, egged on by Henk, and it ended as a friendly enough exchange, although it was clear that the strain of running an expedition, and trying to keep everyone going, was telling on him. This was a critical moment for him: it was fourteen months since his last expedition had dropped off the previous overwintering team, and he knew all sorts of things could go wrong with four people isolated for so long in a tiny camp. Radio contacts had seemed perfectly normal, but Pete would not be satisfied until he had seen and spoken to the team. He felt a personal responsibility since he had selected them in the first place, and it was important to him and Greenpeace that they were a success.

After all the banter over lunch I was still almost late for the helicopter. Liz Carr, who had been ready for hours, was wildly excited about seeing World Park Base, which was to be her home for a year, and kept running in and out of our cabin. She insisted on getting tips from Tim about tape recordings.

From the helicopter the scenery was even more majestic. The air was crystal clear, and from a thousand feet up the sea was dark blue, the sky light blue, with the mountain gleaming white in the sun. Down below we could see the tiny green hut erected by Ernest Shackleton during his 1907–9 attempt on the South Pole where he pioneered the route later taken by Captain Scott. We flew on another ten miles to where we could make out a group of buildings – the Greenpeace base – and a couple of hundred yards away another historic hut, the one used by Captain Scott himself.

There was a lone figure standing on an area of black level land signalling the helicopter to come in. We were greeted rather formally by Keith Swenson, the leader of the four overwinterers. He and the other three seemed very reserved and I felt we were intruding on a private occasion. However, there we were, so we went into the base camp and had a brief look. We were shown into a very attractive living room, stacked with books and videos, and with plants of all sorts growing along one wall, herbs and green-leaved crops like spinach. Sabine Schmidt, the German who was the team's doctor, told me that spinach grew best of all the vegetables and seemed happy to grow year round in artificial light. The team had managed to have something fresh and green almost every day throughout the year. They had eaten a cucumber only a week ago. Since the import of soil was banned in the Antarctic, the plants had been grown hydroponically in continuously flowing water with nutrients.

The *Gondwana* came into view and we went outside into the sunshine to wait. As the ship got bigger the four overwinterers became visibly more excited, hopping up and down and then whooping in anticipation of greeting old friends. None of them had seen the *Gondwana* before, and they were surprised at how big and strong she appeared.

After what seemed a long time the *Gondwana* was close enough to look for an anchorage, and the crew ready to lower the boats to come ashore. The ground here and the beach were made up of boulders and black volcanic ash which at some time had spewed out from Mount Erebus. The volcano was still smoking in the background. Small ice cliffs came down to the beach, in places festooned with giant icicles where the overhanging snow, melted by the sun, had frozen again.

The Greenpeace inflatables finally set off from the *Gondwana*, and the overwinterers stood right at the water's edge. As the boats ran into the sand Pete, Henk, Maggie and other crew members who had been on the previous voyage leapt out and there was much shouting and laughter – relief that the isolation was over. It made me feel very much an outsider, and I went and sat down a little way away (out of the wind) while the Greenpeace family had their reunion. Everyone retired to the base camp with crates of beer the *Gondwana* had sent across. The Cape Evans campers had not had any since September: they had drunk their year's rations in eight months and were delighted with this first taste of the 'civilisation' they were due to go back to. The new team which was to take over was shown round the base by the old hands. They seemed to have hundreds of questions about how things worked and where everything was kept.

The next day, 9 Feburary, was a day for sorting myself out and deciding what to write about next. I spoke to the news desk and worked out a couple of feature ideas, including a piece for the woman's page. They agreed it would also be a good idea to do an eyewitness report about Scott's hut since we were only a short distance away. The drawback to this was that the hut was locked and the key kept by the New Zealanders at Scott Base, fifteen miles away across impossible terrain.

The ship remained anchored in the bay, and there was a great deal of undoing of hatches and checking that the supplies we had brought were still in good shape. Potatoes and apples kept for base camp use were carefully sorted and the bad ones removed. Late in the evening, when I had done all my writing, I popped into the lounge for a beer and found Keith Swenson, the returning Greenpeace base leader, stretched out on a seat ready for a snooze. He was to spend his first night on the ship to allow the new team to move into the base. He was a quiet, soft-spoken man who sat up and asked me about the voyage and what had happened with the whaling. He did not give much away about himself.

The following morning I went up on the bridge to try to contact the New Zealanders and come to some arrangement about the key to Scott's hut. I was told by the watch that this contact was technically difficult because for some reason the radio would not transmit over the glacier which lay between the ship and the New Zealand base. We spoke to the Greenpeace base and found that they could radio the New Zealanders from there because they had a taller radio mast. Maggie offered to run me across in the inflatable and I was glad to be off the ship. Sjoerd Jongens, from the Netherlands, the outgoing radio operator, was explaining to Phil Doherty, whom we were to leave behind, how everything worked. My arrival was an excellent opportunity for him to show off his newly acquired skills by contacting Scott Base. He explained to the New Zealanders, rather grandly I thought, that *The Guardian* and the *New Zealand Herald* (both being represented by me) and the BBC (that was Tim and Sean) wanted to film and write about Scott's hut. The Scott Base commander said he was happy to lend me a key, and a man to accompany it, but we had to provide a helicopter to collect both. After a great deal of radioing to the ship it was finally arranged that I could go the following day, borrowing a helicopter and a pilot for four hours.

Before going back to the ship I walked over and had a look at the outside of Scott's hut. The roof had clearly been repaired, but otherwise the outside was much as it was left in 1914, all the paraphernalia of an Edwardian expedition still perfectly preserved in the perpetual frost. The party had not been very tidy; there were bits of equipment all over the place, a burst bag of nails, old tins and empty boxes on the hillside. This was where the support party had watched and waited for Scott and his companions to return and from where they sent out search parties to look for them, finally discovering their frozen bodies in November 1913, still 160 miles short of Cape Evans.

Scott had known that he was only eleven miles from a depot, and enough fresh supplies for his remaining party, but they were trapped in the tent by blizzards and were so weakened by cold and hunger that they died where they lay.

Both the immense courage and the tragic mistakes of Scott are well documented. He lost his faith in dogs to haul the sledges to the Pole, manhandling them instead, which took a terrible toll on the party. As a reminder of this error there was still a husky chained to the outside of the hut. It had been dead more than seventy years but was still recognisable, standing guard over the other ghosts.

Next to the hut there were bales of hay still stacked up for the long-dead ponies taken by Scott to haul the sledges. They had sunk into the snow and could not cope with the cold, and had to be shot. Up on the hill above the hut, with a splendid view of the bay, was a large cross. It was a memorial to three people who had died during a Shackleton expedition.

I was invited to stay ashore for the rest of the day and make myself useful. Henk had brought a pneumatic drill ashore – the sort used for digging up roads – with the intention of digging out fifty or so empty oil drums that had got stuck in the ice and needed to be returned to New Zealand for disposal. Some of them had been at the base for two years because the expedition was unable to get them out the previous year. The drill made a thunderous noise and seemed to get heavier and heavier as the day progressed. Steve Morgan, Dave Walley, Ian Balmer and I worked on this project for the rest of the day and were worn out, although we still got only twenty barrels free of the ice.

Back at the ship Pete was rather irritated with me for organising the Scott hut business without prior consultation, and we had to have a meeting to discuss it after dinner. Sean and Steve wanted to use the helicopter trip to take some aerial shots of the United States base at McMurdo Sound, which was on the way. This entailed taking the doors off the helicopter to give an uninterrupted view. I said it would be a very cold journey for a guest who was doing us a favour. Why did everything have to be so complicated?

Pierrette, who was going to be the pilot, then chipped in, saying she refused to fly the helicopter with the doors off in such temperatures. Her hands and feet might get too cold to feel the controls. This cheered me up, and the whole filming idea was abandoned.

The next problem was sorting out a visit to McMurdo. Our US reporter, Mary-Ann Bendel, who saw this as the big American story, was very keen to go as soon as possible, probably Sunday or Monday, and have an interview with Ronald R. La Count, the colourful US boss in Artarctica. Paul Bogart also had to go and see Mr La Count, and wanted us all to go the same day, but Mary-Ann insisted on a completely separate interview. She wanted somehow to disassociate herself from Greenpeace. I could understand that, but it seemed to me too late: Mr La Count must know we had been living on board the *Gondwana* for two months in order to get there. After a lot of talking round the subject it was decided that Mary-Ann and I would go and see Mr La Count one day and Paul the next.

I tried last thing before bed to ring my elder daughter, Lucy, who was twenty-four that day. It was 10.30 in the morning in London and her landlady said she had already gone out. I should have to get up at 5.30 our time to be sure of catching her in after college, before she went out again for an evening celebration. My bedtime reading was a refresher course on Captain Robert Falcon Scott, ready for the next day's tour.

When I crawled out of my bunk to call Lucy on Saturday 11 February, it was still the previous afternoon for her and she was drinking champagne. My other daughter, Clara, had been doing the same when I spoke to her on her birthday, twenty-one days before. It must be a reflection of their upbringing.

After talking to Lucy for a few minutes I was too wide awake to go back to bed. Downstairs in the galley Noel Caton, the helicopter mechanic, a quiet, gentle New Zealander, was cooking himself porridge for breakfast before checking over the machines. He had joined the trip at the last minute after someone else had dropped out, and was one of the indispensable professionals Greenpeace needed. He never said what he thought about what was going on, but the helicopters were always in perfect condition. He polished them every time they were used, removing any trace of salt or dirt, explaining that in the cold the lift from the blades was not so great and the shine improved the airflow and therefore the efficiency. When I went up in the helicopters my life was as much in his hands as it was in the pilots'. He gave me plenty of confidence.

After a friendly cup of tea I went back to bed and was woken up a couple of hours later by Tim and Sean bickering about Tim not getting up in the mornings. They were like an old married couple. I decided we were all suffering from a touch of Antarctic syndrome. This is a sort of madness that afflicts people in these extreme climates. Scientists say it is set off by hormonal changes in the pineal gland which cause personality shifts. It was first noticed in 1898, when Adrien de Gerlache and his ship *Belgica* were trapped in the pack ice. His men took their kitbags and began walking home over the ice.

On his first journey to the Pole Shackleton resorted to secret code to record in his diary how much he hated Scott. There were many examples of base and ship crews murderously attacking each other after months of being forced to live at close quarters. Two Britons who walked to the Pole in 1986 refused to speak to each other for two years afterwards. The crew of a US ship which in 1984 rescued seven Argentines from outside their destroyed base on the Peninsula suspected the base commander of setting fire to it. His strange behaviour with fire extinguishers and his habit of stealing the crew's toothpaste made the Americans believe he was suffering from the syndrome.

At around 3 pm we set off for a fine helicopter ride over the intervening glacier, complete with yawning crevasses. After that there was fast ice (permanently frozen sea) dotted with seal families, who live round the holes they make for fishing. They had to keep these open by chewing round them constantly with their teeth. We flew alongside a small range of black extinct volcanoes with small frozen lakes in their craters and then came over a hill crest to see McMurdo, the giant United States base. It had a supply vessel in its harbour. There were oil tanks, pipelines, and all shapes and sizes of buildings. It was ten times the size of any other base we had seen, and filled up an entire black ash valley between two volcano cones, about a mile across. It was the only base I had seen with roads. There was a network of them.

We circled round McMurdo, going slightly out to sea to avoid flying directly over it. Immediately over the next cone-shaped hill we could see another base, tiny and neat by comparison. This was New Zealand's Scott Base. We circled it, checking for any dangers, but could see none, and landed as we had been directed to on the radio the previous day.

As we stepped out of the helicopter, Phil Robins, the New Zealander who had been detailed to come with the key, came running out to meet us. He asked if we wanted to shut down the helicopter and come in, but we declined on this occasion because we were already late. Back at the Greenpeace base I found Sean and told him we had the key if he wanted to film, and then with Phil Robins walked over to open the hut. There was a sizeable snowdrift just inside the door. Phil said the wind forces the snow through the smallest crack because the ice crystals are so tiny. But in any case there was an inner and an outer hut, and the snow had penetrated only the outer, lean-to area. We soon scooped it out. Phil showed me the pony harnesses, with the snowshoes for the ponies still looking brand new. There were long bent poles, which I took to be sled runners, but they turned out to be supports for a bell tent. Alongside them were some very long wooden skis, which looked very heavy and cumbersome by modern standards.

Further in, preserved by the cold, was a large pile of blubber and seal steaks cut to feed to the huskies. Next to them was a bucket full of penguin eggs, also seventy years old. The entrance to the stables was at the back of this outer storage area. These had long ago been filled with snow, but the New Zealanders had begun to dig them out to see if there were further relics. There was an old bicycle hanging on the wall, solid and old-fashioned but looking as if it had been put there only yesterday. The climate played wonderful tricks with time.

Phil opened the door to the inner hut. This time there was not a trace of snow; it was perfectly dry, very cold and dark, and surprisingly big, about fifty feet long and twenty-four feet wide. Phil left me to browse around. Near the door were the stores and the kitchen end of the hut. There was a living area in the middle and bunks on either side. Scott's bunk, with its separate table and chair, was at the far end.

I quote from the piece I wrote for *The Guardian* at the time:

On the dining table it is possible to read in an edition of *The Field (The Country Gentleman's Newspaper)* printed in London on 30 May 1908 that 'There has been more rain than is suitable for the time of year,' and an article on milk yields. By Scott's bunk is *The Green Flag and Other Stories of War and Sport* by A. Conan Doyle, labelled inside the flyleaf 'British Antarctic Expedition 1910'. Underneath is *Stalky and Co.* by Rudyard Kipling. Scott's spare boots, gloves, a shirt and coat are neatly arranged as befitted a naval officer.

The whole hut is stacked with an amazing variety of food, medicines, scientific equipment, sledges, skis, and snowshoes for the ponies that never proved any use in the Antarctic.

It was still possible to smell the Fry's cocoa powder which has spilled from one of the few damaged tins. There was an unopened bottle of India Relish, tins of pickled herring, a box of bloater paste 'guaranteed free of chemical preservatives' and a half-used bottle of Heinz tomato ketchup, looking slightly pale after seventy years frozen solid.

Gone was one feature of Scott's expedition: the line of Huntley & Palmer biscuit tins which marked the boundary between the wardroom, occupied by Scott and his fifteen fellow officers and scientists, and the mess deck for the nine seamen.

Another great polar explorer, Sir Ernest Shackleton, took it down when he visited and occupied the hut two years after Scott's death. He had different ideas on how to lead men.

Otherwise, out of respect for the dead hero with whom he had made the first unsuccessful attack on the Pole, Shackleton left the hut undisturbed.

At the mess deck end are the stove, the cooking utensils, most of the stores, unidentified board games with counters, and a compendium edition of *Tit-bits* from 23 September 1905 to 17 March 1906.

The wardroom contains the darkroom used by the expedition's photographer, Herbert Ponting, with its bottled chemicals needed for making the glass plate negatives.

In Dr Edward Wilson's corner is a perfectly preserved stuffed emperor penguin and many medicines provided by Harrods, including an unopened bottle of chloroform, some refined camphor flowers and some tablets made from the thyroid gland of sheep. Judging by the quantity left, these had not been needed.

The pile of lemon peel, squeezed to the last drop, was probably an attempt to stave off the scurvy which plagued the expedition. . .

There was, of course, much more to see than it was possible to get in a newspaper article. The New Zealanders who had restored the hut had found everything in its place, just as I described. Even though snow had got in through a broken window, it had never been warm enough to melt and so nothing had been damaged. For some unknown reason Captain Oates's bunk had collapsed, and that was repaired.

Standing alone in the middle of the hut it was not difficult to imagine how the support group had lived there during two and a half years; reading, playing games, repairing equipment and carrying out scientific observations and expeditions. It did seem extraordinary that the social difference between officers and men had been so tightly adhered to. The Huntley & Palmer tins which had been used as the hut partition were still there, packed in a corner on Shackleton's orders. I stayed inside the hut for more than an hour, looking at the candles and food supplies, and inspecting the scientific equipment still set up, and the neat rows of jars of chemicals, all carefully labelled. It was Dr Edward Wilson, Scott's closest friend, who died with him on the way back from the Pole, who set up this lab.

These men had taken their science very seriously. They were the forerunners of today's scientists, and made accurate observations from which we are now able to measure clear changes in the Antarctic ice and weather. Dr Wilson dragged his sledge full of rock samples all the way back from the Pole. The sledge was found near his body and the samples recovered. One of the rocks contained the fossil leaf of a fern, the first evidence that Gondwana and the South Pole had once had a temperate climate. It had been a scientific revelation.

I fell to leafing through newspapers and magazines, with articles discussing the prospects for the 1908/9 hunting season – and I took some pictures. The newspapers included copies of the London *Times* all dated 1908, the year the expedition had left London. There was a *Canterbury Times*, dated a year later, from Christchurch, New Zealand, the expedition's last port of call before heading for the Ross Sea and Cape Evans. Considering all these papers must have been read and reread many times they were in surprisingly good condition.

I concluded my piece for *The Guardian* thus: 'Closing the door on the dim interior and walking out into the twenty-four-hour daylight, the husky was still on guard outside, next to the unused bales of hay for the ponies. Looking over my shoulder it was not hard to imagine the ghost of Captain Scott, intrusion over, resuming his seat at the wardroom table, to smoke a quiet pipe.'

When I got outside I found that Phil had gone over to the *Gondwana* to have a look round. Although he was manager of the New Zealand base, his 'real job' was as a pilot in Wellington harbour and he was very interested in a tour of the ship and all its specialised equipment. Maggie McCaw was ferrying people backwards and forwards between ship and shore in the inflatable. I was glad to get back to the *Gondwana*. Phil was drinking large quantities of tea. He said it was far better tea than that at Scott Base. He stayed for dinner and ate every scrap. I was glad he seemed to be enjoying his visit.

At about 8.45 pm we got in the helicopter with Bob Graham, the *Gondwana*'s second mate, who as a New Zealander wanted to visit his fellow countrymen at Scott Base and exchange a few stories about mutual friends. The flight across the glacier and round McMurdo only took about twenty minutes. Phil Robins sat in the front where vision was perfect. It was stunningly beautiful and clear. We could see for hundreds of miles, and Phil was thrilled. It was good to see someone else get excited by such things.

At Scott Base we shut down the helicopter because we had again been invited inside. But we had only just taken off all our outdoor clobber in a sort of cloakroom when the officer in charge came out and said we were not allowed in. This was the first time anyone had been inhospitable in the Antarctic and we were all surprised, especially since New Zealand has always been an exceptionally friendly nation to Greenpeace. But we said it did not matter and immediately got back into our outside clothes. Phil was clearly very embarrassed and insisted on taking us out to the helicopter pad. Outside he explained that this inhospitality was the result of a visit to the base by Ron La Count, the boss of McMurdo, who had arrived just before us. It seemed that our intrusion would not have been welcome to him.

We told Phil that we took no offence and perfectly understood, but Bob Graham was upset. He told me afterwards he felt strongly that he was entitled to access to his own country's base. To be excluded – even because there was a notoriously difficult American present – was not right.

When we got back in the helicopter Bob, Pierrette and I did not feel like going straight back to the *Gondwana*. We were already irritated with the Americans because they had refused to acknowledge us on the radio when we had flown close to their base. It reminded me of the instruction that had been passed to the soldiers at the US air force base at Greenham Common. They had been told not to make eye contact with the women at the peace camp so they could not be engaged in conversation about cruise missiles.

Within sight of Scott Base was the United States ice runway. This airstrip is used to bring in all the personnel and equipment for McMurdo and the other American bases, including the one at the South Pole. It is in fact vital to the communications network for all the bases in the Ross Sea area. As part of the collaboration between nations in Antarctica all airborne visitors to this side of the icecap come, courtesy of US logistical support, on a service via Christchurch to McMurdo. The airport buildings could be seen from where we were sitting in the helicopter. The runway is on fast ice. Since this begins to buckle after a couple of seasons under the influence of cold, tide and glacial movements, US icebreakers are sent in every two years to cut up the runway and allow it to refreeze. This creates a new, perfectly flat surface.

As we had just learnt from our encounter at Scott Base, the Americans' control of air transport allowed them to completely dominate this area socially as well as logistically – even though technically their base was in Antarctic territory claimed by the New Zealand government.

A couple of seasons before, in order to make the point that the Americans could not have it all their own way, Greenpeace had established a small survival hut between Scott Base and the ice runway, near the road from the airstrip to the McMurdo base. Although it need not have been sited precisely there, it had an important practical purpose. The Greenpeace overwinterers often went on field trips for exploration purposes and to check on human encroachment on Antarctica. If they were caught out in bad weather there were enough food, heating and supplies in the survival hut for them to last two or three weeks without help. It was also left open for anyone to use.

Because we were feeling put out at being excluded from the New Zealand base, we decided on a tour of the survival hut, known as Greenpeace Three, even though we were well aware that the Americans would not like us in the area. We again told the US air traffic control that we were taking off and which direction we were going, but again received no acknowledgement. I felt sure that this was deliberate: we could talk to our ship on the same waveband, which was much further away, and we could hear the US air traffic control talking to one of their own planes using the same frequency. As we flew we soon saw a small wooden hut, which was Greenpeace's first survival hut, and then a modern red one which had been added the next year for sleeping because the first one had proved very cold. We landed, walked over, and opened both huts to make sure that all the supplies were in order; took some pictures of each other amid the snowdrifts; and decided to go back to the *Gondwana* since it was late, the wind was getting up and it was becoming very cold.

Once back on board, I was in the mess having a snack when Sean came in and asked if the trip to the American base was all fixed for Monday. I said it was and then realised that he thought I meant that he and Tim would be coming as well. My heart sank, for I suspected that Pete had not included them in his plans. This looked like another disagreement looming. I decided to say nothing and let Pete sort it all out.

Even though the next day was Sunday, Sean and Tim had their usual row about getting up. The row seemed to go on for a particularly long time. The only way round this problem would have been to get up before either of them, but Sean usually beat me to it.

Then, at lunch, a fierce wrangle developed over the trip to the American base, and Antarctic syndrome reigned. I tried hard not to be accused of meddling. Pete had to deal with Tim and Sean, and finally a compromise was reached. The film crew would be dropped separately at Greenpeace Three, with Keith Swenson as guide and field officer. Mary-Ann Bendel and I would be landed at McMurdo to go and see Ron La Count. A telex was dispatched to Ron La Count telling him of these arrangements. Pete and Paul Bogart would be making their official Greenpeace visit later.

Late in the evening a reply was received from Mr La Count saying that apart from Mary-Ann he would not be seeing any journalists. I telexed back immediately, telling him that *The Guardian*'s syndication service reached eighty United States papers including the *Washington Post*. Did he want me to tell them that after I had travelled 12,000 miles to see him he was refusing an interview? What about US freedom of information? I said I would be coming anyway and looked forward to seeing him.

15

A Few Rounds with La Count

THE FOLLOWING DAY Mary-Ann Bendel and I were off to
McMurdo at 9.30 am. We flew the same route as before. Again
the Americans would not talk to us on the radio, and we could
see nowhere obvious to land. Dave Walley was the pilot and did
a careful circuit before settling on an empty flat area near the
shore. We set down all right, but there was no sign of life
anywhere, so Mary-Ann and I struck out for the nearest building
to ask directions. Before we got very far we were hailed by a lady
in red who introduced herself as Ron La Count's helper. She took
us up a long metal walkway to a building called the Chalet. This
was built in an American version of the Swiss style, and contained
Mr La Count's office, the headquarters of the American operation.

Mr La Count greeted us at the door, rather aggressively, but
asked us into his office. He was a big man with a handsome
moustache and a beer gut. He told me he was not seeing me and
not granting me an interview. He knew, he said, that I was anti-
American. I told him I was going to write about McMurdo anyway
and it was better if I got his point of view. While I was about it I
mentioned his air traffic control and their failure to observe air
safety. That lit the blue touch paper, and he banged his desk,
denying it vehemently. Mary-Ann said 'I'm keeping out of this'
and left the room. Mr La Count then claimed that our helicopter
must have been using the wrong frequency, so I offered to go to
the American ops room and test their equipment.

Suddenly he changed tack and produced a file. It contained a
load of cuttings of mine going back several years, including pieces
I had written about the United States during the *Rainbow
Warrior*'s evacuation of the Rongelap people from the Marshall
Islands. I was sitting at one end of his office, which was vast, and
he was sitting at his desk, maybe twenty feet away, so I could not

see all the contents of the file. He kept picking out cuttings and saying 'Anti-American, anti-American' and then putting them down again. I told him I was surprised that the Americans were less free with information and help than the Russians, Italians and Germans. This seemed to stir up his anger again and I wondered if I had gone too far. At length, after leafing through a bit more of the file, which he told me had been sent from Washington for his information, he asked me to wait outside while he had a word with Mary-Ann. I expected a long wait and was given a coffee by his helper, but Mr La Count came out again almost immediately and invited me to join them.

After discussing the size of the base for a couple of minutes, he offered to take us on a tour by jeep. Outside there was a row of impressive four-wheel-drive, air-conditioned jeeps, all hitched up to an electricity supply which in effect provided an electric blanket to keep their engines warm. Even antifreeze is no proof against the wind in the Antarctic.

The tour was very informative. Mr La Count appeared to have changed his mind about me, and insisted on taking us to what he called 'all the hot spots'. He told us he was cleaning up the results of thirty years of the American throwaway society. In the past when machines had broken or passed their usefulness they were simply pushed over the edge of the bay into the sea. This released all sorts of terrible pollutants. When supervising part of the clean-up he had seen a piece of metal sticking up on the edge of the sea and told his men to recover it. They eventually pulled a whole bulldozer out of the sea. There had been no record of its existence, and nobody knew what else was down there. He pointed across to the supply ship we had already seen in the harbour. It was, he said, full to the brim with trash that was to be taken back to Lyttelton in New Zealand to be disposed of properly.

He drove to another part of the base and showed us piles of batteries, all of which he said would be taken home. By now I felt quite sympathetic towards him, and when we came upon two forty-gallon drums of waste oil, both of which appeared to be leaking badly, I felt quite sorry. There was a twenty-yard-long sticky mess on the ground. He was clearly upset and said he would order it all to be dug out and taken back home. I told him that I had seen pictures of McMurdo from previous expeditions and there had then been literally piles of rubbish. He said a lot was still on the site; it was impossible to clean it all up at once and it had been temporarily covered in volcanic ash. There was a $30 million clean-up programme being put before Congress, aimed specifically at dealing with this problem.

At the back of the base a large pile of cardboard boxes and paper were ready for burning in a giant hole in the ground. I thought open-air burning was banned under the Antarctic Treaty and said so, but Mr La Count said that the whole lot would be covered in aircraft fuel. It would burn at a very high temperature, virtually the same as enclosed incineration, which was permitted. A man with oxyacetylene equipment was attacking a dauntingly large pile of scrap metal which Mr La Count said had been brought there from various old rubbish dumps. It was being sorted, stacked into crates, and would be sent home next season for recycling. I taxed him about the sewage outfall which currently just poured straight into the sea. He said the plan was to put it in a pipe 140 feet down in the sound, but before discharge to masticate the sewage so that it would be evenly distributed and digested by the sea.

We went up to the top of the base where he told us there used to be two small nuclear reactors to provide heat and light to the station. All things nuclear, from bombs to waste, had been banned under the Antarctic Treaty, and the United States had responded by removing these two tiny power plants, including the ground they stood on. The contrast between the cost and complete efficiency of this operation and the continued dumping of sewage and machinery in the bay struck me as very odd. We were out for about three hours, ending with a look at one of the brand new dormitory buildings which were of the standard of three-star hotels and took 240 people each. Three were already built and another was due for the following season. There was air conditioning, a cinema, a games room, cigarette machines on every floor, drink and ice dispensers, lounges, laundry rooms and full-time cleaners. Most of the personnel had already been flown out, this being the end of the season, but we were shown round some poor unfortunate's room while he was halfway through packing. Ron La Count obviously showed his staff no more mercy than journalists.

We went back to the Chalet and Mary-Ann bullied him into an exclusive half-hour interview. I sat outside with a National Science Foundation booklet on the US Antarctic science programme. I was astonished at the scale and variety of the US projects. A team was even searching for meteors preserved in the ice. The Americans were also studying the antifreeze in fish blood, and had a complex programme to discover how deep seals and penguins dived below the ice and how they had adapted to survive and hunt for long periods at depths where a man's lungs could not have stood the water pressure. This involved radio transmitters and small movable huts rolled over the seals' breathing holes. When the seals came up for air their breath was captured and analysed for oxygen content. Heart rate and blood pressure were carefully measured.

When Mr La Count emerged from his office with Mary-Ann, he took both of us on to a balcony overlooking the hall of the Chalet and we had a long chat about US operations. McMurdo could accommodate 1,200 people during the summer, and serviced the all-the-year-round station at the South Pole and a number of summer stations, using the US Navy for logistical support. Throughout this conversation he often referred to Greenpeace, approving or not approving, and called them 'your friends'. He obviously enjoyed verbal sparring, and never let a point pass without picking me up if he thought he could. Perhaps he was short of mental stimulation after several months in the Antarctic. I asked him about the Minerals Convention, and he replied confidently that the US was not interested in exploitation. Certainly there was no hint of anything in the science programme that could readily be used in the hunt for minerals: that had been the first thing I had checked for. We discussed other reasons for the United States having put so much money and personnel into the Antarctic over the years. Was it all part of the strategic plan of a superpower to increase its sphere of influence? He laughed and again accused me of being anti-American.

A helper brought him a note. He groaned: 'This is not my day.' Shortly afterwards a number of high-ranking American naval officers arrived, a sort of state visit. The previous day a US Navy icebreaker had been spotted from the bridge of the *Gondwana*. I assumed this was how these visitors had been shipped in. Mr La Count took his leave. I must say I found him very likeable, although I was not sure I would like to work for him.

Since we were banned from entering any buildings unless accompanied by Mr La Count, we now decided to go to the New Zealand base. From the helicopter it had not looked very far away, and Mary-Ann agreed that the walk would do us good. We had at least a couple of hours to kill before our helicopter was due back for us. We walked up the hill towards the back of the McMurdo base where the rubbish dump was, and just as we were leaving the base an American car drew alongside us. Inside was a US lawyer called Chuck Stovitz. He said he was going our way, and would we like a lift? It seemed a bit of a happy coincidence and felt much more as if he was seeing us off the premises. However, with the volcanic dust being blown about and a temperature of around −10°C, whatever the reason for the lift we were going to accept gratefully. Mary-Ann asked Chuck where he came from and he said Beverly Hills, which was close to where she lived. She asked him what a lawyer from there was doing at McMurdo. He said, rather mysteriously, the law, and refused to elaborate.

Chuck dropped us outside Scott Base and drove off back to McMurdo. There was no one about to speak to, so we looked for a way in. The door I had been ejected from on my previous visit was shut, so we went to another entrance. There was a receptionist on the telephone, giving the place the appearance of a hotel. It might have been anywhere in the world. Within a few minutes the head of the New Zealand Antarctic programme, Hugh Logan, who was by coincidence visiting the station, appeared and made us very welcome. There was no mention of the incident two nights previously. We had coffee and a chat about the colourful Ron La Count, and the legacy of thirty years of indiscriminate waste-tipping into the bay. Mr Logan opened the little shop in the foyer from which they sold visitors small gifts to take home, mostly from the US bases, and then gave us a tour of the station.

The New Zealand science programme involved a lot of work on the geology of Mount Erebus and the surrounding area. Hugh Logan told us that 30 million years ago the area across the bay from the volcano was covered in plants, and animals roamed there. Our tour took in the seismic observation post. According to the chart there had been a considerable seismic event that morning. I asked Mr Logan what it was and he said it appeared that the Americans had blown up 4,000 pounds of surplus explosives on the other side of the ice shelf. The throwaway society had not been entirely cured.

The New Zealanders had a television camera stationed at the

top of Mount Erebus, pointing into the crater. It was a twenty-four-hour monitoring operation, and we could clearly see the lava bubbling and smoking gently. The scientists standing nearby put on a film show of recorded highlights from the last four years. There would suddenly be a big blip or vast bubble in the lava lake, and tons of molten lava would be hurled into the air, some flying completely out of the crater. When this happened the whole area was covered in clouds of steam, presumably from the lava melting the snow on the mountain.

I was so fascinated by this that Mary-Ann had to drag me away. We carried on round the base. Staff could get to places like the gym, and even the garage containing the skidoos and other tracked vehicles, without ever having to go outside its shelter. We had the obligatory chat about sewage disposal. They had been tipping sewage into the sea for thirty years, like the Americans, but NZ $400,000 had been allocated for the next season to install a biological treatment plant. We also discussed the use of the US icebreaker to clear ice from a large area of McMurdo Sound each summer. One of the scientists said the removal of the ice covering had caused a much higher uptake of water by the wind and would be increasing the snowfall further down the Ross Sea coastline, in effect slightly changing the climate.

When we left the station after a very enjoyable visit we were again lucky. The incoming manager of the New Zealand base was going over to McMurdo to introduce himself and offered us a lift. Back on the ship we were delighted to find that Merriann Bell, the cook, who was a wonderful baker, had got some white flour from the base camp and had made new bread. It was a great luxury. After tea I gave Pete a rundown of my visits. Although in general I said I'd been quite favourably impressed, he and Paul Bogart were not prepared to give Ron La Count the benefit of the doubt on any point. This lack of charity on their part was uncharacteristic, but if in the past they had been treated as aggressively as I was at first, then this was not surprising.

After a drink I went up to the bridge to say goodnight to Albert, who was on the long lonely anchor watch. We fell to discussing whether it was right for Greenpeace to have a base in Antarctica at all. However careful Greenpeace were, there must be some environmental impact and some pollution. Albert concluded that to establish World Park Base had been a political decision designed to get Greenpeace into the Antarctic talks. But although this plan had failed – the treaty parties had refused to accept nongovernment organisations – Greenpeace still had a base. Albert and I wondered whether Greenpeace should consider closing it down while continuing with their campaign of visiting other bases. Not having to resupply Cape Evans would certainly release more time and resources for this. Realistically, however, as with any organisation, once outposts of empire were built, they were not easily abandoned.

Tuesday was Valentine's Day, a rather special day in my calendar, the day I had proposed to my wife twenty-five years ago. I rang her at two minutes past midday our time, just after midnight at home in Leighton Buzzard, Bedfordshire. Maureen had been asleep but was pleased to hear from me.

The resupply was reported to be going well. Unsurprisingly, however, those who had been working outside were tired with all the hard physical work in the intense cold. Pete and Paul Bogart had been across to Scott Base to do their site inspection and talk to the New Zealanders about the results of the sampling taken last year. It appeared that Greenpeace had found an excess of silver and copper waste in the soils. The silver waste was explained by a spillage of photographic chemicals, but the copper remained a mystery. Otherwise it seemed to be a satisfactory visit. The New Zealanders, with a sixteen-man overwintering team, were clearly doing their best to follow good environmental practices.

Pete had decided it was time we took a break from the resupply and went across to a place on the mainland coast called Marble Point, about forty miles away. The purpose of this trip was to install a survival hut as a field base in the middle of a large flat area of bare ground next to the coast. This hut was the one that had been badly damaged by the French. Henk had all the necessary equipment to weld the damaged bits together and make it weatherproof. We had a crew meeting at 7 pm to discuss the progress of the expedition, the coming trip, and for Pete and Paul to report on their visit to Scott Base.

Marble Point had been discussed by the US National Science Foundation as a possible hard rock airstrip to replace the ice runway near McMurdo. Greenpeace was wholly against this proposal as it would take away another ice-free area available for wildlife. I had asked about the US plans for Marble Point when I spoke to Ron La Count. He told me that the plans for the airstrip had been dropped. Paul was sceptical about this since there was an official record of the proposal and the plans were available in National Science Foundation documents in Washington. He knew a lot of money had already been spent in the area and believed it might be preparatory work for the airstrip project. There was no mention in the records of the plans being abandoned, and he said it might be merely that the final funding had not been made available.

In any case, the Americans already used the area as a staging and refuelling post for their helicopter trips to the interior. A lot of scientific expeditions going to the interior went via Marble Point.

It was decided that we would sail that night for Marble Point. It was a beautiful sunny evening. Arne, who was at the controls, said it would take about four hours to reach the new anchorage. I stood on the bridge wing: the thermometer was in full sun but still registered −6°C. Arne said that the temperature would continue to drop daily now as the sun sank towards the horizon. The summer was almost over. But although the New Zealanders had warned us that the ice conditions further up the Ross Sea were worsening – which meant potentially that ships would not be able to leave the area before the onset of winter – Arne said the up-to-date ice charts faxed to him with the weather forecast looked fairly clear. He was keeping an eye on it, he said, but he was not unduly worried. I was pleased to note that the routine four-hourly checking of the sea water temperature was getting his close attention.

We had a trouble-free trip. There was a small amount of pack ice drifting between us and the coast at Marble Point, but the *Gondwana* made short work of it. We anchored in the middle of a large bay. There was a boulder-strewn plain running down to the water's edge, and behind it an impressive ice cliff, the leading edge of a glacier. A bleak landscape. Through the bridge binoculars I looked for signs of US activity and immediately spotted a bulldozer lying at a strange angle, as if it had keeled over and died. Not far away there were dozens of rusty barrels, some stacked neatly and the rest strewn around in a haphazard fashion. They were probably empty, and looked as if they had been blown about by the wind.

We shut down for the night. Albert was on anchor watch again and I stayed and enjoyed the stillness of the evening. For the first time the sun dropped right to the horizon. It turned the snow on the now distant Mount Erebus a beautiful shade of pink. Then it started to climb again and it was time to go to bed.

In the morning I was woken by the noise of the helicopter taking off. Sean and Tim were still sound asleep. The helicopter was taking Henk and a reconnaissance team ashore to find a suitable site for the survival hut. The helicopter came back to carry over the equipment but did not return. I discovered there were no plans to let anyone else ashore, but eventually talked Ken into putting a boat into the water and dumping one boatload on the beach.

It was a very desolate shoreline, ringed with pack ice moving up and down on the slight swell. A seal popped its head out of the water a few feet away to remind us we were intruding on the family territory. Our party was Tim, Sean, Bob Graham, the second mate, and Wojtek Moskal, who was the Polish member of the outgoing overwintering team. We had only had a few days to get to know Wojtek, but he was a big-hearted cheerful character and a big plus on any venture.

Bob, against the rules, went off on his own into the wilderness, but Sean and Tim with their camera gear, using me and Wojtek as packhorses, walked along a rough track made by bulldozers up the steady slope towards where we thought the Greenpeace hut would be. It was about half a mile to the crest. Then we caught our first sight of the Greenpeace helicopter and the hut, already constructed. They were still some distance away. Alongside the bulldozer tracks was all sorts of litter – old tin cans, bits of wood and metal sticking out of the ground. When we reached the hut everyone was very busy anchoring things down. Henk was welding metal shielding on to the hut to improve insulation, and there was a radio mast still to be constructed and tested. Bruno, who with the rest of the overwinterers would be relying on this hut for a field base, was making sure everything was in perfect working order. During the winter when the intervening sea was frozen the Greenpeace party could travel over on their two skidoos in a couple of hours. My help was not required, so I told Bruno I would walk over to the US helicopter base which I could see not too far away, and on to the bottom of the glacier cliff. I estimated it would take about an hour. This proved to be a vast underestimate. Despite everyone's increasing experience we still made this same mistake over distances, possibly because of a combination of the vastness of the landscape and the clearness of the air.

The US helicopter base consisted of three huts and a parked bulldozer. A little further away were some giant rubber bladders full of helicopter fuel, a self-service gas station for the US helicopter fleet. There was an American flag on a single flagpole standing out proudly in the breeze. I took a picture – another outpost of empire.

As I cut across to the glacier from the US buildings the ground was pretty solid and easy to walk on, gently undulating and rock-strewn but with no pitfalls. What had looked like a small cliff got higher as I approached, and turned out to average about 150 feet. It was an ice cliff. Unlike other ice I had seen in the Antarctic it was full of stones, sand and rock. This was a moving glacier, and I was standing in front of the leading edge.

Along the bottom was what looked like melt water, but what I had thought were big puddles turned out to be solid ice. We were clearly at the stage where the melting glacier had stopped retreating at the end of the summer and was ready to lumber forward again as the winter closed in. Along the front of the glacier were giant icicles averaging twenty to thirty feet, some of them much longer. I could hear the constant tinkle of ice falling. It was clear that during the summer the leading edge of the glacier warmed up sufficiently to melt some of the ice and cause it to retreat. Once or twice giant icicles snapped off and plunged down the cliff, breaking into hundreds of pieces. Fearful of getting speared I retired a respectful distance and took a couple of pictures. It was now so cold that it was impossible to take my gloves off to work the camera for more than about two minutes.

For some time I had been visited on my walk by the odd skua, just flying by to look at me. Quite a large number of them were gathered on a small hill several hundred yards away from the glacier. I had been away from the rest of my party for a long time now, much longer than Antarctic rules permitted, so I decided to return to the hut. I made a detour to avoid the small hill so as not to disturb the birds, but after a while the skuas flying by began to be more and more numerous. They were now buzzing me, about ten to fifteen feet above my head. Standing still and looking round, I could see twenty to thirty skuas going in a great arc to get upwind, and then swooping down towards me. They passed by at enormous speed, squawking, their beaks perilously close to my head. They had a wingspan of about three feet and were shooting past only inches away. This was very alarming, but there was nowhere to shelter or hide so I just had to plod on, moving as fast as possible, keeping my eyes on the ground so as not to fall. After a minute or two I spotted a US marker post lying next to a boulder. For once I was grateful to the Americans for their rubbish. I picked it up and held it above my head to make my escape. The skuas attacked the top of the stick, one or two of them clipping it with their beaks. Then they suddenly called off the attack, no doubt satisfied they had driven me off. I was able to pause for a rest.

There was still a long way to go to get back to the hut, so I set off at a steady pace, still clutching my stick in case of further attentions from the wildlife. I noticed there were a lot of bulldozer tracks and marker posts similar to the one I had been so grateful to find. A suspicious mind would have wondered if the posts were marking out a possible airstrip. I could see no discernible pattern, but I knew that Pete and Henk had sited the hut at what they considered to be the most likely point for the centre of the proposed runway, the object being to embarrass the US government by refusing to move it if the plan was given the go-ahead.

Eventually, topping a rise, I could see the helicopter, more or less in the direction I had guessed, but further away. Somehow I managed to get there by the time agreed for departure back to the bay. It was around twenty minutes' walk, the temperature had dropped to about −9°C, and there was a twenty-knot wind, making the wind chill factor around −40°C. I had two hats on already, a black balaclava and a thick hand-knitted woollen hat. I put my jacket hood up as well. My hands, inside two pairs of gloves with mittens on top, were still cold, and the tiny bits of exposed face felt numb. On the boat journey back, there was quite a bit of spray. It turned to ice before it hit you.

Despite this temporary discomfort I felt a lot more relaxed after my walk ashore. At dinner there was a giant cake again because it was the electrician Phil Durham's birthday. He was twenty-six. He produced some bottles of wine saved up from the trip to the Italian base and we had a very pleasant meal. Life was good.

Up on the bridge there was no time for mellow evenings as Arne had already set our course back for Cape Evans and the rest of the resupply. The wind had blown a lot of pack ice in our path, blocking our way out of the bay. The overwintering party was very impressed as he used the power of the *Gondwana*'s engines to push our way clear. He said we should be back at Cape Evans by 2 am.

The games that nations play over the Antarctic take a variety of forms – the airstrip the Americans planned at Marble Point and the one the French were building at Dumont d'Urville are just two of the political counters. US attitudes were neatly illustrated for me by Ron La Count's robust antagonism towards Greenpeace. He resented the organisation's intrusion into what he already considered his private domain.

Other countries, with less money and manpower, have used other methods to stake their claim in the Antarctic. For example, Argentina and Chile have both established 'colonies' in Antarctica and take great trouble to have children born at their so-called scientific base camps. The British too are using the excuse of their scientific work in the Antarctic to make sure that their influence continues to grow.

To understand how the struggle for influence has developed, it is necessary to examine America's historical attitude to the Antarctic. In 1924 when Charles E. Hughes, then US Secretary of State, issued two statements about the claims of the British and French governments to territory in Antarctica, he made it clear that, for the United States to accept a claim, an actual colony had to be established. In a letter he said: 'The discovery of lands unknown to civilisation, even when coupled with a formal taking of possession, does not support a valid claim of sovereignty unless the discovery is followed by an actual settlement of the discovered country.' This statement of US policy, which became known as the Hughes doctrine, dominated American thinking for the next forty years. It neatly got round the disputatious fact that the United States, Britain and the Soviet Union all claimed to have 'discovered' the continent first. Essentially Hughes said the land was so inhospitable that no actual settlement could be established and therefore no claim would be recognised. In these circumstances the United States would neither press its own claim nor agree to other people's.

This Antarctic policy was an extension of a wider American world philosophy. Instead of annexing other people's territory as had been done by the older colonial nations in the nineteenth century, the United States aimed simply to create spheres of influence in which it could exploit growing markets to the benefit of American industry. The object of the policy in the context of Antarctica was to allow the United States free access in the entire continent should valuable natural resources, oil or minerals, be discovered.

It was this policy that generated the Antarctic Treaty. In May 1958 President Eisenhower invited eleven other countries, all of which were participating in the International Geophysical Year, to talks to find a solution to the political problems of the area. His Secretary of State, John Foster Dulles, proposed 'to establish in Antarctica an international regime which will prevent the mono-polising of any part of this new continent for military purposes but assure an "open door" for the peaceful purposes of all mankind.' The treaty had the advantage not only of limiting the antagonisms between rival claimants such as Britain, Argentina and Chile, but also of preventing the then very Cold War between the United States and the Soviet Union from spreading to Antarctica.

It was a useful solution and a unique international agreement. Nevertheless, as H. Robert Hall, the Tasmanian academic, comments in an article in the *Polar Record* of April 1989, the problems of national interest and prestige may have been frozen but they have not gone away.

Although the treaty is unique, it is not divorced from the pressures of world politics. The large US scientific programme, which ensures a network of bases all over Antarctica, makes it impossible for anything substantial to happen in the continent without the United States at the very least being aware of it. The Soviet Union has played the same game, and both superpowers have made sure by their presence that the territorial claims of other nations cannot in effect be enforced without their permission. The Soviet Union has established a base in each of the claimed territories, while the United States, as well as setting up an equal number of bases spread about in different parts of Antarctica, has built a base actually at the South Pole. Since all territorial claims end at the South Pole, like the slices of a cake, this effectively straddles them all.

Even though the New Zealand base is technically on New Zealand territory, its scientists are wholly dependent on American logistical support for their programme, and are happy for this to continue since they get far more science for their limited resources than would otherwise be the case. And to a lesser extent the Italian and German bases further down the coast are dependent on the Americans too. Although they have their own supply ships, if they need any logistic support by air or rescue services then it is to the Americans they have to turn. Ron La Count sees this as the United States' generous support for its allies and fellow scientists and turns aside any suggestion that it also conveniently reinforces his country's political dominance. He has, however, made it plain that American generosity will not be extended to Greenpeace. 'No beds, no transport for Greenpeace or any that sail with them,' he said.

The Americans use the US Navy for logistical support, thus providing polar training for new recruits and helicopter pilots. The Marble Point solid rock airstrip would be the next logical step in US dominance of the region. Extensive survey work has been done and around $200,000 has been spent on levelling the ground. However, no more money for the project has been provided, and with the slackening of the Cold War the military pressure for such a scheme has gone. The opposition to the Minerals Convention from the Green lobby would make a construction of this size very difficult to get through a hostile Congress, which would have to vote the funds.

Such inhibitions have not affected the United Kingdom, which is hoping to complete its hard rock airstrip at Rothera on the other side of the continent by 1991. This base on Adelaide Island, west of the Antarctic Peninsula, has been operated by the British Antarctic Survey since 1975. It has so far been supported by a fleet of de Havilland Twin Otter aircraft flying from a snow skiway three miles from the station. Significantly, however, although the standard of British science in the Antarctic has always been of the highest quality, the British government's enthusiasm for it (in cash terms) suddenly more than redoubled after the Falklands war. After years of operating on a shoestring the British Antarctic Survey was suddenly voted the money for a new research ship, a hard rock airstrip at Rothera, and a longer-range aircraft. The reason behind this project, according to the British government, was to increase the amount of science done there, and the time scientists could spend in the Antarctic. Instead of the trip to Rothera taking the best part of five weeks from London, it would be possible with the new airstrip to reach deep into Antarctica in forty-eight hours.

The British government is justifiably proud of the achievements of its science teams in the region. In her speeches to the United Nations and the annual meeting of the British Royal Society, Mrs Thatcher repeatedly referred to the British discovery of the hole in the ozone layer. She laid great emphasis on the contribution of British scientists in Antarctica towards understanding the causes and effects of global warming and climatic change.

Despite this, environmentalists remain sceptical. If that was all the airstrip was intended for, it would be difficult for environmentalists to have any reservations about it. But the strategic importance of the Antarctic Peninsula and the control of access to it was too important to be ignored. Indeed, when the British Antarctic Survey had been soliciting the government for money to build the airstrip, it had not only mentioned science in its documents but had frequently referred to the possible mineral resources in the Antarctic.

In April 1990, when the World Wide Fund for Nature launched a campaign to save the Antarctic from the mineral exploitation, they received a letter from Mrs Thatcher's private secretary. The government, he said, was fully committed to the protection of the Antarctic continent, and the only way to achieve this was by international cooperation. The government intended to ratify the Minerals Convention, 'the primary purpose of which is to protect the Antarctic environment'.

The letter went on to point out that the convention did not provide a regime to encourage mining and, in the event of an application to open an area for mining being made, it would give priority to the protection of the environment rather than to the prospective operator. Mining could only proceed under the strictest environmental safeguards known to international law; thus the convention acted as a deterrent to mineral activity, not as an encouragement.

Argentina has probably put a greater percentage of its national effort into staking its claim than any other country. In 1977 the first Argentine colony was established, and the following year the first baby was born there. In the next five years seven more babies were born at the base, establishing Argentina's colonial rights in the eyes of the Argentine government. These are not recognised by anyone else, but just to be on the safe side Chile decided to create a colony too.

Argentina also links this claim with its campaign against the British for control of the Malvinas/Falklands, South Georgia and other islands. As early as 1947 Britain, Argentina and Chile were sending warships into Antarctic waters to emphasise and protect their claims. Two years later the three countries signed an agreement stating they would not send warships to Antarctica during the next summer.

This agreement, although renewed annually, did not stop the tension. In 1952 an Argentine military patrol fired over the heads of a British party attempting to land in Hope Bay, and the following year the British destroyed Argentine and Chilean huts on Deception Island. In 1957 by presidential decree Argentina officially re-established the national territory of Tierra del Fuego, Antarctica and the South Atlantic Islands. Since this date all Argentine schoolchildren have been taught that the territory to the South Pole is part of Argentina and that Tierra del Fuego is the centre of their country, not the southernmost tip. It has even become a criminal offence to publish a map of Argentina without the Antarctic claim drawn in. Chilean and British claims are not mentioned on the children's maps. In fact, Chile, Argentina and Britain have all issued stamps showing the claimed Antarctic territory as their own, with no acknowledgement of rival claims.

Shortly after the Falklands war President Augusto Pinochet travelled to the Chilean air force's Teniente March Antarctic base on King George Island in the South Shetlands to inaugurate the Las Estrellas colony, with six families. By 1990 there were ten children attending the school at the base and eighteen children under ten. It was by then called a municipality of Chile and had its own mayor.

According to the Antarctic Treaty, member countries have to have a serious science programme and a base to become a consultative member and get voting rights. Couples having babies do not qualify as a serious scientific programme, but, as with other areas of the treaty, there seems to be no way of enforcing the rules.

Sometimes, too, the treaty produces curious anomalies. For example, on King George Island the Chilean children meet more nationalities in a few days than many of their fellow countrymen meet in a lifetime. Within a short distance of their homes, on a small peninsula on the island, popular because it is ice-free, there are bases run by the Soviet Union, China, South Korea, and

Uruguay, all with a smattering of visiting scientists from other countries, and all using the airstrip controlled by Chile for getting to and from the island. All the bases remain very friendly and attend each other's social events, as well as running a football tournament.

It appears that all the claimant nations are playing the same game. No doubt Britain will determine who uses the airstrip at Rothera as rigorously as the United States and Chile control access to theirs. At the same time it will all be put forward as an important example of international cooperation. A pointer to British pretensions in this area of sovereignty is that, as the British supply vessel left new crews behind at the British bases during the 1990 resupply, each base commander was sworn in as a magistrate to administer law and order in the part of the British Antarctic Territory under his jurisdiction. Yet Chile has a mayor for the same territory.

What no one knows is where all this will lead in the end. If the Antarctic Treaty remains intact – and everyone says they hope it will – then all the claims and counterclaims will remain in abeyance. The investment in airstrips will still pay off, however, if minerals are ever discovered and mined, even though no government has so far even hinted that this has crossed their minds when they vote yet more funds for 'science'.

16

Message to Congress at Minus Twenty

THURSDAY 16 FEBRUARY: Paul Bogart told me that last night he had a long conversation with the Washington office about Chuck Stovitz, the Beverly Hills lawyer who had given Mary-Ann and me a lift to the New Zealand base from McMurdo. He was said to be personal legal consultant to Peter Wilkness, Director of Polar Programmes in the United States. According to Paul, Greenpeace's Washington office were saying that Chuck could have been sworn in as a federal marshal, and if so would be allowed to arrest US citizens anywhere in the world if the suspect had committed a felony.

There was some doubt about what constituted a felony. It was a more serious offence than a misdemeanour, for which a marshal could not arrest anyone outside the United States. This raised interesting issues for Greenpeace, which intended to demonstrate at the McMurdo base. Deliberate damage to government property was believed to constitute a felony and carried a five-year prison sentence. This raised problems for US citizens aboard the *Gondwana*, like Paul. If anyone was arrested it would break new ground in Antarctic law since no country had ever exercised jurisdiction in the continent, except over their own base staff. Greenpeace in Washington was not keen on allowing the US National Science Foundation to use arrested Greenpeace crewmen as a test case. It would take months of legal wrangling and a great deal of money.

I asked if the problem could be solved by using non-US nationals for any demonstrations. According to Paul non-US citizens could not be arrested, but if positively identified they could be charged and tried in absentia in a US court. They would then be liable to arrest if they ever entered the United States in

191

the future. It was thought unlikely that the National Science Foundation would want to go to such lengths but, Paul said, that was not the point. The US citizens on the *Gondwana* wanted to demonstrate at McMurdo. They felt strongly that what their government was doing was wrong, and that the US citizens in the crew were the people who should say so.

All this was discussed at a crew meeting that night. Paul Bogart, Pete, Sean, Tim, and Bruno, as the incoming base leader, had all gone off in the morning to see Ron La Count. They had recorded the interview, and first they played it back to the crew. It had not been a meeting of minds. Mr La Count, Paul and Pete sparred throughout and were all on good form. Mr La Count was upset that Greenpeace had used the phrase 'cosmetic clean-up' in referring to his efforts to clean up McMurdo.

The crew meeting then discussed Greenpeace's original plan to block the McMurdo sewage outfalls to draw attention to the heavy metals that were routinely discharged into the bay from the base laboratories. There was some discussion about whether direct action was right at this time in view of the considerable efforts the US National Science Foundation had made to clean up. These might seem cosmetic as far as Greenpeace was concerned, but there were promises of further action. The looming threat of Chuck was also considered. In the end, uncharacteristically, it was decided to leave the whole issue to another crew meeting on the following Monday, on the eve of sailing from Cape Evans to McMurdo.

Another item for the crew meeting was the date for our arrival back in Lyttelton, the port of Christchurch, capital of South Island, New Zealand. Christchurch Greenpeace had sent a message saying they wanted to give us a big welcome when we got back but they needed to know the date to make arrangements. Could it please be a weekend so they could celebrate without having to worry about going to work? Currently we were scheduled to arrive back on 15 March, which was a Wednesday. There was a debate about whether we should aim for the 11th or the 18th. Personally I favoured the earlier date to avoid another week at sea, but again there was indecision, and that item too was adjourned until Monday.

As a break from being a journalist I had volunteered to join the work crew ashore the following morning and was up and out at

7.30 am. For the members of the crew who did this every day, it was an opportunity for some gentle mockery, especially because, as it happened, no one was going anywhere: a thirty-knot wind was blowing and it had begun to snow heavily. The temperature dropped to −11°C and we could not see the shore for the blizzard. We were stood down until the weather improved.

As a result I had a quiet morning reading a book, the first time for a week. At lunch time the snow eased, the wind dropped and the day was declared fit for work. We were ferried by helicopter to the shore to continue the clearing-up operation, which involved more than simply the one year's overwintering detritus.

In the first year that Greenpeace had ventured to the Ross Sea, a private expedition called 'In the Footsteps of Scott' had been due to be picked up at Cape Evans. They had erected a small hut to live in and store back-up equipment. The expedition's ship, the *Southern Quest*, which like Greenpeace's first ship was not ice-strengthened, returned to pick them up and, pressing on into the pack ice without sufficient caution, got stuck in it and sank. All the crew and most of their belongings were got off on to the ice and rescued. The Americans from McMurdo picked them up and ferried them by air to New Zealand, charging them for the costs – debts they were still paying off four years later. Their hut, which they had intended to ship out along with all their other equipment, had had to be left behind, and was annexed with their permission to the Greenpeace base. As part of the deal Greenpeace now had to clear up the remainder of the private expedition's gear and return it to Christchurch.

It was sorting out this equipment, now firmly stuck in the ice, that the work party had decided to tackle that day. Using pickaxes we dug out an assortment of timber, scrap iron, and boxes of junk which it was hard to believe any expedition could have needed. We sorted it into piles and put it on to sling nets to be hooked on to a hovering helicopter and ferried back in convenient loads to the *Gondwana*. I was given the honour of standing, arm outstretched, next to each completed load while the helicopter approached to just above my head. I then had to hook the load to the chain hanging below the helicopter. Provided the pilot was careful, this was not dangerous, but the propeller downdraught kicked up a lot of powdered snow from the earlier blizzard. The other inconvenience about this job, and the reason I had been given the honour of doing it, was that the helicopter engines generated a large amount of static electricity. As I hooked up each load I acted as an earth for the electricity and it ran down my arm and into the ground. It was only a small shock really, but the anticipation of it, every time a load was taken away, made the job real fun.

By the time 7 pm came I was very glad to be finished for the day, and feeling healthily hungry. We had managed a lot of clearing up in difficult conditions. While we were waiting for the boat to take us back to the *Gondwana*, Keith Swenson, the former base commander, let us start up the Greenpeace skidoos and have a go at driving them. A skidoo is a sort of motorbike on skis with very fast acceleration, and on the lumpy ground round the hut they were difficult to control. At one point I nearly drove off the ice shelf into the sea.

We carried some waste chemicals back on the boat because they were too delicate to fly in a sling. Werner Stachl, the deckhand, was struggling up the rope ladder on the side of the *Gondwana* carrying a boxful when the inflatable swung out leaving him dangling on the ice-covered rope. He had taken his life jacket off before getting out of the inflatable so he could carry the chemicals more easily, but was now in serious danger of falling in. Pete, who was driving, tried to get the boat back under him. The air temperature was −12°C and the water −2°C. It says something for Werner's dedication that he did not ditch the chemicals in favour of self-preservation, but hung on grimly to the rope ladder until we could get back and help him.

The next day, 18 February, had been designated a day off for everyone, and those normally confined to the ship were to be given a guided walking tour to the edge of the glacier behind the Greenpeace base to a place called Skua Lake. Sadly for them, the weather turned really nasty with the wind at thirty knots. All trips were postponed until after lunch, and eventually abandoned altogether. We settled down to reading, resting and watching a Billy Connolly tape while the storm raged outside. The ship was now down to the last few cases of beer, and it was clear we would run out well before the ship got back to New Zealand. I wonder whether this realization would prompt people to opt for an earlier return to Lyttelton.

The following morning I woke to the sound of the helicopter making runs from the base to the ship, carrying some of the junk we had piled up the day before last. The noise of the crane grinding away just outside the cabin drove me to get up and eventually dislodged Tim and Sean. They were due to go to McMurdo to do some filming, and I settled down to do a long background piece about minerals and whether looking for them and mining them was a serious proposition in the Antarctic. To my surprise Bob Graham told me he had spent a year on a British Petroleum survey ship south of the Falklands. They had mapped the sea bed and come to the conclusion that there was a good prospect for oil. It was on this voyage in 1976 that the Royal Navy research ship *Shackleton*, which was accompanying them, was fired on by an Argentinian gunboat. As a result of this incident, the BP ship abandoned the survey and returned to England.

That evening we had the crew meeting which had been reconvened from three days before. It seemed that most of the resupply and clearing up of the base was complete. There was still a little fresh food to deliver and some rubbish to bring back. One more day should be enough for all this before the visit to McMurdo. Even if we spent a couple of days at the US base, we would still have time to reach New Zealand by 11 March, provided we did not get stuck in the ice. This meant civilisation was only three weeks away, and with it the prospect of going home, which seemed to cheer everyone up.

A two-day visit to McMurdo was scheduled. The first day was to show the Greenpeace flag and allow visitors from the base on board. The second day was for some sort of demonstration. Since the last meeting a lot of hard thinking had been going on about the possibility of arrests and legal complications. Blocking the pipeline had finally been abandoned in favour of filling seven barrels from the end of McMurdo's chemicals waste pipe and placing them in front of Ron La Count's Chalet headquarters. Each of the barrels would be painted with letters so when they were outside Mr La Count's office they would read 'Danger! Cadmium'. Publicity pictures would then be taken. According to the samples Greenpeace had analysed the previous year, the Americans were discharging dangerously large quantities of cadmium into the bay. This kind of discharge is legally unacceptable in the United States and Europe, cadmium being a dangerous heavy metal causing birth defects, sterility and toxic poisoning. Filling the barrels and attempting to shame the Americans was regarded as a more acceptable and a legally safer idea than blocking the pipe.

After the meeting the weather was again bad. Phil Doherty, who had come over on behalf of the other overwinterers to hear what was said and report back to his companions on the base, was unable to leave and spent the night on the ship, probably for the last time before his long winter stint.

20 February: Went ashore to do some more manual work clearing up. Why I volunteered for this when I could stay in a nice warm ship I do not know. Henk found me an outdoor job which involved taking some plywood panels to pieces. At first I thought this was a simple job, but the panels had been put together with screws and nails and would have lasted 100 years. They were needed to provide extra insulation for the winter quarters and were being cut up and remodelled. It took two hours to take them to bits, more time than it took Henk to rebuild them.

Every day now the temperature was dropping an average of one degree as the sun sank lower. The wind never seemed to let up either, so the moment we stopped work we began to freeze. After the panels, Henk found us an old outside toilet to demolish. It was very primitive – a tiny hut with a seat with a hole in, placed over a very large barrel. The barrel had been filled up and the hut abandoned. Fortunately the contents were frozen solid. We transported this barrel on a sledge across to the helicopter nets so it could be taken back to the ship. Henk, who seemed to think of everything, had something to douse it with that would neutralise it when it came back to life on our way back to New Zealand.

Lunch provided a welcome break, and Phil Doherty asked me to accompany him up the first foothill of Mount Erebus where Greenpeace had a radio repeater station. This was equipped with a wind electricity generator, but in the winter the wind was so strong that he wanted to check the structure.

The hill was much steeper than it looked. Where there was new snow, climbing was hard work, but on the exposed parts where the new snow had already been swept away by the wind there was only old ice worn smooth and very slippery. It took two or three kicks with my steel-toecapped boots to make a hole big enough to step in safety. Up at the repeater station the turbine was whipping round in the stiff breeze. Phil managed to dismantle it while I held the tools and admired the view. I had brought my camera, but it froze solid on the second picture. In the bay there was sea smoke, frozen water vapour, a sort of fast-moving fog which runs in dense undulating waves across the sea when a strong wind of very cold air blows off the icecap. It looked like something out of a space adventure film set on an unexplored planet. From our observation post on the mountain the bottom half of the *Gondwana* had disappeared in the sea smoke, but the bridge and masts were still perfectly clear and I could see the man on watch keeping an eye on us through binoculars. I waved and he waved back, all very reassuring. The landscape inland was very harsh, glaciers, black volcanoes, fields of unbroken ice or snow. Not what I would describe as beautiful – too unforgiving for that.

As soon as Phil had finished we started down; it was too cold to hang about. The descent proved pretty difficult – we should have taken ice axes. Thankfully when we arrived back there were no more outdoor jobs to do, and I hitched a ride in an inflatable taking the camera crew back to the *Gondwana*. The sea smoke had encrusted the ship in ice and we had considerable difficulty getting our gear up the side.

We were due at McMurdo by 9 am the following day. At 8.15 am when I got to the bridge the American base was already in view. The ship was ploughing through new ice – the temperature on the bridge wing thermometer was −17°C, the lowest yet. If it went much lower the mercury would retreat into the reservoir at the bottom of the thermometer tube and accurate measurements of temperature would no longer be possible.

The American supply vessel had left in the last few days, loaded with scrap to take back to New Zealand, so the ice wharf was empty. We were obliged to berth at its far end, however, because Mr La Count had claimed the *Gondwana* could damage the wharf if it came too close in. How this was possible when the other, much larger ship had not done so was not explained. As we approached, there were no Americans anywhere to be seen, so the *Gondwana* crew climbed on to the dockside to make the ship fast. Ken Ballard, the first mate, who was normally impervious to discomfort, looked very grey in the face during this operation, and when he came back on board advised everyone to put more clothes on before going ashore. I went back to my cabin and dressed again. Just for the record I was wearing eight layers of clothing on my top half and five on the bottom. On top were an ordinary vest, a thermal vest, a sweatshirt, a thick cotton shirt, three sweaters and an Arctic padded jacket. Below were two pairs of long johns, tracksuit bottoms, and cord trousers topped with windproof trousers. On my feet I had two pairs of woollen socks, boot liners and Antarctic boots; on my hands inner thermal gloves and woollen gloves topped by thick mittens; and on my head a thin black balaclava, and a thick woollen hat covered by a thick green wool balaclava. I was also wearing snow goggles. I was perfectly equipped for a game of strip poker.

Outside, the wind burned the tiny area of my face that was still exposed, but otherwise I was comfortable. A couple of vans from the main part of the base could now be seen creeping along the black ash road towards us, presumably to check out what was happening. About twenty members of the crew were picking their way across the ice wharf towards the shore. It was not particularly smooth ice, at least at the outer end where the *Gondwana* had docked, and it had a large split running close to the shore. The Americans had put a bridge over the split which allowed vehicles to drive on to the wharf from the dirt road which followed the shoreline about a hundred yards from the ship. Pete's plan was for the crew to stand in a long line on the dirt road, holding up a twenty-yard-long banner, with the ugly base in the background. The message on the banner demanded money from Congress for the McMurdo clean-up, and protested about the unfulfilled promises of the National Science Foundation. Taking pictures proved to be difficult in the extreme cold, but Pete's propaganda machine needed them. The crew were soon jumping up and down to keep warm and shouting at Steve to hurry up. American observers, who were now about a hundred yards down the road, watched impassively from their trucks, but made no sign of greeting and no attempt to come any closer.

Not far away from the ice wharf was another historic hut, and I wandered off to have a look. This was Scott's original hut of 1902, built by the first major British expedition attempting to reach the Pole. This hut was a completely different design than the others, being square with a sort of veranda round all four sides. This appeared to be for tethering horses, but surely in this cold they would have frozen to death. It was not possible to find out anything more about the hut because the door was padlocked. The windows were impossible to see through because it was so bright outside and dark in the interior, but in any case the hut had been used by many expeditions since 1902 and none of the original artefacts were still there. It all looked to be kept in very good condition, however. There was a memorial at the top of the bank overlooking the sea next to the hut. It was to an A. B. Vince, 'who slipped and fell into the sea at this point' in 1902.

After lunch Mary-Ann was very anxious to see Ron La Count, and I agreed to accompany her the half-mile up the hill to his headquarters at the Chalet. On the way we met Tim, who was out with Sean filming the dump at the top of the base where Ron La Count had shown Mary-Ann and me the large pile of scrap metal.

Mr La Count met us at the door of the Chalet and invited Mary-Ann in for coffee. He ignored me totally. I asked him whether Washington had sent him the piece I had written about him for *The Guardian*. He did not answer directly, but said he was becoming anti-British.

He then asked us about Greenpeace intentions. We told him that the *Gondwana* planned to be back in New Zealand by 11 March, which meant we could remain at McMurdo and harass him for another week. Since he was due to fly out of McMurdo for home the following day, this was a major blow. He did not say so, but we got the impression he had been given orders to remain at his post until Greenpeace was out of the area. Mary-Ann told him that the *Gondwana*'s telephone system was blocked because Mount Erebus was between the ship's communications system and the satellite, but Mr La Count ignored her broad hint and did not offer to let her use his telephone. She then asked him straight out if he would fly her home in one of the National Science Foundation's planes from the ice runway. He made her ask three times before saying he could not give permission, it was up to a senior official in Washington. To this Mary-Ann replied that she had already made enquiries in Washington and they had said it was a matter for Mr La Count as the man on the ground. He then said he could fly her out if she was sick, but she clearly was not. Then he asked how much she would pay. Clearly he was saying he would not take her – you come with Greenpeace, you go home with them. It was time to go: we were supposed to be back on board by 4 pm and conversation with Mr La Count was not very productive. The walk back to the ship was much more pleasant – we had our backs to the fierce wind and it was downhill. Mary-Ann told me she had gone off Ron La Count in a big way.

Back at the ship none of the other shore parties due back at 4 pm had returned. One party had gone to Scott Base. Another party had climbed a nearby volcano to collect data on a Greenpeace science experiment, dialysis membranes designed to pick up pollutants. A third party had set off to put up a radio mast at Greenpeace Three. Pete was irate. Six of the New Zealand overwintering party from Scott were due for dinner in an hour or so to meet our incoming team, two of whom were in the Greenpeace Three party and showed no signs of returning.

The New Zealand party and a group of six Americans arrived shortly afterwards. The Americans were flying home the next day and told us that very few of their friends had come because Mr La Count was so angry with Greenpeace. By now Pete's irritation with our missing groups had turned to anxiety and we began to organise search parties. It was decided that Dave Walley should go up in a helicopter. He radioed back after a few minutes that he could see people approaching on the road, and a count of heads showed that the whole crew was now accounted for. We were all much relieved, and Pete could feel irritated with them again for being late.

Steve Morgan had been unable to transmit any pictures of the demonstration that morning because Mount Erebus had blocked the satellite, so we now decided to send the helicopter to World Park Base at Cape Evans to use their facilities. I volunteered to go with Steve, only to find when we got going that there were no radio headsets and no ear protectors. Fortunately the heaters were on in the helicopter, so I was able to take off my mittens and stuff them under my balaclava and over my ears. It was certainly worth it, for the views of Antarctica from the helicopter were magnificent. The World Park Base team had finished for the day and were watching a film from the vast collection in the base library. I got the feeling they resented our intrusion. We wired the pictures, a tedious business, and then I spoke to the office. Tim Radford, then *The Guardian*'s Science Correspondent, was standing by the news desk and said complimentary things about the coverage, which was very cheering. It was nearly midnight before we were ready to fly back. Outside, the wind had dropped, and for the first time the sun had actually disappeared behind the horizon. But the top two-thirds of Mount Erebus was still in sunlight and a wonderful pink colour. The flight home was magic, with the helicopter at a height which put the sun just on the horizon. As we swung down over McMurdo we could see the sea smoke swirling off the ice shelf and across the open sea. It was all stunningly beautiful.

Next morning we were woken at 7.30 am to be up and ready for a meeting at eight, but the meeting was in fact timed for 8.30 am: we had all been fooled in order to get us up on time.

The meeting was a briefing for the demonstration which was to begin at ten. We were to meet on the aft deck and were warned that the weather was even colder than the previous day. It was going to be worse for people like me, standing round watching, than for those moving around doing things. At least they would keep warm.

Outside at 10 am the temperature was −17°C with a twenty-knot wind, so it was no surprise that the tractor, which had been brought from the Greenpeace base camp to be used in the demonstration, would not start. The idea had been to use the tractor to haul a trailer full of drums filled from the camp's waste pipe up to Ron La Count's headquarters. There were seven forty-gallon drums from the ship, painted with letters that when lined up would read 'Danger! Cadmium'.

Tempers were beginning to fray on the quayside as the plan looked like falling apart before it had started. Extra batteries were brought from the ship, and a row developed about how best to get the tractor going. A can of starter spray was snatched from Albert's hand and heated words were exchanged. Finally the tractor was abandoned: instead the crew would push the trailer up the hill. The exercise would probably be welcome in the cold. We all followed behind the trailer and walked about half a mile to the waste pipes. Warm water was coming out of the two pipes, and a seal was swimming about amid the sewage and other discharges. There was also a sick-looking penguin standing next to the pipe – but it could just have been moulting. Ron La Count had admitted that sick penguins did congregate at that point and were taken away by his staff. Whether they came for the warmth because they were sick, or got sick after they arrived, was not clear. Either way Greenpeace believed that the heavy metals and chemicals discharged from the pipe would have a serious effect on the ability of the wildlife to breed. The crew were taking the discharge from the smaller of the two waste pipes because when this had been sampled the previous year it was found to have a high level of cadmium, hence the demonstration.

The two pipelines were on supports about six feet above sea

level, built out from the seashore about ten feet so they poured
straight into the water. Initially a barrel was placed in one of the
inflatables and floated under the end of the pipe. The barrel was
not filled, however, because it would be impossible to manhandle
it when full.

Then Ken and Henk discovered the water was shallow enough
not to go over their thigh boots, so the boat was not needed. The
drum-filling operation took some time, and I sheltered behind
the nearest building to keep out of the wind. The building was
empty: it had been erected to house the promised sewage
treatment plant, which up to then had not been delivered.

The barrels were made up into two loads so that the crew could
push them up the steep slope to the Chalet. Tim and Sean had
filming to do, and left some of their equipment behind as we
followed the trailer and struggled up the hill. Seeing me doing
nothing, as they put it, they sent me back for the rest of the bags.
Despite moaning I was rather keen on the idea because the cold
was beginning to cut through even my multilayered outfit. So far
the Americans had not shown themselves, although a car did
drive past the end of the waste pipe when we arrived. Presumably
we were being observed from the windows of the huts. It was hard
to believe that some of the 200 people on the base did not have
at least that much curiosity. With all our varied Antarctic gear on,
it was hard to see immediately who everyone was, but I realised,
after a couple of minutes of waiting for the second load of barrels
to arrive, that Chuck Stovitz, the Beverly Hills lawyer, was
sheltering from the wind behind the same hut as I was. He
greeted me like an old friend, and we stood stamping our feet
together but without having a conversation. Eventually the last
four barrels reached the Chalet and DAN CAD became DANGER!
CADMIUM and the Greenpeace message for the cameras was
complete.

Two people were already using ladders to get on the roof of
the Chalet to erect a giant poster which said simply 'Clean It Up
or Shut It Down'. Paul Bogart, using the megaphone through
which Naoko had addressed the Japanese whalers, spoke to Mr
La Count, who was presumably hiding behind the double glazing
in his office.

Paul said: 'Ron La Count, Ron La Count, this level of
contamination is not permitted in the European Community, not
permitted in the United States, and unacceptable to us in the

Antarctic.' He said Greenpeace had taken the action of collecting the cadmium to put pressure on the National Science Foundation and Congress to clean up McMurdo.

There was much more taking of pictures and filming, and a big cheer as Paul Londrigan arrived on the tractor, having finally got it going. This meant that all the barrels could be loaded on to the trailer at one go and taken back to the ship. Lilian was wandering round looking at people's faces, and she told me I had white patches on my cheeks which were the first signs of frostbite. I must be careful, she said, and return to the ship soon. Pete decided it was time to call it a day, and everyone piled the barrels and themselves on the trailer.

After the demonstration had finished, Paul was called into the Chalet by Mr La Count, who was now prepared to show himself. He was in fine form, promising full information about future clean-up plans and other US programmes in the Antarctic. Paul said that Ron had a copy of Mary-Ann's article about him under the headline 'Pollution in the Antarctic'. It made him pretty mad. He did not seem to have mine to hand, but told Paul he thought I was OK as a journalist but he hated what I wrote. I suppose I have had worse comments.

I said goodbye to Chuck, who enquired about the whereabouts of Mary-Ann. I told him I thought she had stayed behind because of the cold (but she told me later it was because she was frightened of getting volcanic grit under her contact lenses). The trailer went off with a happy band of demonstrators: their job was done and lunch was beckoning.

(On returning to the United States, Paul discovered that Chuck had never been a US marshal, but had been sent out by Peter Wilkness, head of US Polar Programmes, as his personal lawyer to keep an eye on what was happening. He had no powers of arrest and could not have intervened.)

Afterwards I settled down to write my story. The four overwinterers had an invitation to dinner at Scott Base and were taken over there by helicopter about three hours before the *Gondwana* sailed for Cape Evans. The ship was to go out to sea until Mount Erebus no longer blocked the satellite and we could file a story and pictures about the demonstration. The weather had been deteriorating all day, and by the time we reached Cape Evans it was almost impossible to see the base camp. The plan had been to send a helicopter over to Scott Base to pick up the dinner guests, but the weather was too bad. We would pick them up in the morning, or when the weather improved sufficiently.

Davey Edwards, the chief engineer, appeared in the galley for a cup of tea while I was reading there. He was covered in oil and very tired. Apparently we had come from Cape Evans on only one engine. I had not even noticed this. Davey was confident that at last he had found the problem: one of the oil seals in the other engine had failed, letting air in. But now the water used for cooling the engine had frozen and he was having to melt it. He finally got the engine started just before 1 am.

17

Taking Leave

23 FEBRUARY: STARTED to dream a lot of home or foreign warm places. It reminds me of reading about Scott's men, who always dreamed of food. Food is not my problem, it is being stuck on a ship with the weather so bad outside that even going ashore to Cape Evans is not an attractive alternative. I decide it must be Antarctic syndrome I suffer from. Even the full moon, which was visible the previous night, did not seem right to me because, from the angle it is seen in the Antarctic, it seemed to have lost its man-in-the-moon face.

Pete, Paul Bogart and Ken Ballard were using the helicopter in the morning to take the final loads of fresh vegetables over from the ship and bring back the last of the rubbish. The wind was too strong to use the inflatables and by mid-afternoon was up to forty knots, gale force 8, and it was extremely cold. There were worries that the fresh food would freeze before it could be got indoors at the base camp.

On the helicopter's return those who had been working at the base camp while we had been at McMurdo were brought back on board. Marc de Fourneaux, the carpenter, looked very tired; he had completed insulating the whole base. He gave us an energetic description of the new base toilet. This was new technology which it was hoped would turn human waste, and other vegetable material, into organic compost bricks. The toilet was a contraption which involved a throne-like seat on top of a large plastic box. Inside the box were four different compartments. When one section was full it was moved round to allow the contents to rot down while a second section was filled. Marc explained that there was an air-extraction system from the composting area designed to remove any smell and also to pull warm air in from the living accommodation. The compost had to be kept warm otherwise it would 'die' and cease to function. However, the system led to an alarming suction effect as the toilet tried to pull both air and sitter in with it.

Human waste disposal is one of the most difficult problems in the Antarctic, as has already been discussed. Biological methods would seem to be a good solution, at least on a relatively small scale. Theoretically the one Greenpeace toilet would be large enough to take all the human waste from the overwinterers, and the waste vegetable matter, for the year.

By mid-afternoon the work of supplying the base was virtually finished. That night was the formal ceremony of handing over the keys. In fact, there were no keys as such; instead there was a sort of spanner used to open the oil drums for the generator. This was the key to keeping warm and survival, a potent symbol to be transferred from the old base leader to the new. The base itself was continuously manned and never locked: in the Antarctic any traveller was welcome. After the formal handover a farewell party had been planned at the base before the *Gondwana* set off the next day to sail north, leaving the four overwinterers to their twelve months of solitude. Now, on account of the weather, there was doubt as to where the party was going to be held. Eventually it was decided that the weather was too bad to move people to and fro, so one party would be held ashore and those of us on the ship would have to have our own separate celebration.

To my delight Shyama Perera, one of my colleagues on *The Guardian*, who was working on the late shift, rang me for a chat. This was strictly against the rules because of the cost, but I had been starved of office gossip for nearly three months. When I told her I was fed up with being in the Antarctic, she filled in such a dismal picture of life in London that I felt a whole lot better. She advised me to stay away as long as possible. *The Guardian* had not used my last piece, so the editor appeared to have had enough of Greenpeace and the Antarctic. Perhaps it was time for me to relax and read a few books.

On the bridge the weather looked terrible. The snow was going past horizontally, borne by a gale-force wind. I was not prepared to go out on the bridge wing to check the temperature. Instead I went down to the warmth of the lounge, where someone had produced a bottle of whisky and an unexpected luxury – a giant pack of peanuts. It was some hours before we retired to our bunks. I realised that because Sean and Tim were still at the base, with all their equipment, trapped by the storm, I had the cabin to myself for the first time in two months. This was a luxury too.

Sean and Tim arrived back by helicopter at 9.30 next morning, with Tim babbling on as usual despite my requests for silence. I had a terrible headache – no doubt caused by the peanuts. There was to be a crew meeting at ten so that the overwinterers could come over to say a final farewell.

Even though the weather was still pretty bad the wind had dropped to thirty knots, so it was possible to use the helicopters. In the event there was no meeting, but an emotional gathering on the helideck instead. I had grown fond of Phil Doherty, the quiet radio operator who had spent many patient hours trying to line up the Greenpeace computer with *The Guardian*'s so that I could transmit across the world. I would miss him on the return journey. Bruno, the leader of the team, was a different sort of person, less introspective, full of good humour and as tough as old boots. He had won my respect at Dumont d'Urville by throwing himself repeatedly in front of the French bulldozers and diggers but never once raising a hand against the construction workers, although several times flung aside in a violent manner. He generously invited me to visit him in Vienna 'when this is all over'. The two women were more of a mystery to me. Lilian, the nurse, seemed steady and self-contained. On the other hand, Liz, the youngest of the team, had told me she wanted the time and solitude to 'sort herself out'. I hope it worked out for her.

The wind was cutting through us all there on deck as we strapped the four into the helicopter, amid many good wishes, and then stood and waved to them as they were taken ashore.

The wind and the cold had cleared my head and I was well enough to have breakfast. In the galley people were full of tales of the previous night's party on the base. Everyone had got very high-spirited, and the party had reached a peak with a game of bar rugby, in which everyone piled on top of each other in a good-natured wrestling match. It must have been a little too exuberant because, in the first real injury of the trip, Liz had needed three stitches in her lip after someone trod on her.

During breakfast the anchor had been lifted, and now we were under way, not heading north as I had hoped, but southwest to a placed called New Harbour on the Blowers Piedmont Glacier. Arne explained that there were two groups of international support huts there for expeditions, about ten miles apart. Greenpeace had placed food and supplies for its overwintering party in one of them the previous season so they could use it when they came this way on field trips. But when the team had explored inland from this point up the glacier, they had decided that the supplies were in the wrong place and wanted them moved to the other depot.

It took about three hours to sail there, and when we got within range the helicopter was launched to identify the Greenpeace supplies, pick them up and move them. Strangely, after the raging gale of the last few days, the wind had completely died. Not that the weather was good: it was snowing heavily, and visibility was so poor it was hard to follow the progress of the helicopter. Through the binoculars it looked like a tiny mosquito against the grey snow clouds. The sea around the *Gondwana* was covered in new ice, not very thick and broken up into small pieces by the recent winds, but an ominous sign nonetheless, a warning that we should not stay around too long. We checked the sea temperature; it was −1.6°C. So close to the ice shelf, with the ice and snow melt in the recent summer, the sea was hardly saline at all, and Arne calculated that its freezing point would be −1.8°C, which meant we only had a tiny margin of safety. If its temperature dropped by just one-fifth of a degree then the sea would freeze solid in a matter of hours to a depth of two or three feet, maybe more, trapping us for the winter. This had been the fate of many expeditions in the past, men who had not realised how quickly and almost instantaneously this entire vast sea could turn to ice.

Once the food dump was moved and the helicopter back on board, Arne immediately turned the ship north. We were finally going home – although in typical Greenpeace fashion we had some last-minute ports of call up the coast on our way back to New Zealand. The first would be Marble Point, where Greenpeace had placed the new survival hut to make life difficult for the Americans. Henk, and the team putting up the hut, had forgotten to fit a solar panel to provide free heat inside when the sun was out. Marble Point was not very far away and would take only another two hours' sailing time. It would give those of us not involved with operating the ship time for dinner.

It was Henk's daughter's first birthday, and the cooks had made a cake with her name, Ruby, lit up in candles. The big man was missing her badly. We all helped him to blow the candles out, and then shared the cake.

Pete meanwhile had been working at yet another press release to go with a picture of the four overwinterers waving goodbye from the shore. It recorded the fact that the resupply had taken sixteen hours of helicopter flying time using two Hughes 500 D helicopters during which 240 barrels had been airlifted. These included two tons of fuel and six tons of equipment flown into the base. Additionally, new filters specially designed and built for Greenpeace had been fitted to the base generator exhausts to cut down pollution. One generator had been removed from the base for servicing back in New Zealand and replaced with a new one.

In a separate routine update, to the Greenpeace offices worldwide, on the state of the expedition, Pete said it had been a tiring time for everyone on the ship. He went on: 'The base is as neat and tidy as I have seen it, evidence that the decision to backload a lot of material, which has been shown to be excess to requirements over the years, was a correct one.' The *Gondwana* was carrying a lot of bulky junk home, an example of the way Greenpeace practised what they preached. Pete described the leaving ceremony, the handing over of the key and a framed picture of all those on board with our names and good wishes signed on the back. Combining propaganda with a genuine tribute to his friends, Pete summed up the situation thus: 'It's been a great trip and one which will hopefully be recalled in years to come as the one which left the A T C Ps [Antarctic Treaty Participating Nations] in no doubt at all that Greenpeace means business. Keith Swenson, Sabine Schmidt, Sjoerd Jongens and Wojtek Moskal all did a magnificent job; they represented Greenpeace admirably and have enhanced our reputation in the Antarctic.'

By the time we had sent all this off, the ship was stopped off Marble Point. The bay which had been all clear water a week ago was now completely frozen over. It was a reminder of how fast the winter was coming. Now that normal sailing routines were back, Albert was on the look out for volunteers to join him on the 12 midnight to 4 am watch for the journey north to New Zealand, and I volunteered, trying not to think about the mountainous seas ahead.

My first midnight watch was going to be that night, so I went to bed for a couple of hours. I was looking forward to moving through the ice again, this time knowing that the weather would be getting warmer as we moved north and eventually we would

reach green grass and trees. It seemed a long time since I had
seen anything green.

On watch that night we met an astonishing range of ice
conditions. First there was a strange series of discoloured streaks
across the sea: although it looked like some sort of pollution we
knew that in this part of the world it must be a natural
phenomenon. Gradually the streaks thickened, and we realised
they were long lines of ice slush that had been discoloured by
brown algae which appeared to be growing in the ice. Soon we
were heading through continuous slush ice which had turned
white again. It made us nervous that the generator intakes might
block, but all seemed well. We had to reduce speed because it
began to snow heavily and we feared ploughing into an iceberg
lying partly submerged under the slush and invisible to our radar.
Albert sent me out on to the bridge wing to get a better view. The
snow helped in the task of spotting because it settled on any lumps
of ice which stuck out above the general level of the slush. The
snow lay thick on the bridge wing and on the top of my balaclava.
By 3 am the temperature had risen to −9°C and I felt quite warm.
Then the snow slackened and I noticed a white glow in the north,
which even I, as an inexperienced hand, knew meant we were
running into pack ice.

As we approached we could see it was densely packed and full
of small icebergs. Albert turned the *Gondwana* to starboard,
further out towards the centre of the Ross Sea, in the hope of
skirting round it. At this time of the year if we attempted to go
through it there was a danger of getting stuck fast and frozen in.
After half an hour we could see through the binoculars that there
was open water beyond the pack ice, which was tapering off the
further east we went. We continued on until Albert judged that
the band of ice was thin enough for us to break through.
Although it remained daylight for twenty-four hours, the sun was
now below the horizon in the early morning and it was not easy
to see exactly what we were ploughing into.

Much of the ice was lumps of second-year pack, too tough for
us to break up with the ship, but it was possible to push it aside,
using the *Gondwana* as a bulldozer. Our success was short-lived:
the radar showed another lot of pack ice ahead which looked an
even more formidable barrier. We turned again to starboard and
followed the edge of the pack. On the way we met more slush

and then miles and miles of thin, saucer-like pieces of ice. This was new ice which had been broken up by the waves and the edges ground together, making a sort of upturned rim. The technical name was pancake ice. From time to time there were scatterings of pack ice in our path, but the main area remained on the port side, as solid-looking as a piece of the coast. As we moved on we were then dismayed to see the pack ice curve round in front of us, forcing Albert to steer southeast to avoid it, almost going back on our tracks.

Bob Graham came on the bridge at 4 am to take over from Albert. Just then the pack ice began to thin out, and within a few minutes we were able to turn east again and eventually slightly north of east. Before going to bed I rang home to check that Maureen was all right and was able to reassure her that we were at last on the way home.

When I woke again I could feel the ship was moving in a swell, which meant we must be clear of the pack ice. We would be heading now towards Cape Hallett, to look at the site of a joint United States/New Zealand base set up in the 1957 Geophysical Year. It had since been abandoned. Ron La Count had said some work had been done to clean it up and Greenpeace had decided on an inspection.

After breakfast I had a long chat with Wojtek, the Polish overwinterer. I asked him how he had come to leave Poland, and he explained that he had been part of a Polish Arctic expedition to Spitzbergen, to the north of Norway. This is an international free zone, created in 1920 when Europe was reshaped after the First World War. Norway has subsequently claimed Spitzbergen back, but it is still not necessary to have a passport to go there, and the island has a mixed international community. Wojtek had been there as a member of the Polish Arctic Station. He had not liked the routine but loved the climate and had applied at the end of his year to return to Spitzbergen to live. For this, since he wanted to leave Poland, he needed a Polish passport, and he was surprised when one was granted. He had left Poland without delay, and set up home in an old disused whaling hut. He said he had lived there 'just for the fun of it' for a whole winter. One of the friends he made at the time had tried the first-ever crossing on the frozen sea from Norway to Greenland, using dogs. To me this seemed a pointless exercise, but Wojtek was full of admiration.

After some prompting Wojtek, who by now had acquired quite an audience, told us some of his experiences with polar bears, which eat people as well as seals and fish. He only carried a starting pistol, which made a loud noise, and he said it was usually enough to frighten polar bears away. It could also be used to fire smoke canisters to attract attention if he got into difficulties. One day he was sitting at a hole in the ice, which he had made to do some fishing, when he noticed a polar bear coming towards him across the ice. Initially Wojtek was not worried, and confidently fired the starting pistol, expecting the bear to run away. To his consternation it kept coming. He fired three times in all, but the bear seemed completely unafraid. The bear was now only a hundred yards away, no distance at all for such a big animal. Wojtek had nowhere to hide, so in desperation he fired a smoke canister in the direction of the oncoming bear. Fortunately in the still air the smoke billowed out over the ice, and under cover of this smokescreen Wojtek made a run for it, and kept running until he reached safety.

He had had other encounters with hungry bears which would have made me move out of Spitzbergen immediately. On three occasions the hut he lived in had been entered by bears. Once when he was asleep in the back room a bear had come in the front door and had started eating Wojtek's winter supplies. Wojtek loaded the starting pistol, opened the adjoining door slightly, and fired. The bear panicked and ran off. On the other occasions he was out when the bears called. Normally they pushed open the front door, but once the bear had bashed its way through the wall. 'There was just a bear-shaped hole,' Wojtek said. The bears came to eat his stores because they could not find any other food. One had eaten several bars of soap as well and had suffered from diarrhoea before leaving the hut. Wojtek said it took a long time to make the place habitable again.

He said he liked the life in Spitzbergen and intended to return. (This conversation took place a few months before the remarkable changes in Eastern Europe.) At the time Wojtek, who was a member of Solidarity, was very pessimistic about the future. He said he saw little hope for Poland in his lifetime and thought he might have to go into permanent exile. His mistrust of all things Russian was at the heart of these fears.

The weather was calm, and on 26 February we were in sight of

Cape Hallett, the northern arm of the Antarctic continent which forms the northwest shore of the Ross Sea. Davey's troubles in the engine room were continuing. We were running on only one engine again, this time because an exhaust valve was malfunctioning on the other. Our speed had been cut to six knots. The air temperature had continued to rise and now reached −3°C on the bridge wing at 1 pm. A great deal of ice had encrusted the inside walls and ceiling of the bridge, forming almost unnoticed on the metal areas, particularly the inside of the bridge window frames and under the roof as our breath had frozen on the cold surface. It now began to melt, and there was a constant dripping over the chart table and the controls of the ship. Those on watch were constantly busy mopping up and taking off chunks of ice from the ceiling before they fell on people's heads.

Thoughts were already turning to the future. Henk and Ian Balmer were having an argument about creating an office in the radio room for use as a Greenpeace Antarctic headquarters while the *Gondwana* was tied up in Auckland. The ship would be at the quayside preparing for the next voyage. Henk thought the radio room would be an excellent base because he would be on hand to supervise the necessary alterations to the ship and logistics for the next year. Ian was against it because he feared his equipment would be damaged or go missing. He was in favour of mothballing the radio room and locking it up for protection. For some reason I got involved in the argument on Ian's side, and Henk got very cross with me. He was quite right. It was none of my business.

On the radar Cape Hallett was twelve miles away, but from the bridge it looked about two miles. In the background was a mountain called Whewell. Albert calculated that this mountain was forty miles away. According to the chart it was 12,000 feet high. The whole scene was stunning. With the sun at its highest in the sky, the ice was shining white, the sea a marvellous blue, and the mountains in the background looked jet black. The air was so clear it was possible to see every detail of the coastline. The Cotter Cliffs that rose sheer out of the sea were 1,500 feet high. Just to the north of the cliffs, in a bay, was our intended landfall at the abandoned base.

It had been built in the middle of what was now one of the biggest penguin colonies in Antarctica, but since February was the end of the breeding season we did not expect to find many birds there. Pete's intention had been to get the ship into the bay so that we could take a leisurely look at the base in the inflatables, but it was not to be. There was a lot of pack ice between us and the peninsula, and a giant iceberg had floated into the bay and got itself jammed. After an hour of ploughing into the pack, Arne decided we were wasting fuel and time trying to get through and we would have to use the helicopters.

I was rather glad of this because we had a magnificent flight into the bay. Dave was in an adventurous mood and took us high over the cliffs. The ship looked tiny in such an enormous landscape. Dave then swooped down to a flat area about a mile across beyond the cliffs, which was the penguin breeding area. As soon as we opened the door on landing, a rich smell caused by the dung of thousands of penguins, and the carcasses of their young who had not survived, hit us in the nostrils. I was tempted to get straight back into the helicopter. Instead, with the others, I walked over to a giant oil tank and a group of huts I took to be the abandoned base. It had not been used since 1973, according to documents on the ship, but the buildings were very makeshift affairs and could have been any age. There were several hundred penguins standing around in various stages of moulting. They were all very fat, ready for the tough winter ahead, and barely able to waddle. They seemed not to notice the many bodies of their fellows that had been trodden underfoot during the breeding season.

After a while the overpowering smell and the derelict air of the place drove me away. I knew that if I got to the edge of the colony heading into the breeze I would be back into the clean air of the Antarctic. A part of this large flat area was designated as 'specially protected', a patch near the base of the cliffs which the penguins did not use, presumably because it was in shadow. According to the books there was an interesting growth of mosses and lichens, but I did not see any. Gradually as I headed upwind the smell decreased, and I eventually came to a rocky shore where the air was straight off the glacier on the other side of the bay.

The air temperature seemed much colder than it had been on the ship, perhaps because of the breeze off the glacier, and I was glad to get back into the warmth of the helicopter for the return trip. Instead of going back over the cliffs Dave flew fast and low over the pack ice and on to the ship. Arne had turned the *Gondwana* round and was ploughing his way out of the pack ice.

It was more tightly packed than he had realised and we were struggling to break free. Luckily Davey had now fixed the engines. The ice heaved and groaned around us as Arne revved the engines and pushed forward a yard or two at a time. He pointed out that he had not yet had to use the ship's full 8,000 horsepower, with which we could bulldoze our way out if necessary. It took two hours to move about half a mile and reach open water.

It was second engineer Ton Kocken's birthday, and he had requested curry for his birthday meal, the first curry the cooks had served since we left Auckland. It was excellent and we washed it down with the last beer on board. I had half a bottle of whisky stowed away and decided to give it to Ton to help the celebrations. After that there was no more alcohol I knew about on board, and I wondered what a total lack of booze would do to the general temper of the crew.

On 27 February we reached Cape Adare, the northernmost tip of Antarctica on the Ross Sea side of the continent. It was our last port of call before facing the rigours of the Southern Ocean and had been chosen to give the crew a break before the long voyage home. It was another historic site, the first place where anyone had overwintered in the Antarctic, a venture which must have taken great courage, especially since at this latitude the midwinter night lasted ten weeks.

The expedition leader had been Carsten Borchgrevink, a young Norwegian who had emigrated to Australia in 1888, and had come to the spot as an able seaman on one of the first whaling voyages to the Ross Sea. As a whaling expedition it was a failure, but on 16 January 1895 a party from the ship, including Borchgrevink, made history by being the first men to walk on the Antarctic continent. The Norwegian realised the significance of the occasion and collected a number of specimens from the seashore. Back in Melbourne scientists were impressed by his accounts but refused to fund another expedition.

Eventually, with the backing of his employer, British publisher Sir George Newnes, Borchgrevink raised the money for his own expedition. Despite the fact that all three members of the party were Norwegian, Newnes insisted the adventure be called the British Antarctic Expedition. It made records of temperature, weather and ice conditions which were to prove invaluable in the preparation of later expeditions. One member of this 1899 party, the biologist Nicolai Hanson, died after enduring the long winter, probably of scurvy, which troubled many of the later explorers. The other two survived.

On his return to England Borchgrevink did not get the recognition his feat deserved, largely because the establishment feared it might overshadow the British National Antarctic Expedition, which was to set off the next year under the leadership of Captain Robert Falcon Scott. However, Borchgrevink survived Scott and eventually had his achievements recognised thirty years later when he was awarded a medal by the Royal Geographical Society.

Borchgrevink's tiny hut was still standing, and was visible from the ship on a strip of flat land below towering cliffs. The sky was overcast but the weather otherwise seemed good, so boat trips for everyone were planned. By the time I had reached the deck to join those waiting to go ashore Ken Ballard had already left with a boatload to try and find a landing place. He failed to do so, and we were reduced to a tour round the bay instead. When my turn came for a ride I realised why Ken had not attempted to make a landing. The swell, which had looked small from the ship, was fierce close to the shore, rising and falling twelve feet on the beach, and was throwing massive pieces of pack ice against the shore as the waves broke. We took one look and made no further attempts to get ashore.

Above the beach large groups of penguins were standing several hundred yards from the sea, halfway up the steep slopes that led to sheer cliffs. Presumably they were moulting like the ones we had seen the previous day and, because they did not swim when they were moulting, they were keeping well out of the range of leopard seals, which were plentiful in these waters and would regard the small fat birds as easy pickings if they stayed too near the water's edge.

Further along the coast we went underneath an overhang in the cliffs several hundred feet high, a very eerie feeling, especially since the sea was crashing against the cliff face below. The ship called us on the radio, ordering our return, since a snowstorm was showing on the radar. It was drifting across the bay and was so heavy it threatened to block our sight of the ship. Thanks to the timely warning we made it back, but only just. The flakes were huge, and before we had managed to get out of the boat and on to the deck we were covered in them. When it had snowed further south the flakes had been tiny.

The *Gondwana* drifted in the bay, waiting for the snow to lift so that the rest of the people on board who wished to could have a boat trip. As we watched from the bridge windows a couple of dozen pieces of pack ice drifted by, with families of seals in residence on them. There were about thirty seals in all, some black, some grey. In such surroundings it was a constant surprise to see so much wildlife. It was another reminder of how vital the prolific food chain below the water line was in this region.

Finally the weather cleared, the boat trips were completed and we sailed. This was an important transition. We were leaving the calm waters of the Ross Sea behind for the last time and facing the notorious weather of the Southern Ocean on the way back to New Zealand. I took it calmly at the time because I had no idea just how bad it was going to be.

18

Force Twelve

THE MIDNIGHT SHIFT was hard work. We were by then out in the constant heavy swell of the Southern Ocean, which made moving about the ship more difficult. Instead of the easy walk down the corridors and the stairs, it was necessary to hold on and time your movements with the sea. It was colder again at night because the sun had gone completely. We measured −7°C at midnight. It was properly dark, and since we were of course still checking for ice we had to stare straight ahead into the gloom, occasionally helped by the ship's searchlight. In the winter all this would freeze solid, although how that happened if such swells continued I could not imagine. Fortunately we only saw one iceberg during the whole shift, and I was glad when 4 am came and I could go back to bed.

All the inconveniences of the Southern Ocean were back that morning. Because of the roll of the ship, the water from the showers sloshed out and down the corridor before it could run down the plug hole. The drinking water was again a dirty brown colour, and then there was the permanent uneasy feeling that eating might not be a good idea.

Over the last few days I had been discussing with Pete his plans for after the voyage. After ten years with Greenpeace in various jobs, during which he had seen it grow into a very large international organisation, he had decided to strike out on his own. Once the voyage was over he was going to return to London and set up as a freelance environmental consultant. Since he was quite a well-known personality in Britain's growing Green movement, it seemed to me there was a story in this. And if I wrote an article it might help to launch him on his new career, so I sat down below decks in the office and wrote a piece.

At the same time I did my washing before the rust in the water got too bad and stained everything brown. The weather was getting worse all the time, but I managed to finish both tasks. I was thinking of going straight back to bed, only to be told by Naoko that she and I were down for washing the crew's dishes. Fortunately the weather had cut the number of diners (including me), but there were still more than enough of them. The wind had reached gale force 8 early in the evening.

I spent 1 March mostly in my bunk. According to the gauge on the bridge the ship was rolling twenty-five degrees one way and then twenty-five the other. Even the professional sailors were less jaunty than usual. People were counting the days to getting back to Lyttelton and home, and I was deputed to compile a list of names and home addresses of all the people on board, so that we could keep in contact after the end of the voyage. In view of the weather, I put the job off until the next day.

After a terrible night in which I had first given up attempting to sleep, and then given up trying to read, I got up and gave washing a miss too. I was clearly degenerating fast. Tim had said I looked like a wino, and a glance in the mirror confirmed his judgement. I had not shaved for a couple of days and resembled one of those homeless people who live long-term in cardboard boxes under the railway arches in London. We were told, when we were attempting some breakfast in the galley, that the wind had dropped slightly in the night. It did not seem to have made much difference to the size of the waves – they were still very big. Despite this I decided I had to do something, apart from groaning, so I started my task of listing crew names and addresses.

Up on the bridge, checking the watch's particulars, I could see from the charts that we were now quite a long way north, close to the Antarctic convergence, and the watch had seen only three icebergs all morning. They might even be the last of the voyage. We were making about seven knots, running on one engine: Davey apparently wanted to save fuel. It crossed my mind to offer him a bribe to go faster and so shorten the agony. The weather did look a bit calmer from the bridge, but I was shocked by a view of the weather charts. I was told there had been an all-ships warning to make for shelter, but there was no hope of us doing that, as we were now right out in the Southern Ocean. The ship was halfway between Cape Adare and the Campbell Islands, a group of sub-Antarctic islands south of New Zealand.

On one of these islands there was a scientific station, where Bob Graham, the second mate, had once been base leader for a season, and we were now heading for it. We had already radioed the station, and they said they would be delighted to see us, and even had some beer. But on any calculation we could not get there before the new storm hit us, even with both engines. It was a matter of battening everything down and keeping our fingers crossed.

The only good news of the day was that Davey said he had developed a bypass system for the fresh water supply. He hoped this would mean he had avoided the tank that contained the rust and we would soon be able to wash and drink tea whatever the weather. Meanwhile he issued those of us who claimed we were 'crooked' with a bottled water ration from the water maker to keep us going.

I was hoping for a sleep before the midnight to 4 am watch, but Tim and Sean were repacking their film equipment in the cabin now they had virtually finished with it for the remainder of the voyage. They wanted to make sure everything of value was properly anchored down. Instead I watched a very bad film in the lounge, which quickly sent me off to sleep – so it was just as good as being in my bunk.

The watch proved memorable. Although the wind had dropped the previous afternoon to an average speed of around twenty knots, about force 5 on the Beaufort scale, it had quickly begun to pick up again. The swell had not had time to diminish and remained close to mountainous. The sea temperature had risen three degrees, information that had proved difficult to obtain in the circumstances since the thermometer had to be dangled over the side in a small iron cage and was difficult to keep in the water because of the size of the swell. Also, according to the chart, we were still not at the northern limit of icebergs and would have to continue to keep a lookout for them.

Despite the coming storm Albert was his usual jolly self, whipping round every few minutes to watch the wind gauge and check on the downward plunge of the barometer, which in fact was a barograph, one of those drum machines with a pen drawing the pressure lines as it wound round. It had started to drop steeply at about 6 pm and was still going down. Albert kept muttering 'It must bottom out soon,' but it did not. Darkness had fallen, and we all felt closed in after being used to constant daylight for so long. Visibility was bad too, probably because of warmer air over the cold sea, and Albert had turned the spotlight on to show up any ice. Remembering the last storm, when my lookout chair had toppled over backwards and I nearly went down the wheelhouse stairs, he tied the arm and the back of it to the radiator in preparation. I did not sit down immediately but stood and hung on to the bridge rail, scanning the sea for ice. I did not see any.

Although this should already have been done by the previous watch, Albert sent Henk round to check that all the deadlights on the portholes had been closed and screwed down tight. Henk also took what proved to be a last routine round of the helicopter hangar and rear storage. Even with the ropes which had been tied along the decks for the watch keepers to hold on to, it was still very dangerous venturing out: tons of green water were coming over every few minutes.

The wind speed gradually increased, and by 2 am was averaging thirty-seven knots, gale force 8 on the Beaufort scale. Having checked and double-checked everything Albert relaxed and was positively gleeful. We were at last going to have a real sea, he said. He seemed determined to live up to his Viking origins. Knowing the state of my stomach during previous storms, he took pains to explain that there was no need to 'worry' until the wind got to about fifty-five knots (storm force 10), when the ship would have to turn head to wind for safety's sake. An hour later the gusts reached fifty-four knots, but Albert kept the same course – due north for New Zealand – at six knots, with the wind hitting us from the northwest. There was now white water on top of the huge rollers coming across the ship out of the darkness. We were beginning to plunge down the side of the waves before shuddering in the trough and climbing up the other side. The fetch of the waves had become much longer than the length of the ship. By this time I had taken to the lookout seat and shouted to Albert that there was no point in my warning him if I did see any ice because it would hit us before we could get out of the way. He said we would just have to hope we were now too far north for icebergs.

We hung on and watched the spray smack the windows. As the successive walls of green water came towards us I gritted my teeth, but each time, we miraculously rose over the top before plunging down the other side. I was grimly waiting for the end of our shift when, shortly before 4 am, Albert announced that he was hungry.

I thought he was joking, but he sent me down to the mess for some carrot cake to keep him going. This was down two flights of steep stairs. The ship was rising and falling so much that it was vital to hold on with both hands. Every time the ship dropped down a wave I was lifted off my feet, and when the *Gondwana* came back up the other side the climb seemed to double the weight of my body.

Somehow I made it down to the galley. The carrot cake had been jammed in the fridge, and I managed to chop a piece off, put it on a plate, and start off, reaching the bottom of the stairs just as the ship got to the top of a wave and plunged down the other side. I held myself down with my free hand but forgot the carrot cake, which lifted off the plate. To catch it I had no option but to leap up the stairs after it. Because of the speed the ship was dropping down the wave I was able to take the twelve stairs in two bounds. The carrot cake, which had flown up the flight in front of me, landed neatly back on the plate.

I repeated this performance for the next flight of stairs on the next wave and was up on the bridge in a flash. Albert remarked that I seemed finally to have got my sea legs.

Henk roused the next watch, although they were already awake. The wind was still rising and the barometer falling. It was very close to the bottom of the drum – down to 960, very low pressure indeed. Bob was still discussing with Albert the merits of going head to wind when Henk and I were dismissed. It was hard work just walking along the corridor. Inside my cabin was a terrible mess. The two chairs were tipped over, and sliding about the floor with every wave. Mixed in were books and papers, shaving gear, a bar of soap, a bottle of shampoo, and anything else that had not been tied down. It took ten minutes to gather up everything and jam it in the narrow space between the bunk and the wardrobe. We would have to sort it out after the storm.

Shortly after I got into bed the metal ladder up to Tim's bunk lifted off its hooks and crashed across the cabin. It was weighted specifically so it would not do this. As I lay listening to the wind and the crashing of the sea we suddenly lurched over much more on one wave than any previous one, and as a result three drawers of the wooden chest we used for our clothes flew out. I discovered later that Sean had ill-advisedly greased the runners because the drawers were too stiff.

He and I, both unable to sleep, now got up and together

crawled about the floor trying to anchor things down, only to have
them break loose again. We gave up and went back to our bunks.
Despite the board along the edge, I felt as if I might be thrown
out on the floor. I braced myself against the side of the bunk and
wedged myself in with blankets. This worked for a while and I
fell asleep, only to have the movement of the sea work my body
loose and wake me again as my head smacked against the side of
the bunk. Things eased a little quite suddenly a short while later,
and for a moment I thought the storm had abated. Then I
realised Bob must have turned head to wind. It meant we were
rolling less but pitching more. I tied myself to the bunk with my
covers and tried to get some sleep.

After the tough night it would have been easier to stay in my
bunk than to get up, but I had promised to ring home and let
Maureen know my schedule for coming back. At 11.30 I made
my way over the scattered debris to the communications room. I
still had to hold on all the way, otherwise I would have been
thrown off my feet. It was clear the sea had not abated. It seemed
strange that the telephone should be working perfectly normally,
and Maureen be sitting in bed 12,000 miles away in a warm house,
unaware of our plight.

Over the howling wind I heard her say she had been trying to
finalise my flight details for the homeward journey. At my end
the doors on one of the cupboards on the other side of the room
swung open and snapped off their hinges. My chair was chained
to the floor, but with the terrific noise of wind and sea and the
stuff rolling about the floor I had trouble hearing her. I was
holding myself still and keeping the receiver jammed close to my
ear. Maureen was alarmed, and asked what was going on. I said
we were having a bit of a storm, and she comforted me by telling
me it would soon be all over. She might have been right in ways
she hadn't meant if the weather had got much worse. I promised
to ring back when things got a bit quieter. The call over, I sat
contemplating the mess and realised that I was no longer feeling
sick. Like Albert, I was actually enjoying the excitement.

I went up the stairs to the bridge. The gusts had been building
up all night. The speed had reached sixty-six knots on the wind
gauge, more than seventy miles an hour. The wind was logged as
storm force 10 to 11, gusting to hurricane force 12. The seas were
impressive. There was now an enormous distance between one
wave crest and the next. The ship was still steering straight into

the wind. We first hovered on a crest, with the spray whipping past, and then tipped forward and rushed steeply down to the bottom of the trough as if it were the side of a hill. When we got to the bottom I thought the *Gondwana* would plough on down into the looming wall of water, but her head came up and she swiftly climbed the other side.

Albert appeared for his noon watch in high spirits. The barometer had finally bottomed out, and Bob Graham was going to send it off to the meteorologists' museum in New Zealand to see if it had registered a record fall.

The wind was still increasing, but there were no reports of any leaks or damage. As I stood enjoying the spectacle I heard someone say they were going for lunch, and was surprised to find I felt hungry enough to attempt some myself. Eating in such conditions was not easy. We had marvellous rubber mats designed to stick to the table and hold the crockery down, but nothing held down the cutlery. Food had to be held on the plate until it could be manoeuvred into our mouths.

The crew were very quiet after lunch. Tim and I were able to have a game of chess with the magnetic set he had had the forethought to buy in Hobart. About six people were settled down to sleep around us. The lounge, being in the centre of the ship, was by far the most stable place. Some people had taken to sleeping here on a regular basis, but the disturbances as they shifted about and tried to get comfortable were probably as bad as being in their own bunks.

Soon curiosity drew me back to the bridge. I found that the largest gust so far had just been logged – seventy-three knots – and the wind was now entered as hurricane force from the northwest. We were quite a long way off our original course and well behind schedule.

We could see an increasing number of squalls coming on the radar. They passed over, pelting us with hailstones and then with rain. Bearing in mind that we had seen nothing but snow for three months, this was a real sign we were back in warmer climes. The captain, Arne, and I watched the wind gauge as the squalls hit us: it climbed to seventy-seven knots – off the top of the Beaufort scale altogether, beyond hurricane force. The sea was white foam.

Arne, who had spent seven seasons in the Antarctic, and had crossed this sea many times, said this was the worst storm he had seen. We were lucky that this had happened near the end of the voyage when the ship was so light. Having used 2,000 tons of fuel, the *Gondwana* was riding the waves like a cork. It would have been much tougher if we had met these seas on our way south when, heavily laden, we had wallowed low in the water.

As the waves towered about the wheelhouse Arne made out the daily weather report for New Zealand Met Office. He recorded average wave heights of fifteen metres – forty-five feet. Even though I was looking at them out of the bridge windows, the figure astonished me. On the good side, the temperature was much higher, and had reached 8°C.

Despite the exhilaration of the storm I was becoming increasingly exhausted. As darkness fell again, I retired to my bunk to read *The Vicar of Wakefield*. Set in eighteenth-century England, it was a charming antidote to gale-force winds. After hours of being tossed about I finally began to feel that the wind noise was less noticeable and the ship's pitching marginally less violent. I read to the end of the book – all was well, a happy ending. It had kept me occupied until the worst of the storm was over and I fell asleep at last.

On 4 March the seas were still enormous, but the wind had dropped to just below gale force and we were back on course. We had lost twelve hours' sailing time because of the storm. I decided to wash and shave to show that I really had got my sea legs. I felt a lot better for being civilised, and found everyone else was also in much better spirits when I went down for lunch.

Bob Graham had worked out how many miles we would have covered on the expedition before we reached Auckland again. We all guessed (mine was 4,000) and were all wildly under the real total. Bob's measurement was 9,922 miles, the equivalent of three times across the Atlantic. It seemed a great deal, even taking into account the rushing around after the Japanese whalers.

Contemplating these distances, and still hearing the waves crashing about outside, I remembered something I had written about earlier in the trip – towing icebergs from Antarctica to Australia to use them to water the deserts. This was a scheme that had been looked at seriously several times. The ice was so cold it would last a long time even in a warm sea, and it was estimated that two-thirds of the iceberg would arrive unmelted on the Australian coast. One technical difficulty was the erosion of the front of the iceberg by the waves, and scientists were considering a large protective skirt slung round the leading edge. On paper it had sounded feasible, but after the last few days of storms I would not have put any of my money on it succeeding.

The bridge passed down the message that the barometer was falling again, and everyone went off to bed early to get some sleep, in case we were in for another long storm. As it turned out it was merely a gale and a minor inconvenience.

On the midnight watch again. I spent four hours walking from the lookout chair to the radar screen, checking that a dot was gradually getting bigger as the shift wore on. We were within striking distance of Campbell Island, only six days out from New Zealand, when I went to bed. At least, when I woke up, the ship would be at safe anchor.

19

Last Resting Places?

6 MARCH: GOT up early despite the lack of sleep and was delighted to see we were well into Perseverance Harbour, four and a half miles from the open sea. Campbell is a big green island, with the emphasis on green, a colour I have not seen out of doors for months. It has a dense woody scrub rather than trees, and has grassy hills, the highest of which is Mount Honey, 1,876 feet, according to the New Zealand Pilot book on the bridge. We anchored about 300 yards from a jetty which looked like a landing stage in a Scottish loch, and soon had the boats in the water. On the way across we could see unpleasant-looking giant jellyfish and some small fish. We were met by two friendly New Zealanders, two men of the team of three men and two women who are spending a year on Campbell Island. The two women are meteorologists. There had been a sixth member of the team, the cook, but he had fallen and broken his arm. The last ship which had called in had taken him back to New Zealand. This is the fifth month of the New Zealanders' tour and we are to be the last visitors of the season. There is no ice here to inhibit winter visitors, but it is too far south to be on any shipping routes, and only fishing fleets hitting rough weather might seek shelter. We walked up to the base's main building, which turned out to be much bigger than I imagined.

It had in fact been built for much larger numbers of personnel. The science programme had been cut as an economy measure, and the base staff reduced to a token number in the winter. We all sat round exchanging news and drinking tea made with rust-free water. Tim was giving the chocolate biscuits a hard time. The officer in charge, a chap called Paul, suggested if we wanted a trip to see the wildlife we should go over to the other side of the island to a place called Sandy Bay where there were families of rare Hooker sea lions and elephant seals. The route was marked by regular posts, but one of the New Zealanders, Royston, volunteered to come with us to be on the safe side.

229

The Hooker is seal-shaped but much heavier in the chest, with big front flippers and a whiskered blunt nose. These creatures hide in the long grass with their pups. Royston did not warn us, and we were terrified when a female Hooker rose on her flippers, roared very loud, rather like a lion, and then charged. All of us ran off except Royston, who stood his ground, knowing from experience that most sea lions are all roar and no bite, and will normally stop before mounting any attack. He was right and we all strode sheepishly back and took the sea lion's picture. She stood protectively between us and her small pup, but without charging again.

The island was tough walking country, reminding me of the Scottish Highlands, with wet peat bogs, long tufts of grass, and small trees in the sheltered hollows with clumps of ferns. It all seemed very lush after the bare rocks and ice of the Antarctic. We soon discovered that the Hooker sea lion, although a very rare animal (there are only about 5,000 left in the world), was very numerous on Campbell Island. Several times they rushed at us unexpectedly from hollows, and more than once I fell over backwards in the wet peat. Royston always stood his ground; he said it was very rare that they actually bit anyone. Later on the walk he pushed his luck too far with a young bull which left several teeth marks in his hand and forearm from a single bite. It needed a bandage when we got back to the base.

It was two and a half hours' walk to the other side of the island. After months on the ship it was really enjoyable but tough going: the ridge which ran down the centre of the island was about 1,000 feet high, and Royston set a cracking pace. I was just beginning to feel I would have to drop behind when Royston stopped and pointed to a great white bird sitting in the grass. This was a royal albatross on its nest. Even though I knew these birds often had a twelve-foot wingspan and weighed twenty pounds, I was amazed at how big this one looked close to. It had a great yellow beak and pure white plumage. Royston said they were not afraid of humans, and we indeed walked right up to the nest without the bird moving.

Once at the top of the ridge, we were hit by a powerful westerly wind of which I had had no hint when we were climbing up the long path from the base. The scenery was terrific, towering cliffs, the sea churning below them, and albatrosses soaring in the wind. As we walked along the top towards Sandy Bay we passed a number of other albatross nests, all just below the ridge on the sheltered side. We stopped to look at another bird, gratefully stepping down the hill to be out of the wind. Royston explained that it was chick-hatching time, and he held his hand just above the head of one of the birds. This was a trick he had learned, and for some reason it often made them stand up. It worked now, and we could see a tiny white chick sitting between, and on, the bird's feet. Royston said the chick was only a day or two old. He said the young stayed in their nests for ten months and the total rearing time was 360 days. The parents took turns to sit on the nest while the other flew to the feeding grounds off Sydney Heads in Australia – the return journey took three days.

By the time the young had left the nest and learned to fly, the adults needed a year off before they bred again. That explained why around half the nests on the hillside were empty. Pairs used the same nest every two years, adding a new top each time. Some of them were now quite high, about a foot off the ground, and many years old. In New Zealand an albatross first ringed forty years before was still coming back to the same nest. Royston said last year's young could still be seen practising diving and soaring round the cliffs of the island. When they finally left their breeding area they spent a year at sea in the huge expanses of the Southern Ocean, feeding and resting on the waves. He believed they circumnavigated the globe in that time. It was eight or nine years before they came back and started looking for a nest site and a mate. In my months of watching these birds from the ship I had never seen one flap its wings; they just used the air currents to stay aloft.

We carried on along the ridge until we could look over the edge of huge cliffs at the far end of this island. Fur seals were resting on the beaches below. These were the seals that had once been thought to be extinct. Royston said they were seen on the Campbells frequently. We eventually descended from the ridge to reach a beach where we were attacked in a half-hearted fashion by a number of young Hooker sea lions. When the sea lions were due to have pups they went a long way inland, presumably to protect them from predators. They left the pups hidden in the long grass when they went hunting. Royston said he had been exploring about a mile inland a month or so previously, about 500 feet up on a hill, when he had encountered a mother and her pup.

When we reached the survival hut on Sandy Bay which the New

Zealanders had built on this side of the island, we all needed a
rest. The *Gondwana* crew members were all wearing far too many
clothes and carrying survival bags, whereas Royston, who had
done the trip many times, was wearing shorts. One of the reasons
why the hut had been built on this spot was that the bay was one
of the few known breeding grounds of the world's rarest whale,
the great right whale. This species breeds in shallow bays and
coves and moves through the water at only about five miles an
hour, which makes it the easiest whale to trap and kill. From
prehistoric times it has been killed by man as it came inshore to
breed. It is known as the right whale (to hunt) because it contains
so much oil that it continues to float for some time after it is dead
and so can be towed to the beach to be cut up.

It was the first whale species to be brought close to extinction
by man. Only the remoteness of breeding sites such as this one in
Campbell Islands, and another better-studied colony in Patagonia, has allowed the species to survive at all. For a long time
experts doubted that there were enough left for a viable
population. Best estimates now are that there could be 2,000 left
in the world, in two populations in the northern and southern
hemispheres. Sadly for us, it was not the breeding season, so we
were not able to see these rare animals. They live in close-knit
family groups, and can be watched playing for hours in shallow
water. They have a distinctive double 'blow' when they breath out,
making them very easy to identify. Families come in every third
year to breed, but where they go to in the meantime remains a
mystery. Bob Graham got very excited earlier in the trip when we
were on watch together and I believed I had spotted one out at
sea. He was anxious to send the sighting off to a researcher friend
of his, but I was not experienced enough at the time to be
confident.

Royston told us about thirty great right whales visited Campbell
Island each breeding season and spent many days in the shallow
water. They grow up to sixty feet long and can weigh a hundred
tons. The adult males have the distinction of having the largest
testes in the animal kingdom, weighing over a ton.

To my surprise there was a flock of sheep grazing on the edge
of the beach. They charged off at high speed at the sight of us.
These are descendants of the animals brought here by the
Shetland islanders who came in the last century to farm the island.
Conditions proved too tough even for Shetlanders, and when

they abandoned the island it was assumed that the sheep would die out. But they survived. They were evolving now into a separate breed and were ruining the native vegetation and the habitat of the native birds, including the albatross. There was a dispute locally as to whether they should be preserved or wiped out. In any event their numbers were getting too large, so 600 of the 1,200 population had been shot and a fence had been put across part of the island to try to confine the remainder to one half.

There were four enormous bull elephant seals stretched out on the beach. They weighed more than a ton each and were so covered in blubber they had no real shape apart from that of a great fat cigar. They seemed very docile and unafraid of us, as all the wildlife seemed to be, apart from the sheep. I remembered Bob's story about sea elephants, however, and remained a few yards away, but Royston, keen to show off, stood close until one reared up and roared at him. The smell of its breath was so terrible that we all fell back in horror. This must be the elephant seal's ultimate weapon.

Towards the water's edge there were several families of Hookers and more elephant seals. Some of the Hookers which had appeared to be asleep got up and chased us ten yards or so up the beach. The skuas here, although of the type which had given me such a hard time at Marble Point, were not in the least aggressive. Instead they were patiently standing about, very close to the sea lions. We quickly realised why. The sea lions had obviously come back from fishing and, as is their way, were regurgitating all the bits of fish bone and other parts of their meal they did not want. As they worked up to being sick the skuas would jostle for position and wait for their warm free meal to be delivered on to the sand.

Eventually we turned for home. On the way back Royston pointed out a rocky island in the bay. It was the only nesting place of the Campbell Island teal, a flightless, ground-nesting bird, once numerous on the islands, which had been virtually wiped out when rats were accidently introduced from a passing ship. The rats had so far not reached its last refuge in the bay.

As we walked we quickly realised how unfit we had become during our three months on the ship. I set off to go up and over the ridge. The wind was blowing even more strongly than before, and my legs were so weak that I was literally blown off my feet two or three times. I was not the only one, and we all lay down for a rest. Even after that I had to stop again, and one of the New Zealanders, obviously anxious to get on, offered to carry my pack. This was the first time I could ever remember being thought too feeble to carry my own equipment, and it hurt my pride. I asked them to go on ahead and leave me to catch up in my own time.

It was another hour before I finally got down to the shoreline, and by then it was raining hard, but I was recompensed by the sight of a family of Hooker sea lions playing in the shallow water of the bay. They were very swift and graceful animals in the water, diving and rolling over each other.

Ten of us stayed at the Campbell Island base overnight to have a few beers with our hosts and take advantage of their snooker table. They had dormitories for visitors, and I slept better than I had for weeks. I was up early, woken by the sun shining through the window.

We were due to sail directly after lunch, but Ian, Wojtek and I decided we could fit in another walk. We went up the hills in the opposite direction to the one we had taken the previous day. The first mile or more of this path had been improved with boardwalks so that visitors did not sink into the peat bogs. These made the going easier, but it was still a long way up the mountain. Eventually we saw white dots all over the hillside in front and we knew that these must be sitting albatrosses. It took us another hour and a half to get among them. They watched us carefully but did not move. We had been told there were 5,000 nests altogether, mostly royal albatross, but there were also some wandering albatross among them. In the distance we saw some birds landing and others taking off, presumably the three-day shift change. We reached the top of one of the smaller hills and looked out towards the north of the island, which was covered with virtually impenetrable scrub. We sat down and shared an apple, the only food we had with us, and marvelled at the beauty of the scene.

When we got back, later than we had been instructed, we found everyone unusually relaxed. Arne, for the first time I could remember on the trip, had come ashore. He had gone up the hill on the path we had taken yesterday to look at the albatross nests.

While we were waiting we did some bartering. We gave the New Zealanders a large quantity of surplus butter and two dozen cartons of cream, in exchange for a few crates of beer. (As I had expected, the lack of alcohol on board the *Gondwana* was getting everyone down.) We also agreed to take the cook's belongings back to New Zealand, because there were no supply ships due back to the island on which he could hitch a lift and so finish his tour of duty. We loaded up our beer and the cook's crate of clothes and shipped it back while we watched for Arne to return.

When we sailed I was reluctant to leave such a lovely place and stayed on deck with several others taking pictures of the yearling albatrosses, which buzzed us in dozens as we pulled out of the harbour. We were soon forced off the deck, however. Outside the harbour the sea was as rough as ever, driven before yet another gale. In the lee of the hills we had not been aware of it, but once we were out of their shelter we were forced to close all the doors and prepare for another buffeting. It was a force 9 gale by the time we had finished dinner that night.

We were heading towards the Auckland Islands, an uninhabited group which like the Campbells is controlled by New Zealand. Landings of any kind there are banned in order to protect the wildlife. According to the books, this is even better than on the Campbells because by some fluke there are as yet no rats.

Even in this remote part of the world no one knows how long the unique wildlife on these islands can continue to be preserved. It is not just the possibility of stray sightseers or fishermen landing on the islands and not realising the damage that they are doing that must be guarded against – the problem is much more fundamental than that. The Hooker sea lion, for example, a rare and wonderful beast, which only breeds on the Auckland and Campbell islands, should be thriving. It enjoys total protection, and yet its population, estimated to be 5,000, is going down. Many adults are clearly being caught in the nets of the fishing fleets increasingly operating in this part of the ocean.

The same is true of the albatross. All over the Southern Ocean this wonderful bird, which is universally wondered at and loved, is suffering a decline in numbers. Although as yet no definite reason has been established, the number found dead in fishing nets is thought by scientists to be a clear sign of their basic vulnerability.

But this is only part of the story. The whole ecosystem of the Antarctic area is threatened by man's over-exploitation of the fish stocks. Although other nations have shared in the harvest, the biggest single culprit is the Soviet Union, which has wiped out large stocks of fin fish. But the fishermen cannot take all the blame. An international organisation was set up ten years ago by the Antarctic Treaty nations to solve the problem of overfishing and to safeguard the recovery of any endangered species, but it has been sadly lacking in strong political will.

A convention designed to control overfishing was set up with the best of intentions. The Convention for the Conservation of Antarctic Marine and Living Resources (CCAMLR), to give it the full title, came into force in 1980 'to protect the ecosystem'. It was agreed by fifteen nations, including the Soviet Union. A special commission was to control the exploitation of all living organisms in the Southern Ocean, except the seals and whales, which are already dealt with by different international agreements. The stated aim of the convention remains very much in the forefront of modern thinking: it focuses on what was in 1980 a new and bold idea, looking at the health of the entire food chain. No part of the chain should be so over-exploited that any other animal or fish dependent on it is adversely affected.

So far CCAMLR has manifestly not succeeded in its aims, and disaster threatens much of the wildlife in the Antarctic unless urgent steps are taken. The Soviet Union and other fishing nations will not accept annual quotas on various species, no decisions are reached, and meanwhile the fishing goes on.

Commercial fishing began in the Antarctic ten years before CCAMLR was negotiated. The convention was thought necessary because of the disastrous consequences of this first full-scale harvesting by factory ships. In the 1969/70 season the Soviet Union caught more than 400,000 tons of marbled rockcod from around the British-controlled islands of South Georgia, but only just over 100,000 tons could be caught the following year. By the end of that season, in fact, the factory ships had completely exhausted the stocks of the species in the area – it had been wiped out as a commercial fishery in two years. In the late 1970s another species, the mackerel icefish, was targeted by the Soviet fleets in the Atlantic sector of the Southern Ocean. Successive catches of 240,000 tons, 220,000 tons and 100,000 tons by the factory fleet wiped out this stock too.

Gradually, as each species has been depleted, the fishing nations have investigated and harvested alternative species. Another species that seems likely to be wiped out is the Patagonian toothfish, a very long-lived fish that inhabits the shallow seas round South Georgia. It is caught on long lines which are also known to kill numbers of wandering albatross which dive for the fish they can see caught on the lines. The commission, although aware of the problem, cannot reach a consensus on what to do about it – and so the fishing continues.

The key problem is the same as that faced by the International Whaling Commission. Nations keen to continue fishing argue that stocks are much higher than those calculated by the nations which favour conservation measures. Thus at the November 1989 meeting of CCAMLR in Hobart, Australia, the Soviet Union argued that mackerel icefish round South Georgia were three times more numerous than the Commission's scientists claimed. This disagreement was not resolved, so the Soviet Union concluded there should be no management of stocks. The Soviets also rejected the scientists' suggestion that mesh sizes of nets be increased to allow small fish to escape and so save some breeding stock. They said that, in the absence of more detailed historical and current biological data from fishing vessels, new management procedures for stocks should not be enacted.

A more serious long-term threat is the intended harvesting of krill. In the same season that I sailed on the *Gondwana* there was a total catch of these tiny shrimps of 370,663 tons. The Soviet Union took 300,000 tons, and Japan the rest. Fortunately for the krill the Japanese have found little market for these creatures at home, but the citizens of the Soviet Union, with their permanent food shortages, are less discriminating. The Soviet Union did have technical difficulties in processsing such tiny creatures into acceptable food, but after the 1989 season it announced that it had overcome this problem and was planning to increase the harvest dramatically. To this end a new fleet of large integrated vessels for catching and turning fish and krill into fish cakes was being built for the Soviet Union in Finland.

A working group of the Commission recommended in 1989 that krill catches 'should not greatly exceed the current level until more is known about the predator requirements and local krill availability'. In other words if the Soviet fleet wiped out the krill in certain areas, as they had already wiped out the fish, then the penguins and other birds which rely on them for survival would starve to death. One important factor is a lack of understanding of the life cycle of the humble krill. No one knows for sure how it survives the long cruel winter to thrive and swarm in millions in the short summer.

Will excessive harvesting cause a crash in the population which destroys the entire ecosystem? Rather than wait for an answer to that question the Soviet Union has decided to press ahead with harvesting on the assumption that it will not. This is contrary to the spirit and the letter of the convention which the Soviet Union signed. In the Antarctic this policy of harvesting first and assessing the consequences afterwards has proved disastrous for virtually every animal and fish so far exploited by man, from the seals and whales onwards.

The obvious failure of the Antarctic Treaty to deal with the problem of overfishing is used by conservation organisations as proof that the whole treaty system is weak. They say it allows nations to do what they want. This was one of the reasons why Greenpeace believed that the French felt they could get away with destroying the penguin colonies at Dumont d'Urville, and the Americans with tipping chemicals in McMurdo Sound. The failure of CCAMLR is also being used as an argument to show that the Minerals Convention will not work either. Conservation groups argue that inability to reach a consensus over mineral plans could mean that countries would simply go ahead, ignoring the feeble protestations of other nations.

Supporters of the Minerals Convention argue that the two conventions are completely different. The fishing convention is to establish quotas for catches and repair damage to overfished species after the damage has already been done. The Minerals Convention, on the other hand, has given each of the claimant states the veto over anyone prospecting or mining on their claim. Each proposed development would have to go through a detailed environmental analysis at every turn, and any infringement could result in a veto by any one of a number of organisations on a management committee.

Despite the obvious differences between the two conventions, the fact that CCAMLR has not succeeded in its stated objectives must inevitably cast a cloud over the ability of the system to make its other agreements work. The conservation lobby, which is growing ever stronger, is not convinced it can trust governments. As a result public confidence in the politicians' ability to protect the Antarctic is low. Until governments can at least make the fishing convention work, it will not begin to rise.

20

The Last Lap

ON 8 MARCH the Auckland Islands were still twenty-eight miles away according to the radar, and the weather continued to be rough. Even so, people were talking all the time of their plans when they returned to Lyttelton or Auckland, or about travel arrangements to Europe or the United States. There was also acrimony between people who had previously managed to get on well together. Ian Balmer and Pierrette Paroz were having a pointless argument in the galley about how some people on the ship did more campaigning than others. Pierrette defended herself by saying that she was a pilot and a translator, not a banner carrier. I said we all had our place, even a drone journalist.

Going through the lounge I found Tim Fraser, with whom I had amicably shared a cabin for three months, having a fierce exchange with the ship's carpenter, Marc de Fourneaux. Suddenly they set about each other, fortunately not coming to blows, but ripping each other's shirts off. They were both a bit embarrassed by their stupidity and this successfully defused the argument. I never found out what it was about.

Having been burrowing through the *Gondwana*'s library I was reading *One Flew Over the Cuckoo's Nest*, Ken Kesey's book about life in a mental institution, and I was beginning to notice similarities between the behaviour of people locked up for a long time in hospital and those on board the ship. During the day I had talked to Paul Bogart about the quote I had used about the krill jumping out of the water as a result of the oil spill from the Argentinian ship. He had magnified the incident in his mind and was very nervous about the reaction of the staff at the US National Science Foundation to him when he returned. These scientists said krill could not jump, so they would accuse Greenpeace, and Paul in particular, of fabrication. It seemed to me such a small thing to worry about. I read to him from the Kesey book: 'Some things are true even if they never happened, some things could never be true even if they did happen,' but I do not think it helped.

Marc now found an outlet for his surplus energy. The ship's flagpole had been snapped during the great storm, even though it had not had a flag on it at the time, and Marc was charged with making another one so we could fly the Greenpeace flag when we came into Lyttelton harbour. We had also discovered that the main lifeboat on the port side had been stove in by a wave, and we had lost the floodlight off the top of the helicopter hangar.

After lunch we came into calm water in the lee of the Auckland Islands, two very large bright green wooded islands with a long, sheltered fiord in between. We were going to anchor and rest for a few hours, but unfortunately the echo sounder chose that moment to blow a circuit and we could not immediately find somewhere suitable. We did not wish to go too close inshore because of the absolute ban on landings. Instead we cruised very slowly up and down, accompanied by Hooker sea lions and dolphins playing in the water round us. There were also a lot of ducks and an Auckland Island shag, of which there was a sub-species in the Campbells, although the difference was not immediately apparent.

Late in the evening we sailed for Lyttelton. The wind had dropped and the sea was calmer. I hoped that we had endured our last storm before getting home.

That night Pete and Paul Bogart were composing a telex to Mrs Thatcher, urging her not to ratify the Minerals Convention, in the hope that it would persuade me to do one last story to mark the expedition's return to Lyttelton. I sat down to write the article, only to discover that they could not send the message because they could not find out the telex number of 10 Downing Street. Pete said he would sort it out.

On the bridge there was alarm because someone had miscalculated on how long it would take us to get to Lyttelton. We had planned to arrive on Saturday 11 February, but the *Gondwana* was still travelling on one engine to save fuel, and at the seven and a half knots we were making we would not arrive until Sunday the 12th. This would be disastrous for those who had organised our reception for the previous day. On further calculations we could still make it in time if we speeded up, so our revs on the one engine were immediately increased. Davey was preparing to get the other engine going later so that we would meet our target arrival time of 10 am on Saturday.

Talk was still of what people were going to do at the end of the trip. Both Phil Durham and Dave Walley were going to get married. Others, the Greenpeace rolling stones, had made no plans at all and would stay living on the ship until the mood took them to go elsewhere.

This was the last night I would have to do the midnight till 4 am shift and I was beginning to feel quite nostalgic. It was a beautiful night, with the Southern Cross directly above and the Milky Way very clear and strong. We had a great display of the Aurora Australis for about half an hour.

Later as I was staring ahead into the darkness I noticed a faint glow on the far horizon. Albert could not explain it, but when we looked on the chart the light was directly in line with Dunedin, the southernmost town in New Zealand. According to the chart it was 120 miles away, and Albert at first said it would be impossible to detect lights at that distance. But as the night wore on the glow got more noticeable, and he eventually conceded that there could be no other explanation for it. He said there must be a cloud or water vapour above the town to reflect the light because the town itself would be out of sight below the horizon. As I went to bed we were only 300 miles away from Lyttelton, just under thirty hours sailing.

In the morning I finished my washing, and sewed a button on my green shirt. Sabine had been recommended as ship's barber and made a good job of making me look respectable again. Everywhere people were washing walls, polishing and cleaning, ready for our arrival the next day. Ken Ballard was going on about things not being clean enough and urging people to do better, a typical first mate. We were now travelling up the coast of New Zealand, although we could not yet see it because it was misty and raining heavily. There were fishing boats passing by, and at one point we had to thread our way through a fleet of thirty scallop boats. Having been so long in an empty sea it seemed strange to see other boats and to be able to wave to people on them.

Pete had finally obtained Mrs Thatcher's telex number and sent off his message, so I dutifully dispatched my story, but with no expectation that it would be used. Having not used money for so long, I had to find some in the bottom of my suitcase to settle my bar account, which was for all the beer I had drunk on the trip. Greenpeace were charging only wholesale prices, so that, combined with the gaps when I had not been able to drink because of seasickness, the bill was so low it was a disgrace to my profession.

Saturday 11 March was the big day and we were all given an 8 am call. The showers were all busy, even though Davey's tank bypass had never worked and the water was still dark brown.

We were in the approaches to Lyttelton by the time I got on deck, the engines idling because we were waiting for a pilot to guide us between the tall bare cliffs and hills guarding the entrance to the harbour. We travelled sedately down the sound, and as Lyttelton came into view strained to see if there was anyone on the quayside to meet us. We were not disappointed: there was a small crowd shouting and waving – with a big sign saying 'Welcome Gondwana' and a lot of other banners I could not read from so far away. As we got closer we could see a man dressed as a clown conducting a small band and a group of Maori people, some in traditional costume. Considering the size of Lyttelton, which apart from the dock is a scatter of small houses on the hillside behind a couple of shops and a hotel, it was a very respectable crowd.

As we pulled into the quayside friends, wives and lovers leaned perilously out to get first touch, welcoming home crew members who were in return hanging far out over the rails. No one could actually go ashore until the customs and Ministry of Agriculture officials, in this case conveniently rolled into one person, came aboard to give us clearance. The gangplank, which had not been moved since we left Auckland eighty days before, was untied and the crane lifted it into place.

The band played on, a television crew filmed and the New Zealand official smiled and gave the go-ahead to disembark. Phil Durham and Dave Walley fell into their fiancées' arms, and Carol Stewart, the New Zealand Antarctic campaigner, and a few friends came aboard with boxes of fresh fruit, flowers and beer as consolation for those of us with no one to hug. I found Davey Edwards and a couple of others skulking in the galley. Like me, they were finding it hard to take the emotion without anyone special to share it with. We ate a couple of new season's apples and welcomed people into our retreat. They kept telling us how well we had done and how much good publicity there had been until we all felt better.

Just as we were about to get stuck into the beer I remembered that I had decided to travel overland to Wellington and then Auckland from Lyttelton and needed to make arrangements. I had to get to Christchurch by noon to get tickets before the coach station shut for the weekend. One of the well-wishers offered a lift and I was able to arrange my trip for the following day. I was then whisked back to the ship in time for the fish and chips Davey had organised as a homecoming lunch for the Brits on board. Even more people had by then arrived to welcome the crew, many of them with no connection with Greenpeace, simply wanting to wish the campaign success. Having been isolated for so long it was a little overwhelming, and after lunch a group of us walked over the hills to Christchurch to have a quiet wander round the Victorian granite houses and get accustomed to civilisation.

We went for a Chinese meal, the ultimate proof that life was back to normal, and then returned to Lyttelton to a hotel called the British, a clone of an English pub. The landlady, having hosted previous welcome-home parties for Greenpeace, had been on the quay to welcome us that morning. She was not disappointed with the extra custom. In the relief of being away at last from the unpredictable and exhausting sea, all the tensions and irritations of the last three months were washed away in a tide of beer and good humour. It was a memorable party.

The next day, with a thick head but a light heart, I set off by coach to explore South Island, New Zealand, before getting on the ferry to go to Wellington, the North Island, rejoining the ship briefly in Wellington to watch a final Greenpeace demonstration. While I had been enjoying myself as a tourist, the crew had unloaded and disposed of the rubbish accumulated during the voyage and sailed the ship north to the capital. But the barrels of cadmium waste collected at McMurdo had been saved and were wheeled from the dockside through the city to be dumped in a short ceremony, for the benefit of the press, outside the American Embassy. The United States staff refused to take any responsibility, and the New Zealand authorities finally removed the barrels after Greenpeace had gone. The public health department took no risks and treated the waste as toxic. Greenpeace got charged with leaving litter but judged that the extra publicity was worth it.

The ship then sailed to Auckland to be refitted for another campaign the following year. Some of the crew, like me, left immediately to go back to the lives they had left behind. Others went to find summer jobs until it was time to return to Antarctica and continue the campaign. The overwinterers all passed their psychiatric tests with flying colours and went on a tour to drum up more support for their cause and get used to dealing with people again.

On my return to England I had a week's holiday in Spain with Maureen, so that we could get to know each other again. We had unseasonable snow. Shortly after returning to work I was made Environment Correspondent of *The Guardian*. This means I have continued writing about the Antarctic, the Minerals Convention and all the other related problems the continent is connected with – global warming, pollution and the receding icecap. Information comes from the scientists stationed in the Antarctic, who analyse the measurements of the ice and atmosphere and try to interpret what they mean so that politicians will understand what needs to be done. Can they all be persuaded to halt the rot before disaster overtakes us all?

Despite mounting evidence that the Antarctic should be preserved for science, there remains a strong resistance to the idea of turning the Antarctic into a World Park. The British, United States and Japanese administrations in particular still favour the Minerals Convention. And meanwhile the whales, seals and other wildlife remain in danger of over-exploitation from other nations. The struggle to convince the Soviet Union that its short-term plunder of the fish and krill stocks has to stop still goes on. The concept of sustainable development, so willingly accepted on paper by the Antarctic Treaty nations, continues to be ignored in practice.

While it seems difficult to move governments, Greenpeace appears to be winning the battle for public opinion. A large number of environmental groups have now started their own campaigns to save the Antarctic, including the World Wide Fund for Nature. Other organisations, much more part of the establishment, also support the idea – including, for example, the British Women's Institute and apparently its most distinguished member, the Queen of England. In June 1990 Her Majesty, in her capacity as representative of Sandringham Women's Institute in Norfolk, attended the annual meeting of the national organisation at the

Albert Hall when a proposal to make Antarctica a Wilderness Park was overwhelmingly approved.

In 1985, when Pete Wilkinson took on the Antarctic campaign for Greenpeace, I told him he was trying for the impossible, the continent was too remote to get people interested enough to try and save it. Five years later he has proved me wrong. But the battle is still far from won, for if the Antarctic is saved it will be the first, and only, part of the world that man has chosen not to plunder. The *Gondwana* and her crew still have much to do.

Index